ONE WOMAN'S JOURNEY

Sharon M Jordan

First edition published by Reach Publishers 2013

ISBN 978-0-620-55080-2

eISBN 978-0-620-55079-6

Published by Reach Publishers, P O Box 1384, Wandsbeck, South Africa, 3631

Edited by Gail Kruger for Reach Publishers

Cover designed by Reach Publishers

Website: www.aimtoinspire.com

E-mail - reach@webstorm.co.za

I have used a number of 'snapshots' in this book to illustrate my stories. Many are old photographs and in some instances the photographer's name escapes me. I apologize for this but would like to thank you as earnestly as I thank those whose names appear in alphabetical order below:

L. Guastella
P. & P. Hanegraaf
L. Jordan
D. Majeweta
R. Stanton
C. Tomson
A. Van Luyk

Sharon M Jordan
wildcoast.s@gmail.com

A meandering story of an African motorcycling odyssey, interwoven with trekking expeditions in the mountains, murder in paradise and extraordinary sailing escapades

Special Thanks

To my long suffering family, Lara Jordan, Thana Jordan, Justin Kaiser, Daphne and Jeff Bompas and the Hanegraaf clan for your love and support through the years; it can't be easy having a mom/daughter/family member who periodically has crazy ideas but knowing you support me, no matter what, is important to me. Lara, I loved your idea for the cover and appreciated your final 'read through', comments, suggestions and corrections.

To my brother, Paul Hanegraaf, for your invaluable help with making sure that my motorcycle was in tip-top shape. You spent many hours making sure of this while your family gracefully hosted my stay in your home in Cape Town, so thank you Pam, Kelly and Wendy.

To my friends, Reinet Cavanagh for her tireless faith and enthusiasm in this book and her help with the proofreading as well as her partner, Mike McEwan, for providing the inspiration for the name of this book.

To Rob Stanton, my hiking pal and friendly neighbour of 21 years, for your patient help in reducing my various meanderings to meaningful lines on a map.

To Tanya Hall who dragged me out of my shell when I needed it most, for your pep talks, your unflagging friendship, your infectious joie-de-vivre and the fun we always share. Let the good times roll!

To my adventure buddies who joined me on these outstanding trips. Sometimes my daughter, Lara, and my youngest son, Justin, joined me, and often members from the Mountain Backpackers Club to which I belong and have the privilege of being a hike leader, accompanied me on one of my explorations. There are too many of you to mention individually without running the risk of accidentally omitting someone – but you all know who you are. These outings would not have been the same without the enjoyment you brought along, your support and your camaraderie.

To the Mountain Backpackers Club in Durban which has helped keep me motivated and fit. Quite apart from the numerous hikes always on offer, the bi-monthly slide presentations and talks by adventurous people have not only been fascinating but inspirational as well. The Mountain Backpackers Club was instrumental in 'getting me going' by putting out bait in the form of an advertisement for a Wild Coast hike. I have since undertaken numerous hikes there and have become an accredited tour guide for the Wild Coast.

Contents

Prologue

About 18 years ago I was at a *braai* (barbecue) where I was encouraged by my friend, Reinet Cavanagh, to tell my Palmyra story. At the end of the narration one of the guests, Michael Green, a lecturer in English at the local university, urged me to write a book about this and my other sailing adventures. In the past I flirted with the notion of writing and had got as far as jotting down and organising the chapters of the book-to-be, but that was as far as it went. I protested that my grammar might not be up to scratch, that I had no knowledge of writing a book and that I might mess up. In short, I didn't have the confidence to give it a go. He told me to write as I speak and not worry about the rest. These words have stuck in my mind all though the years and now, after many others have written about the Palmyra incident, I am finally writing my own account; not only about Palmyra but about all the other unexpectedly great adventures I have had along the way.

Actually I love writing and have messed around writing stories for myself, mostly half written, about life and love and several going nowhere stories. I have spent many pleasurable hours putting together presentations which I hope have been motivating; presentations I've done at schools and my hiking club. At one of the schools at which I spoke, all the children listening sent me letters commenting on my presentation. I was taken aback at how much they enjoyed hearing my stories and the impact they had on them. I have scanned a few of these and included them at the end of the book. A thoughtful question posed by an 11-year-old girl was, "Well Miss, your life has been so exciting, I wonder, what you do now for fun?" What, indeed!

Apart from Curt Rowlett, other people have written books which include my experiences, so I've never bothered to do this myself; one such book being 'And the Sea Will Tell', a riveting account by Vincent Bugliosi. He interviewed me about the Palmyra case and I have no desire to duplicate any of his work, delve into the background of the story or get into any of the courtroom detail as he has so painstakingly done. This was also made into a two part mini-series movie by the same name. It was strange to see myself being portrayed by an actress!

FBI Files, an American television docudrama series, screened an intriguing episode entitled *Deadly Paradise*, all about the same incident and more recently a friend phoned and said that he was reading about me in a book he had taken out of the local library. So it was high time I wrote my own book and included my own version.

Many people contacted me, thinking that my 15 minutes of fame had somehow translated into earning a fortune; truth be told I never received one cent from anyone and never thought anything of it. If what I have read is to be believed a handful of people made money with this tale.

At the time my husband, Rob, and I did receive something special though, which meant a great deal to us. We had been deliberating on applying for residency in the United States which we mentioned to one of the attorneys involved in the legal proceedings as a consequence of my find on Palmyra. He was from the Criminal Division of the U.S. Department of Justice and of his own accord sent a letter to the U.S. Ambassador in South Africa recommending their favourable consideration of an application by us. He said, "I wish to report that the government of the United States is indebted to the Jordans for their service in assisting our government to bring a dangerous criminal to justice." As it turned out my now ex-husband and I did not emigrate to the U.S. at that time, although after many years sailing Rob has settled there permanently.

Anyway life continued, as it does, and I went on have many more incredible and unusual experiences; so much so that I am going to include a significant portion in this book. Fortunately I took the precaution of requesting my mother to keep all my letters to her, which she did. These took the form of a diary, so I have an accurate record of my sailing days. I am using those letters to refresh my memory and assist me in the veracity of my recollections.

Apart from being satisfying, writing 'One Woman's Journey' has been cathartic as well as stimulating. I feel that I have almost relived certain parts of it, parts that otherwise would have remained buried in the recesses of my memory. It has also been motivating for me, so much so that I am in the process of reorganising my life in order to 'smell the roses' once again.

This book, a collection of stories, is not in chronological order, but is rather a series of windows into periods of my life that I thought were worth sharing; periods covering what I have done in terms of occasionally challenging journeys of exploration. I hope this book will motivate others, women in particular, to follow their passion... because if I can do it, anyone can!

I apologise in advance for any discrepancies that might have crept into this book; they are unintentional as I have tried to stick to the truth as closely as possible.

— 1 —

The Birth Of An Idea, Preparations And Departure

The birth of an idea

In the days leading up to Christmas, which is a notoriously lonely time for some, I found myself feeling decidedly down in the dumps. My teenage son, the last child still at home, was happily snowboarding in Austria so I was left to my own devices. I missed my son's cheerful company as well as that of my ex-boyfriend. As a result of the timely ending of this relationship my emotions were roller-coasting and it was high time I pulled myself together and got on with the business of enjoying life. My energetic, clever, high-profile, unpredictable, mountain-climbing, surfing, paddling, cycling, constant but totally-unsuitable-in-the-long-term companion was now out of my life and so had ended a tumultuous, emotional and passionate one and a half year relationship.

In the past my love of the outdoors kept me fit and sparkly but as a consequence of this break-up I had allowed myself to chill longer than I should have. Let me correct that; I had wallowed in the loss of this man's companionship, a loss that was actually a blessing and I knew it. Of course the big question was – what should I do with myself now as I dearly needed to get away for a while? I had accumulated leave so work wouldn't be a problem; besides business was quiet at the moment.

My general philosophy is 'enjoy life, no one gets out alive' and to this end, over the years, I have planned regular escapades. Apart from the feel-good factor I feel that it's essential for me to shake off the little comforts and luxuries I have become accustomed to, in order to appreciate them fully on my return.

I have sailed extensively on pocket-sized yachts, visiting exotic destinations and deserted islands – hmmn, too much *moola* needed to buy a cruising yacht although that would have been terrific. Also, could I navigate the oceans single-handedly? Was I capable enough? Is that what I genuinely wanted to do? I didn't know.

Climb a mountain or two? Mount Everest base camp and Mount Kenya were still fresh memories… move on. Hike through Central America? Now there is something I could do or maybe cycle Vietnam, Laos or Cambodia. Decisions, decisions! While pondering a plethora of ideas, my work, family, social commitments and general everyday activities kept me in my rut, in my comfort zone, and kept me from being serious about making a decision regarding the next grand undertaking.

That is, until the day I went Christmas shopping with my daughter, Lara. I hate to admit to this but the day we went shopping my smile was fake. I was still feeling sorry for myself and instead of being the pillar of support I should have been for my daughter I think some of my sadness must have rubbed off on her. Her boyfriend, Clayton, had been working away for a while and she needed cheering up. Anyway while browsing through travel books in the bookstore, I had the moment Oprah calls 'the light bulb moment' and what a flash it was. As Lara ambled over I grabbed her hand and said, "That's it – we're going to escape into the unknown on a great motorcycling adventure."

Lara and I had small, 125cc off-road motocross bikes totally unsuitable for a journey of any significant scale but what the heck, never say never, just do it. "Excellent idea," said Lara with tremendous enthusiasm and that was it – the concept was born! She was up for the challenge and we understood that at times it was going to be tough, demanding, wild, maybe dangerous but a once in a lifetime experience. We also knew it would be stimulating and as novices we were aware that our motorcycling skills would improve immeasurably en-route.

Now we had to nurture this concept and flesh it out. "So where are we going to ride to?" queried Lara. My initial concept was to find our way to Mount Kilimanjaro, climb it and return home but Lara vetoed this suggestion with a derisive, "Uh, uh, no mountain climbing for me, I'd prefer snorkelling – how about Lake Malawi?"

"That's it, a motorcycling circumnavigation of Lake Malawi," I said. Christmas shopping forgotten we now scoured the shelves for books with information on travelling off the beaten path. We quickly deduced that we would need to leave from South Africa, go across the border into Swaziland, through Mozambique, into Tanzania, around the top of Lake Malawi, back through Malawi into Mozambique and finally home to South Africa. Rather a tall order for two little, unlicensed, unroadworthy motorbikes. We did a quick, rough calculation and guesstimated that this journey could be around 8,000 kilometres plus, and ideally we would need about two months to do it in as we not only wanted the riding practice but also wanted a chance to take in the sights en-route.

We spent the following weeks tossing ideas around and playing with logistics. We also had to take a long hard look at our bikes. My logical reasoning was to use my Yamaha XT 660R, a dual purpose bike well suited to this sort of riding. That notion didn't last long – "Oh no you don't," emphasised Lara, "you're not leaving me in the dust and anyway, where's the challenge in that!" So, on to finding out about lighting coils, rectifiers, voltage regulators, batteries, headlamps, tail-lights, brake-lights, indicators and hooters (horns) to make our 125cc motorcycles road legal. Now that might sound relatively simple but we received conflicting advice from 'experts' with a few even saying that it was impossible on these particular bikes. After googling various websites and educating ourselves on the topic, we were confident that this would not be a problem. My supportive dad and brother assured us that it could be done. It took no less than 10 phone calls to motorcycle shops and auto electricians before finding one, M. Motorcycles, who said that they could do the conversion. The next obstacle would be licensing these vehicles, which apart from being bitterly tedious would entail being sent endlessly from one department to another trying to unravel (or ravel?) the paperwork required for this.

We pored over maps, looking at various routes, doubtful as to whether they were do-able or not, checking these routes on the web, trying to scavenge additional information on road conditions, the whereabouts of border posts, and trying to establish if there were bridges or ferries over rivers and distances between petrol stations. We heard that a fuel known as 'superpetrol' is available throughout Mozambique but no one seemed to know if it is leaded, unleaded or diesel. We were told not to request *petrolio* because we'd get paraffin. Route planning proved to be an interesting challenge; one of the consulates didn't know where the border post was or even if they had a border post in a particular province bordering another country. The helpdesk person's instruction was to ask someone when we were in that province. Luckily we eventually found this information after scouring the internet. A helpful South African travel agent contacted a lodge owner in the Niassa Wildlife Reserve and informed us that it has a road running through it to the border post and motorcycles were not allowed in the reserve. Well, that seems like a sensible place to have a border post! So now we'd have to find a way around that one. The Niassa Wildlife Reserve apparently has a lion population of roughly 1,000 head; elephant, sable antelope, Cape buffalo, Lichtenstein's hartebeest, eland, zebra, warthog, lion, leopard and spotted hyena abound and there are smaller populations of kudu, bushbuck, impala, wildebeest, waterbuck, reedbuck, and hippo as well as the endangered African wild dog.

We queried a particular ferry across the Rovuma River at the alleged border into Tanzania. We had heard that it had sunk and no one in authority was able to tell us if it had, in fact, sunk or was still operational and suggested that maybe a bridge had now been built or was that the one that was bombed in the war?

It didn't appear much better on the other side as an official at the Tanzanian Consulate advised us against riding at night. We assumed that it was a safety precaution as a result of the usual problems of domestic animals and pedestrians or maybe other vehicles without lights on the roads at night but that was the least of his concerns. We were somewhat mortified when he said it was because of the danger of being attacked by wild animals.

Could a 125cc out-perform a charging lion or elephant? That is assuming you still have your wits about you sufficiently to accelerate off at speed! With this in mind we put mace onto our growing list of items to buy. I had watched a TV show where a man hiding in a pile of rubbish trying to film a rummaging bear from close up got a little too close. He whipped out his mace spray, sprayed it in the bear's face and the distressed creature couldn't get away fast enough.

Interestingly enough I discovered that the big cats apparently see a human being on a motorbike as prey and will chase you. I was even sent a photograph of a cheetah chasing a completely oblivious game ranger going about his business on a motorbike in a South African game reserve. (Unfortunately, despite trying, I have been unable to track down the photographer of this photo so full credit goes to the anonymous photographer.)

Now the one big problem that we faced was the lack of fuel stations in the far-flung areas we would be travelling through. The only way around this was to carry extra fuel. No matter how we looked at it, a 125cc off-road motorcycle does not have the tank capacity to make some of the long distances between fuel stations. In addition to fuel we would also be carrying water, food, spares, tools, a medical kit, small tents, a stove, mugs, plates, cutlery, cameras, a GPS, diaries, sleeping bags, sleeping mats, rain gear, clothing and a teeny little bag of toiletries.

Reality took over and suddenly the mom and daughter undertaking was now elevated to expedition status as we identified the importance of a 4x4 primarily to carry the additional fuel. Of course this opened new doors for us and we thought that we might as well welcome whoever wanted to be part of our expedition. We had long toyed with the notion of somehow helping women along the way and having a 4x4 seemed to make the idea more feasible. Perhaps we could carry medicine or prostheses to remote rural clinics. But what was needed?

This time it was Lara who had 'the light bulb moment'. "HPV vaccines Mom!" (The HPV vaccine prevents infection with certain species of human papilloma virus associated with the development of cervical cancer.) Many of our female friends have had the big 'C' scare and have gone under the knife or laser to remove all traces of abnormal cells from the cervix. A friend of mine died a long and painful death from cervical cancer, detected too late. This is now a preventable disease as a vaccine is available. Is this vaccine going out to isolated rural clinics? Are women in these areas even aware of this vaccine? Do they have regular pap smears – probably not? How many deaths can be attributed to cervical cancer in these areas? Could we help? We needed to do our homework.

As we neared the end of January with our sights set on departing South Africa in August, I had a setback. Ugh, I felt so sick. My head was spinning, I was nauseous and my left hand stung and throbbed at the same time. I had been in hospital where the ruptured ligament on the inside of my thumb was repaired after a spectacular wipe-out on the Springfield enduro track. The accident happened about a month beforehand and as luck would have it, it was the first day on the course on my 'new', pre-owned motorcycle. The dirt trail was fairly rough with overhanging branches, clumps of long grass, steep mounds, switchbacks, soft sand and concealed obstacles lying in wait for the unlucky motorcyclist. A strategically hidden rock stopped my bike in its tracks but I continued on over the handlebars and with my helmet I thwacked from side to side on the neck brace; the helmet and neck brace although separate are designed to work together to restrict any extreme range of movement of your neck which can damage your spinal cord. At least my chest protector did a sterling job of saving my boobs from roasties. The rest of my protective gear did what it was designed to do but my gloved thumb bent backwards and the intense pain at that moment had me seeing stars! After a while Lara became aware that I was no longer with the pack and she came back to find me sprawled across the track in agony.

I had my hand X-rayed at the local (private) hospital where I was assured that there were no broken bones and that all was fine – I was directed to the casualty department for a check but they said there was nothing a pain-killer and an anti-inflammatory or two couldn't sort out. Yeah right! In retrospect I'm childishly glad I stomped mud all over their clean floors. A month later I was still in pain with a swollen hand. Finally I made an appointment with a specialist for a second opinion and after an ultrasound examination he immediately booked me into the hospital for an operation to reattach the thumb ligament which had ruptured.

I was not able to continue riding as although I tried to ride with the plaster cast, pulling in the clutch was too painful and it seemed as though the recuperation period was going to be a minimum of six weeks. So there I lay on my couch, left hand in plaster and airborne to stop the swelling while brainstorming with Lara and trying to work on our budget.

While doing the numbers we spotted the latest Bike SA magazine lying on the table. Aha, now we could raid the pages for information ranging from motorcycle insurers to communication systems. We scanned the used motorcycles section as we were still keeping our eyes open for street legal motorcycles so as to save ourselves the hassle of conversion from unlicensed and unroadworthy motorcycles to licensed and roadworthy. I drank tea and swallowed painkillers, Lara sipped a stronger and altogether more suitable drink and we had a fruitful evening covering many different aspects of our planned jaunt. Helping women get HPV vaccines was top on our list of possible causes to support. We realised that because we wanted to include something really meaningful we'd gone beyond what a few bucks in the bank could support and we needed to start looking for sponsorship. Our planned activity had escalated from bundu-bashing girls having fun in the sun to bundu-bashing girls having fun in the sun AND doing their damnedest to enable other girls to live their lives – and have fun in the sun too! Lofty ideas but we didn't recognise this at the time.

Through my lounge windows I idly observed the pouring rain and the wind whipping the trees around and as I wrote this chapter I couldn't have been more contented. My thumb injury was giving me a break from work so I could use this down time to brainstorm with Lara, write and reminisce.

My affair with motorcycling goes back to when I was around 15 years old. A neighbourhood friend and I pooled our limited resources and together we bought a clapped out old Yamaha 100 twin which had just enough grunt left in it to make learning to ride a possibility and was enough fun to keep us riding. We zoomed (in reality, spluttered) around the 'burb', had a few entanglements with hedges and dogs and generally rode the area flat! As soon as I started working I bought a Yamaha DT 125 and took the next step riding wise – the sugar cane fields. Here my friends and I, all on our scramblers, raced each other through the narrow paths separating the fields of sugar cane. Dust, mud, sand, rain or shine we were there on weekends. These were the carefree days when crash helmets were not mandatory and suitable scrambling destinations aplenty. The Umgeni Valley was particularly attractive and presented some challenging riding as well as river crossings and steep hill climbs which invariably had most of us taking a tumble at some stage.

In those days you rode your bike into the ground before casting around for your next boney. The same went for spares – why change a part if it still had some life in it?

A popular pastime while riding through town was to dice all the other bikes from traffic light to traffic light. I knew the time had finally come to change the sprocket when I revved , dumped the clutch and instead of shooting off the mark I remained on the same spot with the rrrr, rrrr, rrrr noise of the chain desperately trying to get a grip on the teeth of the sprocket which were now worn down to vague stubs. Ignominiously I would have to assist by pushing with my legs still astride the bike before the tenuous grip of chain on stubs would get me going again!

My new but actually very second-hand DT 175 never went as well as the DT 125 despite a talented friend painting flames across the tank and painting my helmet to match. Although I considered myself to be as hot as the flames on my helmet and motorcycle, this bike was a disappointment. Thereafter I shared my love of bikes as well as the bikes, with my husband, Rob. We had a Honda Elsinore 250cc two stroke, which carried us, as well as our luggage to Cape Town and back, a distance of 3,500 kilometres. At some stage we had a Kawasaki Big Horn 350cc, fondly known as the Kwaka – this was the hardest to kick-start, and if you didn't get the compression just right, which sometimes took a bit of manoeuvring, you would be unceremoniously launched and could count yourself lucky if you had remembered to fold back the passenger foot peg and didn't cut your heel open on the peg's serrations. Many a chivalrous guy came to grief after witnessing me positioning the kick-start lever and then insisting that he knew the correct way to kick-start this bike. I would stand back and observe the action, trying hard not to laugh.

Then we made a decision that we wanted to sail around the world and much to friends and family's utter disbelief we packed up, sold everything off and relocated to Canada where we proceeded to build the boat we would eventually put to sea in. While living, working and building our boat in Vancouver we bought a Honda XL 350cc and travelled to Toronto and back to visit South African friends, camping en-route in our two man tent and scaring ourselves to pieces with visions of marauding bears whenever a twig snapped. Eventually we realised that all that twig snapping while we cowered white-knuckled and pop-eyed in the tent was caused by foraging squirrels! Before leaving Vancouver, Rob welded up a luggage rack which he theorised would double as a backrest for the pillion passenger. Unfortunately for us the combination of the weight of the luggage and the vibration of the motorcycle proved fatal for the rack, which cracked and broke within the first few hundred kilometres. The luggage was too heavy for me to carry on my back so I rode the motorcycle the rest of the way to Toronto and Rob was pillion, the unstable load on his back periodically causing me to weave alarmingly across the road. We froze across the Rocky Mountains, stopping long enough to thaw out in a motel, in a bathtub filled to the brim with hot water, before continuing our crazy jaunt.

It is interesting how we adventured with an attitude of "no worries mate". We didn't think twice about doing this 8,500 kilometre round trip in Canada. Now it seems that in order to have a great adventure, great planning is necessary. I guess that can in itself be exciting but not having spontaneity can also be a drag. We seem so weighed down by our commitments to careers, work, children, pets and homes, and I know that as a result I have allowed my passion for wild exploits to dim from time to time. Now and again I force myself to take stock, examine my life, recharge the batteries and give myself a reason to get excited.

Thereafter motorcycling became something of the past. Rob and I built our yacht, Moya, over the next three years and with abundant jubilation set sail for Hawaii one fine spring day. Cruising through South Sea island archipelagos was the stuff fantasies are made of; I imagined I had found heaven. Every so often my dreams became nightmares and heaven became hell when I couldn't overcome severe seasickness and when extreme weather conditions made sea and sky indistinguishable.

Unbelievably we later exchanged our lovely Moya for a smallholding in Australia complete with motorcycle! This motorcycle was special, a real bling machine – the ex-owner had boosted the 750cc Honda to 820cc's, chromed visible parts and had upholstered the seat in plush red velvet! It was perfect for my antenatal visits to the hospital in Adelaide about 30 kilometres away. My growing tummy rested comfortably on the tank, the going was smooth, and the bike an absolute treat to ride. Life was good. Although we didn't know it at the time as we shunned the notion of finding out the baby's sex via ultrasound, this was to be our daughter's first introduction to motorcycling, in-vitro motorcycling!

A dry motorcycling spell followed and it wasn't until about 10 years later that I had the opportunity to circumnavigate Los Angeles on a borrowed bike. This was, at 1500cc's, by far the biggest bike I had ever ridden – a Honda Goldwing. It had gigantic fairings and a sound system that had the music volume increasing as speed and wind noise increased. It was exuberating; it was a challenge and pleasurable but this big bike was too cumbersome for me so my motorcycling juices weren't stimulated into flowing.

Many long and difficult years followed. My marriage fell apart as my husband's only true love was the sea and sailing. By that stage we had two children, so my focus was on trying to be the finest parent I could be for my children. Necessities were the order of the day and I never thought about motorcycling again. Many years later, at the age of 53, all that changed. (Maybe this was my somewhat delayed midlife crisis, or more aptly, a menopausal crisis). I had been involved in a reality show and in a conversation with the producer he mentioned that he might like to do a documentary on over-landing through Africa on Harley Davidsons. My response was so enthusiastic I think the poor man had no option but to suggest that I come along if I wanted to. I suspected that a Harley would not be suitable for traversing Africa and seeing as I hoped to be in a support role on this production I didn't need to be filmed on a Harley and could choose whatever I wanted. I started surfing the net, gathering information on suitable dual-purpose motorcycles.

Eventually I determined that the best bike for me and the one most suited to the task would be the Yamaha XT 660R, so I went ahead and bought one. Disappointingly the production was canned but I felt so thankful to the producer for giving me justification to buy this bike in the first place; I had no intention of getting rid of it.

Marvellous times followed. I was befriended by a group of knowledgeable off-roaders who believed that we could ride anywhere on anything… and we did. We rode in isolated areas, river valleys and boulder-strewn forgotten service paths; alongside railway tracks, gravel roads seemingly covered with marbles they were so slippery, and through vegetation and sand. Of course I was completely out of my depth in terms of skill and know-how but I adopted the attitude of "if they can do it, I will do it too", and I never slowed them down and gamely kept up whatever the terrain.

On the island of Pemba, Tanzania, I rode pillion on a bike which anywhere else in the world would have been destined for the scrap-heap. However, nothing can keep a Honda CG 125 down, especially one with flames on the tank! With our backpacks strapped on to the luggage carrier, we clattered around the island on pot-holed tar roads, dirt roads and beach sand. We fell off once at relatively low speed and the driver, Mountin' Man sustained

a minor burn on his leg from the exposed exhaust pipe. I leapt out of the way with alacrity!

In Nepal I once again rode pillion with Mountin' Man, again on a 125cc motorcycle with the alluring name of Yamaha Enticer. This little machine, fully loaded with the same two backpacks, purred all the way from Kathmandu to the Chitwan National Park via Pokhara and back, faultlessly. It took all sorts of horrible terrain in its stride, including stony passes and fairly deep river crossings.

Back in Durban I continued my pleasurable, sometimes challenging weekend riding on the Yamaha XT 660R. Many, many falls later, while attempting rides that should only be attempted on motocross or enduro bikes by someone with more proficiency than I had, I adopted Lara's advice and bought a lightweight, trail bike and joined her on the track and in the bush.

My brother helped source the right bike, a Suzuki 125, wrapped it in bubble wrap and sent it from Cape Town to me in Durban. When the freight truck arrived at my office with my 'gift wrapped' bike I was as excited as a kid on Christmas Day and couldn't resist ripping off the bubble wrap and trying the bike out in the parking lot, high heels and smart office attire notwithstanding. At the first possible opportunity I joined Lara and Clayton on the track… and promptly ruptured my thumb ligament.

Lara astounded me by being a biking 'natural'. She learnt how to control a motocross bike in about half an hour and immediately joined us on a variety of bikes for a four-hour off-road enduro. This little group included my brother, Paul, a motorcycling veteran and his motocross competing daughter, Wendy. His other daughter, Kelly, also rode with us. Lara had a great time and this stimulated her into buying her first bike, a Honda CR 80R, a two stroke suitable for track riding and the one she considered using for our trip.

Lara joined me with this diminutive motorcycle for a ladies' biking day; I was on a Yamaha TTR 230, kindly sponsored by a Yamaha dealership for the day. We raced around the motocross track, flying into the air off tabletops, and we scared ourselves to smithereens with bad landings which we somehow miraculously righted at the last moment. We splattered each other with the mud flinging off our knobbly tyres and only stopped when our arms and legs became too shaky with fatigue to continue. With our plastic breast protector plates we looked like filthy Madonnas but we couldn't wipe the smiles off our faces. After topping up our energy reserves we attempted the enduro track, racing each other along the narrow, twisty paths, slipping and sliding through streams, one with a challenging vertical bank on the other side. This exercise showed us just what the bikes were capable of and most importantly what we were capable of; we were awed by these little machines and pleased by our own performance. The day ended on a high when we each won a much-needed pair of riding goggles. We were exhausted by sundown but also invigorated by the excitement of the adrenaline-inducing riding.

Of course Lara's boyfriend, Clayton, was not immune to the motorcycling frenzy now building around him and eventually succumbed after Lara sourced a coveted two stroke motorcycle for him. So when Clayton started exploring the possibility of joining us I wasn't in the least surprised. Initially he was anxious at the thought of attempting the unfamiliar; then he felt that it was a pipe-dream but as time passed by he could no longer resist the allure of an expedition of this magnitude. He realised that this opportunity might not present itself again and that he should grab it while the going was good. He also understood that he would be stepping out of his comfort zone into the unknown as he had never done anything like this before, but ultimately

I think that his personal growth on this lengthy sojourn outstripped ours.

Preparation

Our planned excursion kept on snowballing. We had done our homework and we discovered that our initial contemplation of HPV vaccines wasn't feasible. This was disappointing news but after much consideration and investigation we decided that condoms and contraceptive injections might be a more achievable idea.

These we would take to difficult to access clinics for distribution. A recent World Health Organisation press release stated that 'almost half of the 600,000 pregnancy-related deaths occur in Africa which has only 12 percent of the world's population', and that 'the highest levels of adolescent pregnancy are in Sub-Saharan Africa where every second woman gives birth to a child before the age of 20'. Saddening statistics! Eventually we would not be able to get a donation of, or raise the sponsorship required for, the purchase of contraceptive injections. However a family operated concern, RRT Medcon, generously donated many large boxes of condoms which we hoped to carry in an accompanying 4x4 vehicle and distribute at remote clinics. Unfortunately the 4x4 backup vehicle that we needed never materialised, but we had a volunteer who kindly helped us later with the distribution of these condoms in northern KwaZulu-Natal.

I often sensed that Lara was cracking the whip and I was jumping. However that was not necessarily a negative factor. So when she insisted I do the 'marketing' side of the expedition I took this task on to my already overflowing plate. I can now state with authority that trying to market this and actually achieve some degree of success was very, very difficult and more time consuming than you can imagine. I applaud all those adventurers out there who sell themselves so successfully that they end up with solid, see-the-project-to-the-end sponsorship. Apart from the condoms, the sum total of our sponsorship was two Leatt neck braces supplied by Leatt Brace for which we were grateful.

While working on all of this I tried to keep up some semblance of a social life and not disappear altogether on my friends. This created tension between Lara and me, with her feeling that I wasn't giving enough attention to her or my kin and that my friends were getting too much attention. I began to feel down-hearted as this project was all about spending time with Lara and I speculated on how our relationship would progress once we were on the road facing real challenges. Sometimes I even doubted if our relationship would take the strain. Clayton's role at this stage was not really defined, possibly because this excursion had initially been a mother/daughter plan. At this time I also began to doubt their commitment to the project. I so badly wanted things to turn out well. I thought that I must always remember to retain a reasonable sense of humour even under trying circumstances but as you will see later in the narrative I let myself down a few times.

Together Lara and I trawled through maps, magazines and books, the internet and Google Earth for information which was all part of the preparation but we knew that at the end of the day the only thing that was going to work was simply to get on the bikes and go and find out for ourselves. We decided we needed to have at least a rough blueprint of where we wanted to go, but we needed to be flexible and be prepared to change the route as we went along. Getting off the beaten track was one of our priorities but what we failed to realise was that some of the main roads in Mozambique and Malawi were so bad we felt as though we were completely off the beaten track anyway.

The ongoing debates over the wiring and registration of the bikes became an irritation and I opted to sell the 125cc Suzuki and buy a slightly bigger bike which I'd probably prefer. After having read Lois Pryce's excellent book, 'Red Tape and White Knuckles', I determined that a Yamaha TTR 250 would be perfect. I quickly discovered that these bikes are like hens' teeth in South Africa so redoubled my efforts in obtaining one. Eventually I unearthed 'The Bike', a 2005 model, only used (thrashed is probably the right word) off-road. It had no lights and was unlicensed and somewhat beaten up but perfect. I was able to license it without any hassle and then took it to a motorcycle shop, M. Motorcycles, in a nearby southern suburb for a wiring loom, speedometer, lights, indicators, neutral pick-up light, hooter, carry rack, a service, a thorough check for any problems and sundry other bits and pieces.

I instructed them to be sure to spray the air filter with air filter oil as I had washed this filter and it was bone dry. This company agreed to do the job for a specified price which I paid. At the conclusion they reneged on the deal and I had endless problems with almost everything they had done. I must give them credit for the carry rack they fabricated. It was simple and it worked well. They took about three weeks to complete the job and within a few hours of collection the headlights and indicators stopped working, the neutral pick-up light flickered in all gears and the hooter was intermittent, so I returned it. This happened again the second time around, so a large male acquaintance took it back and this time things worked. I guess the mechanic decided that he was not the right person to mess with! They couldn't even fit a clutch lever. The one they had used didn't fit as it was the wrong shape and prevented the lever from being fully pulled in. They fitted such a huge back sprocket that I think I'd still be riding if I hadn't changed it for a suitable one – at my expense of course as they refused to change it even though the bike hadn't been ridden. Ultimately though, everything they had done packed up and despite checking with them twice when the bike was in their workshop, I discovered in Mozambique that they hadn't even sprayed the oil filter; it was still bone dry and worryingly sandy.

We were running out of time. The vitriolic arguments with M. Motorcycles had to stop (they had their bucks and I wasn't getting anywhere with them) and a decision had to be made – do I take my chances and go on this bike as it is? I cogitated long and hard about this and no alarming noises being present I made up my mind; we were good to go.

As luck would have it Lara popped into Cyclecraft Yamaha and there it was. The bike for her, a Yamaha XTZ 125cc! It was in fair condition, the price was right so she bought it. She was then the proud owner of two motorcycles.

In the meantime Lara, Clayton and I got down to the serious business of learning for our motorcycle drivers' licences which we all passed on the first go with no problems whatsoever. This was a startling event as we had heard stories of many people not passing on the first try unless a little gratuity changed hands beforehand. We had driven 150 kilometres to a small town north of Durban to do our licences as the backlog in the city was many months long. On our way back to Durban, Clayton bought a 'pre-loved' Yamaha XTZ 125cc, the owner threw in a helmet to sweeten the deal and Clayton had his first ride on this schoolboy commuter bike. He now also owned two motorcycles so between the three of us we had six bikes!

On May 20, 2009, we posted this on our motorcycling madness website:

Escape in August – September 2009

Are you a mad, adventurous motorcyclist or 4x4 owner who has what it takes!!!

SIX WEEKS OF MIND-BLOWING ADVENTURE MOTORCYCLING AND 4X4 EXPERIENCES

It's going to be tough, fun, demanding, wild, challenging, and at times dangerous but the best trip ever! This is a once in a lifetime experience!

We would especially like women to join us in our mission to promote "women have the right to choose". We will be riding small capacity dual purpose motorcycles and will be travelling the less travelled route.

"Enjoy life; no-one gets out alive".

...... to which we had absolutely no response at all, so it was down to the three of us.

Departure

The rough outline was to leave from Durban and head for a meal of prawns washed down with the local beer, Dois M, in Maputo, Mozambique, then set off up the coast, taking little sand roads to who-knows-where along the way. From who-knows-where to somewhere well after Vilanculos and just before Beira we planned to head inland and cross the Zambezi on the Dona Ana Bridge, the longest railroad bridge in Africa. From there the plan became a little vaguer but the general idea was to head for Lake Malawi, the southernmost lake in the East African Rift system, board the famous old ferry, the M.V. Ilala, with the motorcycles and disembark at the northern side of the lake which would be about the right time to start heading for home. Of course we planned to visit an island or two and to snorkel amongst the famed cichlids (small, brightly coloured fish) at Cape Maclear before meandering back to South Africa.

Meanwhile I bought heavy duty tubes and brand new tyres from East Coast Kawasaki, who gave me appropriate tyre advice, bought a few spares and two 10-litre jerry cans, tested the loaded bike the day before we left and I was 'A' for away! We wore minimal protective gear but did feel that proper riding boots were essential and we would definitely recommend boots, gloves, neck brace and helmet as the absolute minimum requirement. I wore a jacket most of the way as well but sometimes it was uncomfortably hot. I kept it on regardless as sun protection must be taken into consideration.

We made decent progress with all the last minute running around. Lara concentrated on her and Clayton's packing arrangements while Clayton and I concentrated on detailed route planning. This itinerary was to provide a skeleton for our big ride with many changes along the way.

"I need a stiff vodka," were Lara's words as she climbed off her bike having test ridden it for five kilometres, fully loaded!

I laughed and responded, "Only about 7,995 kilometres more to go, La."

August 3, 2009

Our friends gave us an initial send off from North Beach in front of Joe Cools one Saturday morning at 8:00 am and then an awesome send-off after a very late breakfast at Beach Bums at Casuarina Beach on the KwaZulu-Natal North Coast. Lara wobbled her way to Richards Bay where our friend, Tjaart, adjusted the rear shock-absorber to the hardest setting which solved the wobbling problem. In the meantime Clayt discovered his packing arrangement didn't work as his bike was so top heavy it simply fell over when he put the side stand out in an attempt to park it!

Gales of laughs later we ended up at Bushbaby's Campsite, which is about eight kilometres along a dirt road outside of Hluhluwe. We watched the rugby in a festive atmosphere in a large thatched communal lounge area. Even with the teething problems we managed to cover 320 kilometres on our first day.

The following day was the first of only two rainy days while on our holiday, so August is certainly the month to do it in if you want to avoid the rain. However I think we received five days worth as it poured all day, so we only got as far as Golela on the Swaziland border. Clayton's spark plug popped out on the muddy, slippery, dirt road but he managed to pop it back into its place without a problem. We were cold, wet, grimy and happy, and thankfully stumbled across a warm chalet at the Sodwana Angling Club to put the finishing touch to the day! The chalet even had a verandah for our bikes! We were turned away by the KZN (KwaZulu-Natal) Campsite because we were on motorcycles. A good thing too as tents wouldn't have provided the warmth and comfort that we had in the chalet. We took advantage of the fireplace and dried our clothes to a smelly, smoky crispness.

The KwaZulu-Natal Campsite as well as the Sodwana Angling Club chalets are tucked away on an insignificant road just off the main route to Mozambique. The key attraction here is Lake Jozini or Pongolapoort Dam on the Pongola River, which supports a massive population of fish, hippos and crocodiles. It is popular as a tiger fishing destination with the lake supporting the southern-most distribution of these predatory fish. The Pongola Game Reserve borders the dam and buffalo, wildebeest, giraffe, zebra, kudu, bushbuck, duiker, steenbok, hyena, cheetah, wild dog, serval, warthog and even the occasional leopard can be seen. The birdlife is fantastic with sightings of over 350 different species. Years ago my son, Justin, and I spent a pleasurable weekend camping in the reserve, brushing up on our bird identification skills. We both ended up with tick bite fever but we had been careless in that we had relaxed on our backs directly on the dry grass, making it easy for ticks to gain access to our bodies.

Generally the weather behaved itself. Of course the further north we found ourselves the hotter it got and I longed for my ventilated motorcycling jacket, which in the interests of saving space, I had left at home. I sweltered in the hiking jacket that had taken preference as I planned to use it for my ascent of Mount Mulange in Malawi. I had brought three sets of clothing and a sarong – one set of riding/hiking clothing, one set of non-riding, relaxing clothing and one set of 'jolling' (going out) clothing which I only wore once so they could have been left behind. My advice here is taking as little as you can get away with but don't forget the sarong which has a multitude of uses.

My sarong was used for what it was intended, as a wrap, as well as a towel to dry myself and to lie on, on the beach. I have used it as a headscarf on a Moslem island, a neck scarf and as a shawl to stop my arms from getting sun burnt; on hot nights it doubled as a sheet, and on hot days where there was no shelter I rigged it up to provide shade. It's been a tablecloth, it hauled gear on Mount Mulange when I wore it backpack style and it's even carried a baby when used as a sling over one shoulder. I have read that it can be used to filter water by folding it in such a way that the water strains through at least eight layers. Apparently this cuts down on the chances of being infected by a water-borne disease! No wonder it's used in so many communities – sarong, pareu, kapulana are some of the names this simple length of fabric is known by.

— 2 —

Sashaying Through Swaziland And Into Mozambique

Riding through Swaziland was an absolute pleasure. Most of the time we seemed to have the well sign-posted road all to ourselves. The smooth tar surface was unblemished and we surmised that either the roads are regularly resurfaced or there's not much traffic to mar or damage the roads. Fences line the road on either side and we came across the occasional restaurant along the way. We had a forced roadside stop when Lara discovered that the nut, bolt and lock washer arrangement on her rear sprocket was working loose. This was problematic as it was not possible to screw it back into place, despite considerable joint effort.

We weren't unduly worried as the riding was easy and there was minimal strain on her rear sprocket but we kept a sharp look out for a suitable shop at which to buy another bolt. We crossed the border into Mozambique at a somewhat chaotic Namaacha where we stopped for a relaxed lunch before continuing on the now very busy road to Maputo. Eventually, just outside Maputo, at a greasy roadside spare parts shack we bought an old bolt which solved the problem. The predatory vendor, seeing Lara's desperation, charged her the exorbitant price of ZAR 70.00. (ZAR 20.00 would have been too much.) Lesson learnt – carry a modest selection of nuts and bolts with you.

We wove our way through the heavy traffic, dodging the rest of the drivers-with-a-death-wish and luckily I avoided a close call with a bus, much to Lara's heart-stopping distress. Then at last, Maputo and heaven in the form of gigantic tiger prawns, fresh barracuda and ice cold Dois M's, a fine local beer. I hauled out my kapulana (the Mozambican name for sarong), wrapped myself in it and felt right at home! The weather was balmy and the temperature perfect.

From here on down the coast we could look forward to seafood and Dois M, hopefully ice cold, at the conclusion of a hard day's riding. We rode nearly every day, covering distances up to 488 kilometres (our longest day). On our 'relax' days we would invariably ride anyway – there was so much to see and do!

Four days after departure the bulk of my 'new' just-installed-by-a-motorcycle-company, electrics packed up. The only other mechanical problems were minor; Lara and Clayton's chains needed adjusting a lot of the time. The chains seemed to stretch very quickly, fly off the rear sprocket and then jam in the front sprocket. Clayton became a master at the art of the quick fix.

Bilene, on the shores of the calm Uembje lagoon, made up for it with its good gravel road and protected camping spot. The lagoon had been closed to the sea for years and on closer inspection an uninviting algae was growing thickly in the lagoon. As we gingerly walked on the slimy bottom, gaseous bubbles rose to the surface and discharged their foul odour. As a result the area was suffering a decline in tourism so we had the place to ourselves. We took a refreshingly long walk on the beach, along the shores of the lagoon and were perturbed to see a fake coconut palm being erected at a new development while the real thing lay chopped up on the ground next to the fake one. The market in Bilene was quite well stocked with food and assorted sundries, where we were able to buy fresh fruit, fish and veggies and finished off the day with a succulent fish *braai*.

I have heard, over a year later, that the lagoon has broken through into the sea and this area has, once again, become a swimming, snorkelling, fabulous holiday destination.

On our fifth day on the road, the pot-holes began and according to Lara the 'near death' incidents also began. We negotiated an extremely challenging soft beach-sand road, from Quissico to a deserted beach on the coast. It was swelteringly hot and the powder-soft sand was all churned up.

Many spills later we were all okay but exhausted. At one point I misjudged the curve, my front wheel twisted to one side in the sand and over I toppled, crashing down in a billowing cloud of sand with my leg trapped under the bike, the luggage tie-down clip on my knee supporting the entire weight of the bike. I screamed in agony and the lone old man impassively gazing at me from the side of the road didn't flinch. I carried on yelling until Lara and Clayton arrived and lifted the bike off me. The weathered old man observed all this with serene detachment, annoying in the extreme.

With a sense of relief we finally arrived at the appealing campsite between a lagoon and the beach, shaded by coconut palms. My indicators had packed up and while trying to find the problem, I found out that M. Motorcycles had also neglected to spray my air filter which was dry as a bone. Luckily I detected this early on and immediately sprayed it but unfortunately couldn't fix the electrics.

The camp, neatly tucked into the lee of the dunes and the impressive beach was well worth the taxing ride in. Once again we had the place completely to ourselves and revelled in the exquisite isolation. Whales were cavorting offshore, the sea was a magnificent blue, the surf was creaming in to the shore and the white beach stretched endlessly in both directions. Conveniently, in addition to our tents, we had the use of a baraka (a thatched roof supported by poles encircled by a half-height wall) and for two relaxing days we did nothing in addition to swimming, walking, eating and drinking milk stout around the fire.

In the owner's absence the person looking after the campsite chopped wood for us and had thoughtfully conjured up a crate of milk stout as he had been unable to fill our beer order.

(We were in such a remote area that the unthinkable had finally happened – no beer.)

I saw that the caretaker's companion was using an instrument to shred coconut, an instrument I hadn't come across since my cruising days in the Pacific many years ago. The shredded coconut is then squeezed in a muslin bag and the thick fatty milk extracted.

The early push out on damp sand was easier. I noticed that coming into these places on soft sand in the late afternoon was tougher than leaving on the same road in the morning.

In the afternoon the sand is dry and churned up by other vehicles. The dappled light through the trees makes judging the surface very difficult. In the morning you are strong and full of beans and the damp sand is fresh and feels much firmer. Also with the shadows at a different angle, one's judgement of the surface is more accurate, and there are no spills.

Our favourite lunch stop in Maxixe, pronounced Ma-sheesh, was fully booked… by the Mozambican president and his entourage! At least we now know we have fine taste. Maxixe, a thriving town, is situated in a bay opposite the town of Inhambane and throughout the day picturesque ferries and dhows can be seen crossing between the two. We had lunch at the nearby restaurant in the caravan site and then continued on the EN1 to Morrungulu.

We rode across the Tropic of Capricorn, an exciting milestone which elicited a "Whee hah, we're making good progress!" from Lara. At the 212 we turned right and once again headed for the coast on the hard-packed sand road and to our camp for the night.

We pitched our tents at the newly renovated, expensive but well-positioned Morrungulu camping grounds. The campsites were all grassed and we had an electrified thatched baraka to use as a kitchen. A sunset stroll on the white sandy beach topped the day off in style. Later, feeling a little restless, we made our way up to the communal area where we sat and caught fleeting glimpses between the rustling coconut palms of the full moon, which was at times obscured by scudding clouds. We could hear the wavelets gently lapping the shore and when the moon came out from behind the clouds it cast a silvery gleam over the water. It was all so romantic that I felt somewhat bereft at the thought of sleeping alone in my little tent with only my luggage for company!

From Morrungulu it was a fairly quick zoom to Vilanculos, dodging the ubiquitous pot-holes along the way. En-route we fuelled up at a quaint station where the pumps were hand operated. Once the tanks were full the operator extracted a calculator from his pocket, read off the number of litres from a meter on the pump and worked out what we owed him.

Vilanculos was a town we had been looking forward to visiting again but we were initially sadly disappointed.

Now it seemed like a rip-off joint, expensive (no value for money) and many places charged in U.S. dollars.

We were told that this was as a result of the devastating cyclone that had hit this area a few years ago and the locals were trying to recoup their losses. We felt sorry for them and their difficult circumstances; however we didn't feel that this justified fleecing tourists and in the long run, chasing tourists away by overcharging would be detrimental to them.

My pet hate is places that charge in U.S. dollars. This is not America, this is Africa – stick to your own currency! I have come across this quite often in my excursions here in Africa and it usually happens in the touristy areas. I have come to the conclusion that it is simply another way of lightening the tourist's pocket.

After arduous searching, riding minor roads, being chased by dogs and being offered dreadful, unhygenic litter-strewn campsites at over-the-top prices, we stumbled across an unofficial, appealing, clean, correctly priced camp on the beach which looked out over impossibly white sand and blue sea with dramatic views of the Bazaruto Archipelago in the distance and of picturesque dhows at anchor in the foreground.

We settled into Sid's campsite, unpacked the luggage from the bikes, erected the tents and felt right at home. This was our ninth day on the road, we were a little fatigued and the camp was so nice that we declared a rest day. After a well-deserved lie-in we washed, and then fiddled with and generally attended to the bikes. Clayton's front tyre was showing disturbing, uneven wear and he needed a new one. The camp owner, Sid, helped Clayton to more or less fix his dented rim which was causing the uneven wear, with a rectangle of wood and a hammer and gave me a bolt I needed for my exhaust guard. I didn't know it at the time but had I looked carefully for the missing bolt I would have found it jammed between the clutch cover gasket and the swing arm. I'll leave it to your imagination to guess what happened as a result of this.

After attending to these little chores we rewarded ourselves with heaps of steamed clams followed by a lazy siesta. We concluded the day with a gentle stroll along the beach. It was a lovely, relaxed day. On our return we luckily happened upon fishermen at the gate. Clayton haggled gamely and we had fresh fish for supper.

I reflected on where we would all be had we not done this trip and I considered myself so fortunate and privileged to be exactly where we were at that moment in time.

"Today was a challenging 407 kilometre ride to the shithole that is Inchope." That was Lara's opinion. I didn't mind it at all – just another grubby, crowded town with numerous hustlers out to try and make a fast buck. We met Roy Sadan, an around the world bicyclist and owner of a big red beard, and had a pineapple lunch with him in the shade of a huge tree. His positive attitude and his spellbinding stories were inspiring, his faith and trust in fellow humans humbling and we deemed ourselves lucky to have met him.

There was hardly any petrol available in the area we were going through, but we worked it out well and supplemented from our jerry cans when necessary. We camped under the Milky Way in the Inchope town park, between a run-down and busy intersection and a dingy restaurant. This overnight stop at Inchope was to prove a crossroads for Clayton; up until then we had always managed to find campsites that were clean, picturesque and quite 'First World'. I think if Clayton could have, he would have gone home at that point. We had even looked at some overnight rooms; Clayton merely blanched while rapidly beating a retreat to the 'campsite'. While he sat glumly on his bike, Lara and I put up the tents, hoping that the browsing goats didn't include tents in their diet. This 'campsite', for which we were charged, was covered in refuse, did not have a toilet or running water and the last straw for Clayt –the beers were over-priced! Well, as it turned out, he survived this 'campsite' and nothing fazed him after this; he was invincible! Later, he even ate a roadside purchase of a suspicious-looking kebab being waved around by a ragged vendor, something he would never do at home.

From Inchope we had an awesome ride, on this our 11th day on the road, 411 kilometres including a 132 kilometre detour to Chimoio, for Clayt to buy a new front tyre. Chimoio is the fifth-largest city in Mozambique and the capital of Manica Province. We stopped for fuel on the outskirts of Chimoio and while waiting our turn a disturbing scenario played out in front of us.

A stick-thin blind beggar woman was being led by her equally thin, ragged young son. He seemed to be about 14 years old and was clearly an angry young man. His leading consisted of yanking his mother along or pushing her in front of him. She stumbled rather than walked and kept up a steady stream of physical abuse and spittle-flying verbal abuse. She screamed and slapped, cackling when her slap met flesh but then paying for it by being violently yanked, pushed or kicked for good measure. They were driving prospective donors away with their behaviour and everybody shrank away as they approached. Eventually she indicated to her son that she needed to go to the toilet. He took her to the edge of the embankment where he pushed her over and she fell down. A few minutes later she reappeared and then with lightning speed and deadly accuracy, shoved her son over the edge of the embankment. He lost his balance and landed in the steaming pile of excrement she had deposited. They continued on their pathetic way and we felt heartbroken for both of them.

Clayton found a spares shop with ease and bought a tyre for less than he would have paid in South Africa. There is a lot to be said for riding a small bike in Africa where all the motorcycling inhabitants ride bikes of around 125cc's and under. He strapped the new tyre on top of his impressively towering load, to be used when the one on his front wheel died completely. Then we went food shopping in a large well-stocked supermarket. Outside the guarded supermarket an unsuspecting Lara and Clayton were swindled by unscrupulous money changers.

We passed gigantic baobabs, refuelled from our jerry cans at a fuel station that had run out of fuel and had a superb meander around Mount Gorongosa, but were saddened by large areas of deforestation and wood burning for the charcoal industry. I have since read that this region is being reforested in a carbon off-set initiative; however I gather that this is a temporary measure as eventually the trees die and release carbon dioxide and methane in the decomposition process which is actually worse for global warming. This area is worth exploring but unfortunately for us we had time constraints. Heaven was waiting for us at the end of the road from hell in the form of James Whyte Camp. We spread out in a delightful wooden chalet, luxuriated in the hot showers and indulged ourselves with delicious food in the restaurant after relaxing, ice cold beer in hand, around the outdoor fire. This is what makes an undertaking like this so worthwhile!

The next day was memorable; we had one pot-hole crash involving Clayton and Lara, I had a head-on collision while spanning the longest bridge in Africa, an interesting if somewhat primitive ferry transfer, disappointing hot springs, nightmarish roads and finally accommodation that Clayton hopes to forget. Crossing the Zambezi on the Dona Ana Bridge has to be one of the most exciting things I have done in a long time.

This astounding 3.7 kilometre railway bridge which links the towns of Vila de Sena and Muturara has a narrow, maybe one-metre wide, pedestrian lane alongside the tracks. Lara and Clayton accepted the helping hands that lifted their bikes up onto the bridge walkway, but I tried to ramp my bike up onto the bridge via a narrow shiny plank. Halfway up the wheels started spinning, I lost all traction and gazing with horror into the brown, churning, crocodile and hippo infested river below I started falling over. I was immensely grateful to the guys who caught me; obviously this is how they earned their daily living. This crossing was legendary. Halfway along, a 125cc motorcycle zooming from the opposite side and loaded with a toddler

on the tank, dad driving, mom hanging on for dear life, baby on her back in a sling and incredibly, some suitcases behind her, crashed head-on into me. They all fell off, got up, dusted themselves down, hopped back on and expertly wobbled off, exhaust spluttering. I, in the meantime, was trying to extricate my trapped, bruised and painful wrist from the bridge railing where my bike and I had been knocked on impact. We were all helped on our way by the locals who are, without fail, hospitable, friendly, super people. Apart from pedestrians carrying goats, chickens, and so on and other motorcyclists, there were numerous bicycles, mostly carrying cargo.

When we eventually reached the other side we were somewhat alarmed by the fact that there was no road. Of course we hadn't thought it through – there was no justification for a road and to illustrate the point at that moment we heard the blast of a train's whistle. As it passed we looked along its tracks hoping to see a path of some sort, but we saw nothing.

In my awful, broken Portuguese I asked someone the way to Mocuba and they pointed out a meandering pedestrian path through the huts of the village. This joined up with a track and eventually a corrugated dirt road.

We bounced along for kilometres on red earth and without warning arrived at the Shire River, a tributary of the impressive Zambezi River and the major outlet for Lake Malawi. We were offered passage across on tippy looking dugouts, whose owners assured us that motorcycles were no problem, but decided that this wasn't the time to save a few meticais and opted to cross the river on a rustic-looking ferry. The thick clumps of water hyacinth impeded the ferry but three men with long sticks were employed as water hyacinth deflectors and slowly, slowly we made our way across. This hand-operated, wood and iron ferry even transports massive container trucks across. We were told that this river, like the Limpopo, abounds with crocodile and hippo.

Not long after the river crossing Lara had a minor breakdown; her chain came off the rear sprocket and we stopped so that she could repair it. Within minutes hoards of children materialised and stood quietly scrutinising us. In order to access the tools Lara had to remove all her luggage and put it on the ground, so in effect, her gear was spread out around her mixed in with kids everywhere. To their credit and to our relief, not a thing was touched. One little boy, Mario, was particularly captivating and I thoroughly enjoyed our interaction without a word being spoken.

En-route we visited and were disappointed by the hot springs, which turned out to be a convenient laundry and body-washing spa for a local

village. People were hanging around naked or semi-naked, green soap was being used in abundance, the bushes were festooned with items drying, dogs, goats and chickens were listlessly scratching around and rubbish littered the immediate surrounds. This spot was shown on the map as 'hot springs' and I was proud to have found them as I was so looking forward to relaxing in their soothing, restorative warm waters. Hah!

Finally, after our eventful day we arrived in Morrumbala and battled to find accommodation. While riding around the town one of Lara's luggage tie downs came adrift and a piece of luggage fell off. She was unaware of this but when glancing in her rear view mirror she saw a boy running behind her. He was waving his arms and trying to get her to stop. He had been desperately trying to return her luggage! Later we were advised to sign ourselves in at the local police station, which we did, why I don't know and I don't think the police knew either. They were helpful and suggested we try for accommodation at the World Vision Aid Centre where we ended up spending the night on bunk beds in a cubby-hole sized room. We fell asleep to the crunching sound of minute insect mouths busily chomping away at the woodwork of the room we occupied. (Maybe this was the reason for Clayt's intense dislike of this place.) A memorable day indeed!

The following day was absolutely exhausting with some very tough but character-building riding. As usual it was clear skies and sunny, hot weather but it was one of those days that never comes to an end, a day when you keep saying to yourself, "How much further?" We rode until our behinds were throbbing and then we rode some more. We had two lengthy bike chain adjustments with the interested locals crowding around us as usual. This started getting on Lara's nerves. We weaved, we slid, we cursed but still, we wouldn't have it any other way. In the end we all agreed that the 200 kilometres to Mocuba through deep corrugations, soft sand, wash-aways and pot-holes was the hardest section so far.

Finally we were on to black, fresh tar but it only lasted a pitiful five kilometres and then upsettingly it deteriorated into the worst road we had yet seen and that's saying a lot given what we had encountered so far! Later we were agreeably surprised by the last 100 kilometres to Gurue on good tar, which was a blessing as by this stage we were driving in the pitch dark with only Clayton's headlight providing any satisfactory illumination. We broke our own rule of not travelling after dark and noticed that Lara and my headlights were so dim as to be useless. Clayton's headlight was good, so we had to stick behind him in 'V' formation into Gurue.

By the time we reached Gurue, where we stayed for two nights, we were utterly exhausted. The accommodation in Gurue was predictably dismal.

There was no camping ground or anywhere suitable to pitch our tents in this bustling town so we went and had a look at the local hotel, which we simply could not bring ourselves to stay in.

Even worse, we'd have to leave our bikes out in the street as they had no suitable parking. Diagonally across the road was a building even more dilapidated looking which had 'Backpackers' written down one wall. The writing was chipped and faded and clearly had been there for a long time. On enquiring, we discovered that no one actually knew what the word

'Backpackers' meant or why it was written on the building. However, they had rooms to rent and most importantly, a safe, locked yard to park our bikes in.

Tired as we were it was difficult to ignore the night-time business being conducted in the alley-way alongside this building. The sole member of this one-woman business had a steady flow of customers, most of them lustfully noisy, drunk or both. Periodically screams and shouts would erupt and we imagined that a dispute over the price of services rendered was taking place. The next morning we felt as exhausted as she must have. Luckily by the following night the weariness was so intense nothing could have kept us awake. Possibly the same applied to her.

On day 14 we had a wonderful time messing around Gurue. We explored the colourful market, were amazed at the entrepreneurial abilities of some of the stallholders, ate a few street delicacies and took a few photos.

Second-hand shoe stalls do brisk business. The shoes had all been

washed, renovated and polished to a shine. Those that weren't sandals had been stuffed with old newspaper to keep or perhaps give them shape. We speculated as to where they had all come from.

Later we indulged in exploratory riding through the hills in the manicured tea plantation where we had an easier time of it without the cumbersome luggage. We came across a carefully tended oasis, clearly a small sanctuary with religious artefacts, and we stretched our legs hiking while looking for a cave depicted on our map of the area and found a stately picturesque home in ruins, overlooking Gurue. We were taken aback when a man in his underwear and a scantily clad young woman came out of the house and beckoned us. We chatted to them and it seemed as though they were having a saucy afternoon tryst. When they told us that the roof of the outbuilding had been stolen the day before, we felt as if we were in South Africa. Then they suggested we come inside and join them in drinking alcoholic spirits. We graciously declined and continued our sightseeing through the hilly tea plantation.

When we got back we joined the queue at the fuel station for about half an hour before our turn at fuelling, then washed the bikes, cleaned the air filters and enjoyed a few beers while Lara and Clayton messed around with adjustments on their bikes. We planned to head for Malawi the following day as we were no longer catching the Saturday ferry in Cobu.

'I am almost too tired to press the buttons on my cell phone to sms Calvin today's blog' were my words at the end of the day. This is how it played out; we had a spectacular bump and bounce to Malema on a road best described as a bicycle track. We could see the fabled Malema Peaks in the distance. The surface of this track appeared firm and most of the time we kept up an acceptable speed and raced across it.

Now and then one of us would suddenly break though the firm crust and then battle to keep the front wheel from digging in and twisting in the soft sand below. At one point, the track suddenly disintegrated under me, my bike spun around 180 degrees and I took a headlong dive into the bushes. Lara and Clayton are still laughing, but were there in a split second to help me.

In the afternoon we took a challenging ride on footpaths, across rock faces, through streams and over boulders into the Malema Mountains where we were surrounded by breathtaking scenery.

Lara hoped we could find a suitably wild space to camp for the night but no matter how secluded the area appeared, within five minutes of stopping, people would materialise out of the forest or the bushes or maybe even the rocks and stare at us. The longer we stopped the larger the crowd became. It was disconcerting and disappointing.

Eventually we gave up and headed back to the unremarkable town of Malema where we rented a comfortable room in a large, fully furnished house which we had all to ourselves for the night. We were amused by the over-the-top space-ship light fittings and the abundance of kitsch decorations.

On the way to Mandimba, on the Mozambican side of the Malawian border, we came across an extraordinary building, more of a large block-shaped monument really. It was straddling the road even though there's nothing else there, no town, not even a visible village. Of course we stopped, took photos and appreciated the unpredicted break. As usual the weather

was perfect, the sun hot, the sky blue and the clouds prettily puffy.

This was another hard and hot day on horribly corrugated, dusty tracks which could hardly be called roads. I found I had to concentrate all the time on evaluating the road's surface, as well as looking out for pedestrians, animals, bicycles, contraptions that passed as vehicles, as well as each other. The bikes performed well and the carriers held out nicely.

In Malema we had made the decision to aim for Malawi but overnight at the border town of Mandimba en-route. We were forced to change our initial plans as our attempt to reach the ferry traversing Lake Niassa at Cobu on the Mozambican side had not been feasible. We simply ran out of time. After Mandimba we had hoped to indulge in sightseeing and maybe head on to Monkey Bay in Malawi instead of hanging around waiting on the ferry's schedule. Good thing too, as later, when we were on the ferry we discovered that it no longer came in to Cobu and we would have waited there in vain. The schedule had changed about a year ago but no one had thought to update the website or inform the tour operators.

As a matter of interest the lake is known as Lake Niassa (or Lake Nyasa or Lago Niasso) on the Mozambican side and Lake Malawi on the Malawian side. At its widest point this impressive 570 kilometre long lake spans 75 kilometres and is the third largest and second deepest lake in Africa and apparently the ninth largest in the world! It is shared by Malawi, Mozambique and Tanzania. Water enters the lake chiefly via the Ruhuhu River.

As for Mandimba, it was a dismal, uninspiring place and we were quite disappointed. After chatting to some of the informative, salt of the earth characters we met coming out of the local watering hole, our decision to press on through the border into Malawi was confirmed.

Once again we faced chaos at the border post resulting in a delay of three hours. Efficiency is not a strong point here but hey, this is Africa!

One of the things we had noticed in poverty stricken Mozambique was that many of the women of child-bearing age were pregnant and many had a breast-feeding toddler and a few youngsters in tow as well. This seemed to be the norm. We were quite shocked to find out later that the women in Malawi, equally poverty stricken, managed to outdo their fecund Mozambican sisters.

— 3 —

Malawi, The Warm Heart Of Africa And The Long Ride Home

The delay meant we had to proceed in the dark. Once again we ended up travelling at night with Clayton leading the way. We knew by the climbing and the twists and turns that we were missing out on spectacular scenery so we came back and did it again the next day and were well rewarded by the scenery.

Our first night in Malawi was spent at Palm Beach Campsite where we were happily introduced to the local beer, Kutche Kutche. Before we could take our first sip, the large resident dog had to have his share in a bowl placed on the counter at the pub! We were instant converts and like the dog, this beer became our sundowner of choice. We were amazed that at some places we paid the equivalent of only ZAR 4.00 for one quart of this beer. We were also introduced to the local hippo population here and judging by the loud grunts, we had camped way too close to their haunts, so midnight saw a somewhat panicked Lara urging us to drag our tents and shift our bikes to a safer section alongside the restaurant.

We woke up in a spectacular campsite with the lake 20 metres away. You'd think we would take a break from riding, but no, we then wandered back up the mountain pass to view the scenery which we'd missed the night before. Malawi seemed more organised than Mozambique and quite geared towards tourism. The biggest plus for us was the smooth tar road – at last!

We decided to catch the ferry up the length of Lake Malawi on the Friday, departing from nearby Monkey Bay. This gave us some much needed time to explore the area and do some work on our poor deserving bikes.

The highlight of our stay at Palm Beach was a visit to Liwonde National Park, a stopover to cherish. There is something a little nerve-wracking riding one's (very small) bike along a treacherous deep sand track with steaming elephant dung liberally scattered around. One almost expects to whack into an elephant around the next bend. We booked ourselves on a river tour and weren't disappointed; it had a Jurassic Park like quality, with animals in abundance – enormous crocodiles sunning themselves on

the river banks, well camouflaged monitor lizards hanging off bushes, rafts of bellowing hippo cavorting in the shallows, herds of elephant languidly grazing as they tramped along, warthogs snuffling around the mud, looking comical on their knees, and a variety of buck to fill the picture.

We'd been on the move for 19 days and sadly the time seemed to fly past in a blur. We were delighting in the trip so much and didn't want to think of it ending as we had established a happy rhythm to our days that could go on and on.

The next day dawned sunny and cloudless, a superb day for snorkelling, but that wouldn't be here so we left Palm Beach early in the morning with two goals. One, go to Monkey Bay and book our cabin on the M.V. Illala, the ferry across Lake Malawi to our destination and turn-around point, Chilumba, and two, snorkel off Cape Maclear. We had booked and paid for two private cabins by 10:00 in the morning and then spent the rest of the day exploring Cape Maclear.

Cape Maclear is busy, not the sort of place that would normally appeal to us but we wanted to visit it because we were hoping to see some of the numerous cichlid species which can be found nowhere else in the world. They can be divided into two main groups; the Mbuna cichlids which inhabit the shallow and rocky areas and the Peacock cichlids which can be found in the open waters in Lake Malawi.

Unfortunately, as with Vilanculos, Cape Maclear is completely over-touristy and the locals harass you constantly and talk in U.S. dollars. It really is a scenic place and one I would not like to have missed. There is plenty to do here but you need a tough hide. Even so, we enjoyed ourselves and had an unforgettable time there.

We motored in a local boat to a nearby island and snorkelled in a sheltered bay. The fish were like a myriad of jewels... sparkling turquoises, deep purples, luminous greens, bright yellows and 'dayglo' oranges.

Although the water was cooler than we had anticipated, we lazily drifted around for a couple of hours amongst these striking fish and the boulder-strewn scenery. If that was not enough, we were treated to a fish *braai* which attracted cheeky colourful lizards that were bold enough to snatch titbits from your hand. All the while the Fish Eagles called out for their share which they swooped down for. A sunset cruise back and an ice cold Kutche Kutche put the finishing touches to another perfect day in paradise!

Lake Malawi is like a sea. It has beaches with beach sand and islands and

when the wind blows it has big waves. I had to keep reminding myself that it's an inland lake, especially when I felt seasick in bad weather later that night. We had boarded the M.V. Ilala at her home port of Monkey Bay for the three day excursion to Chilumba, stopping at other ports en-route. Once again we believed that lightweight motorcycles were the way to go as they had to be manually lifted from the dock onto the foredeck of the ship, and then manhandled into place. We had reasonably luxurious but cockroach infested cabins, which forced Lara, who has a profound cockroach phobia, to pitch her tent on top of her bunk.

The stops were raucous and entertaining with about an hour of squawking, quacking, bleating and shouting madness, loading people, animals and goods on and off. Order was only restored upon our departure. At the stops we grabbed the opportunity for a flying visit of the local sights. I found the ideal way to do this was to hop on a bicycle taxi and be pedalled around by a young man with calves and buns of steel. This I did on our first stop of the day at Chipoka and ended up sharing cool drinks with a bunch of friendly locals we met on the way.

Then it was on to Nkhotakota, followed by a brief stop at a small village called Metangula on the Mozambican side of the lake. Our next stop was Likoma Island, where we walked up to St. Peter's Cathedral which deserves special mention as it is so out of place and such an architectural masterpiece. It was strange to see a building that looks like it belongs in Europe but was in the middle of a reed and thatch village. So many people got on board the dinghy to be ferried to the M.V. Ilala, that a woman with a baby strapped to her back lost her footing and fell awkwardly off the overloaded dingy. Luckily she was swiftly rescued although neither mom nor baby seemed the slightest bit disturbed. The mom shook herself off and the baby blinked rapidly and that was that. From then on there was a serious space problem on board the M.V. Illala. As Lara tried to get out of her cabin later, she almost stood on a sleeping man lying in the gangway and across the entrance to her cabin.

We were constantly assailed by a variety of interesting and intriguing smells on board. In fact, smell is part of the biking package. The acrid smell of smoke, the dank smell of wet foliage, the variety of smells as we passed markets or gatherings of people, the familiar smell as we approached the sea, the soft smell of dry sand… the list is endless and oh so enjoyable. Overall, the smells, the people and the country of Malawi truly deserve the title of "The Warm Heart of Africa".

Early the next morning we were awoken by the blast of the ship's horn signalling our arrival at Nkhata Bay. We waited until we thought the off-loading mayhem was over and stepped down to the lower deck to disembark. After 10 minutes of pushing and shoving, we gave up and resorted to climbing through the railings and over the side, then jumping onto the dock.

We ambled around Nkhata Bay, bought some fruit and a few lengths of colourful cotton fabric suitable for kapulanas and all too soon we headed back for the next leg of this splendid 'Out of Africa' voyage. During the night the wind and waves picked up as a storm hit us. At the next stop, the waters were stormy and violent, there was no moon, and it was pitch dark. We stared as people, chickens and goats were loaded into the heaving, overcrowded dinghy and chugged off into the darkness. Around midnight, we arrived at Chilumba where our bikes were swiftly and efficiently off-loaded.

The voyage on the M.V. Ilala had been an extraordinary experience and one of the things I had been dying to do for years. She really is a rust bucket of a ship and I say that most affectionately. I didn't trust the water from her tanks and used my reliable MSR ceramic water filter, nor did we trust the food being sold aboard so we cooked our own food, using our camping stove. This ferry's role on Lake Malawi is a crucial one as she is the link the secluded villages depend on for their survival.

As soon as we were deposited on shore we checked the bikes, located the correct road and managed to find our way in the all-encompassing darkness, lit by our unsatisfactory headlamps, to the unfriendly Sangilo sanctuary. This was not a sanctuary at all but a campsite. We battled to erect the tents and in the morning I discovered that my tent was on a stinky mound of dog faeces. Our 1:00 am arrival did not endear us to the grumpy camp owner, who, one would think, was acquainted with the M.V. Illala's timetable and would welcome customers at any time of the day or night.

By 7:00 the next morning we had struck camp, packed up and were off to Livingstonia in the mountains, accompanied by rain. Our first bombshell was the shocking state of the road which continued deteriorating the harder it rained. Eventually we were reduced to walking speed as our tyres, boots and bikes clogged with clay and we started sliding around. The locals obviously knew the drill. They were out in force in the downpour, kindly

helping to push the bikes as we tried to power our way up.

Many hairpin bends later we reached Livingstonia exhausted, filthy and ravenous. At the renowned Stone House, where we had hoped to spend the night, we ordered breakfast and its arrival was our second nasty shock. A 'full English breakfast' on the menu, which we checked and double-checked with the waiter as consisting of eggs, bacon, toast and jam with coffee arrived as tea bags with a thermos of cold water and some sort of oily, fried brown item on the plate. Disgusted, we left, and still hungry, had to face going back down that intestinal nightmare of a road. Luckily the rain had stopped and although hazardous the road wasn't as bad as it had been coming up.

Along the way we turned off to Lukwe Eco Camp where we were welcomed and treated to a real breakfast. The generous owner insisted we have a cabin for the same price as a camping site, which had a bird's eye view down the valley. Close to the camp we passed through an enchanting permaculture garden which I hoped to emulate at home, then we hiked through lush rain forest in spectacular mountainous terrain to the highest waterfall in Malawi, the 125 metre high Manchewe Falls. Feeling happy with life we finished off the day with a few cold ones around the fire. This is a campsite we can definitely recommend.

The next morning we noticed that the road had thankfully dried out, so we had an easy time of it. We passed through many police checkpoints, with friendly and inquisitive policemen manning them. Our ride took us past a rubber plantation, banana plantations, a coal mine and sugar cane plantations. We stopped at Flame Tree Lodge at Chintheche, just past Nkhata Bay where we had an early night for a change. Mosquitoes are a nuisance along the lake and all the campsites seemed to have their fair share but this campsite was plagued by these zizzing little monsters.

I lay in my sleeping bag reflecting on events so far. It was day 25 and we had reached our furthermost point at Chilumba and were now homeward bound. Although we still had loads of exploring and the unknown in front of us, given the option I think we could all quite happily have kept on riding through Africa. Malawi was terrific and the Malawian people, as with the Mozambican people, had been friendly, informative and helpful. There were times when our gear was spread all over the road while we searched for an elusive spanner and although we were consistently the object of fascination for the locals who tended to crowd around us, nothing was ever so much as touched. Violent crime seems to be a rarity and unheard of in most areas. We never felt in any way threatened or nervous as we do in South Africa. I wonder why this is so? Even the police at the numerous roadblocks were courteous and simply waved us on our way after a few basic enquiries.

There were many occasions when we were truly grateful to have small lightweight bikes. I feel that these bikes are perfect for the African roads and the surprises which kept popping up in the form of the dodgiest ferries across fast flowing rivers like the Shire River, planks laid haphazardly across gaping holes in the road, the talcum powder soft sand to the Quissico Beach Campsite, and the 19 hairpin bend road to Livingstonia that turned into slippery clay on the only other day it rained. My Yamaha XT 660R was safely parked in my garage at home and I never once regretted my decision to leave it behind. Only now and again did I think, "However, on my next trip where I anticipate better roads… "

We continued heading south along Lake Malawi, partaking in a spot of kayaking, swimming and hiking. I had developed a worrying oil leak which I diagnosed as a leaking clutch cover gasket. My remedy was to top up to the halfway mark when it needed oil, which was roughly every second day. Clayton's tyre was showing canvas as the wheel was still dented and the tyre was wearing unevenly. Lara's many spills were starting to take their toll on her bike's plastics, but luckily not her body.

We realised we needed money – kwacha. We rode into a dodgy looking little town and were directed down a dusty road to a sugar factory. Strange, we thought. Lo and behold, we rounded a corner and there was a Standard Bank with an ATM! We tried our ABSA bank debit cards, not anticipating much, but to our astonishment the machine started spewing out fistfuls of cash! Problem solved. On a different note, we were amused by a conversation we had with a local tour guide who we met while standing in the queue at the ATM. He said that the people there knew about our South African President Zuma and his famous shower episode and that the locals said they were glad he was not their president.

We came across a marvellous campsite at Fish Eagle Bay, right on the beach, which we had all to ourselves. After pitching tents and having a glorious, cooling swim we settled down to a good old South African *braai* while being treated to yet another magnificent sunset. We were unanimous in thinking, "Whew, can it get any better than this?"

We woke up to the perfect day – sunny, warm and clear skies. So we forgot biking and said hello to kayaking! The gentle swell provided entertainment as we explored the nearby, rocky outcroppings. Later Clayton worked on changing the tyre, which was showing canvas patches. Finally he was going to use the tyre he had bought in Chimoio and reduce the bike-toppling height of his load. Two local dreadlocked artists adorned Clayton's T-shirt and my bike with traditional art while keeping their eyes red and their creative juices flowing with puffs of 'Malawi Gold'.

Our going was good down the coast to Selima where, at a fuel stop, we spent some time chatting to George, a fellow overlander travelling all by himself on his well-appointed motorbike, riding from Cape to Cairo and loving every moment. Later we were to hear that sadly he had had a nasty accident and had returned home with his health intact but no motorbike.

We pushed on to Senga Bay on Lake Malawi and found Cool Runnings Campsite – true to its name. The campsite was shady, cool and grassed (excuse the pun) and had a homely restaurant overlooking the lake. Clayton had his sights fixed on chilling at the beach while Lara and I taxied to the one and only internet café in the town. We tried to upload our photographs onto our website at this impossibly small internet café but unfortunately in Malawi, as with Mozambique, the internet connection hardly functions and we were unsuccessful.

We arrived there on the pillion seats of two bicycle taxis. These bicycle taxis are such a clever idea. The industry is regulated and the operators all have their discs visibly displayed. I reflected on how the congestion could be eased in my hometown's city centre. Then I remembered the average girth of the mamas at home and I understood why we don't have bicycle taxis.

We got up bright and early for the start of our fifth week on the road with our sights set on reaching Blantyre in the daylight. We waved goodbye to Cool Runnings and started getting into the rhythm of the day's ride. It was at about this point that I developed a sincere respect for Clayton. As we rode along I had noticed street vendors on the roadside waving sticks at us with something impaled on them. Clayt, feeling peckish, stopped to investigate. To my and Lara's absolute disbelief he said, "I'll have one of those," and proceeded to eat a scrawny sparrow-like bird off the skewer and followed up by using its crispy little toe-nails as toothpicks. Well, when in Malawi…

Along the way we bumped into Roy Sadan again, the lone cyclist bicycling around the world, now pedalling for Tanzania. He was happy as usual and regaled us with horror stories of his stay in Tete Hospital after coming down with a life-threatening bout of malaria as well as some other strange ailment. He said that the government hospital in Tete was the ghastliest hospital he has ever been in or could ever imagine. Being fit obviously helped him with a quick recovery and maybe the hospital wasn't quite that bad after all! Nothing could wipe the smile off his face though and it shone with his love of life. He is one amazing guy!

On, on, to Blantyre. The traffic increased dramatically. Now, besides the usual surge of bicyclists, pedestrians and animals, we also had to contend with trucks, buses, cars and taxis. We swished into Doogles Lodge in a down-at-heel part of town but it turned out to be an unlikely oasis. Happily they served food on demand and we relished the delicious French fries. It was relaxing to shower, socialise with other vacationers and watch the rugby.

La and Clayt puttered off to buy a new chain for Clayton's bike and they were thrilled to find a Shoprite supermarket where they were able to buy milk, soap, cheese and all the little luxuries they had missed.

This tiny motorcycle spares shop had everything Clayton needed

At the ungodly hour of 4:00 am we were awoken by a rampaging Bulls' supporter, terrorising the backpackers. He threw our door open, yelled, "What are you people doing here? Why don't you leave this friggin' hole?" and ran off, swearing, into the night. Apparently he was annoyed by the pathetic stream of water from the shower head which he felt ruined the thorough rinsing he was looking forward to.

Thanks to this loud tirade, Clayt was angle grinding links off his new chain at the crack of dawn. After a successful job we set off for the Mulange Massif, also known as Mount Mulanje, in the Mulanje Mountain Forest Reserve and the supposedly largest monolith in the world. It surpasses even Uluru (Ayers Rock) in Australia. It is the highest mountain in Malawi and high enough to induce rain clouds to form, making it a significant source of water. We hoped to summit the 3002-metre Sapitwa Peak. It was a three-day round trip and we stayed in mountain huts along the way. Sadly, two weeks before our arrival an experienced Brazilian mountaineer perished on this mountain. Three thousand and two metres does not sound like much, but here, as on all mountains, conditions can deteriorate quickly and high winds, plummeting temperatures, sheer drops, treacherous terrain and poor visibility make Sapitwa Peak just as dangerous as higher mountains.

Let me tell you a little about my love of climbing mountains before continuing on with my account of our ascent of Mount Mulange. This appeal had its infancy in the Drakensberg Mountain Range in South Africa. Often I would pack my stove, sleeping bag and warm gear into my backpack and join fellow hikers for a strenuous weekend in the mountains. We would hike all day, plunge our tired, hot bodies into an icy stream and then retire to a cave, more often an overhang of rock, for the night. There we would toast each other with 'Obies', a local brand of cheap but popular sherry. Sleeping on our thin foam mats with the night sky clearly visible felt like a privilege and I loved snuggling into my soft down sleeping bag, cosy in the cold night. It is such a pleasurable and healthy pastime!

When the opportunity came to hike up the multi-summited, jagged Mount Kenya, the second highest mountain in Africa, I was thrilled. (Mount Kenya is an ancient and extinct volcano second in height to Mount Kilimanjaro.) Mountin' Man chose the longer but spectacularly scenic Chogoria route which is acknowledged as one of Africa's finest treks.

Two weeks before departure date saw me hiking in the Drakensberg. I was walking rapidly along a narrow mountain path with a drop off on my left and was fiddling with my GPS, so I didn't notice the hole on the path in front of me. The next moment I was cart-wheeling through the air with enough presence of mind to try and hold my GPS in a protective way so that when I landed it wouldn't get damaged. I ended up wedged in the rocks below, a tangle of gear around me, with a twisted ankle and the GPS slightly scratched. After my extraction I pretended that it wasn't too sore and hobbled along behind my fellow hikers, worrying about how this was going to affect my Mount Kenya expedition. Luckily I was able to purchase a neat, unobtrusive ankle brace that fitted snugly into my boot. Problem solved!

From Johannesburg, Mountin' Man, another friend and I winged our way to Nairobi, a large, bustling African city. Marabou storks, huge birds at 1.5 metres tall with a 2.9 metre wing span weighing in at a hefty nine kilograms, drooped menacingly on top of the light posts. They are one of the largest flying birds in the world and many consider them one of the ugliest, with their balding, scabby head and pendulous pink air sac. The carrion-eating Marabou also has an off-putting habit of squirting excrement onto its own legs. Despite all that I find them curiously mesmerising.

We drove to Chogoria, stocked up on supplies, collected the guide and porters and then the final leg to Meru Bandas at 2,800 metres was in a clapped out old Landie owned and driven by a man named Frederick, on a dreadful road pitted with pot-holes and scarred by wash-aways. Frederick piloted his pride and joy with the expert ability of a man who has done this many times before. The Kenyan National Park, only 200 kilometres from the equator, is rich in flora and fauna.

Fresh buffalo dung was scattered liberally around the huts we were to sleep in. That night I battled an altitude headache of note, drinking gallons of tea in an effort to curb it, but thankfully after that I was fine.

As we trekked upwards with our sights set on Point Lenana at 4,895 metres, the trekking summit on Mount Kenya, we realised that this was indeed an ecological paradise boasting Afro-Alpine scenery and weird rock formations, rugged pinnacles, waterfalls and tarns.

On the second night we camped near the Nithi Falls at Nithi (3,200 metres) and dunked our sweaty bodies in the pool of icy water at the base of the falls.

The remarkable scenery continued and we had uninterrupted views of

Vivienne Falls and Lake Michaelson. Hall Tarns, at 4,300 metres, was our third camp and a day before we summited, one of my companions came down with an even worse altitude headache than the one I had had at Meru Bandas. By the next morning he seemed to have recovered enough to continue with the trek.

The last hour of trekking before we reached the summit was the most difficult and I sensed that I hadn't acclimatised fully and that was the problem. My speech was slightly slurred and my legs felt leaden; they weren't reacting to the signals from my brain as quickly as they should have. I kept trudging along, one weary foot in front of the other, determined to make it.

I was elated to finally reach the top and revel in the all-round magnificent views, including that of the rapidly shrinking Lewis Glacier.

Mountin' Man and I had the privilege of sleeping next to the glacier at Austrian Hut where as luck would have it, gale force winds nearly blew our tent to smithereens. After losing at a Ching Chong Cha challenge (rock, paper, scissors) I was gleefully pushed out into the icy blackness to collect rocks to secure the flapping sections of tent, and while I was out there he suggested that I might as well collect some water and check on our mate in the hut who was struggling with sleep apnoea. The following day we took the Naru Moru route out, surfing down the long shale slope and then sloshing through the bog further down.

I have spoken to people who have hiked both Mount Kenya and Mount Kilimanjaro, and while Kili is a definite notch on the belt, Mount Kenya is certainly the prettier of the two. Also, Mount Kenya is not overrun with hikers and while there we felt as if we had the mountain to ourselves.

Mount Everest base camp at 5,300 metres was entirely different. Flying into Kathmandu with peaks in excess of 7,000 metres showing above the cloud line was truly awesome and gave us a taste of the enormity of the undertaking to climb one of these giants. From a vibrant and exciting Kathmandu with its temples, body burning and frenetic shopping, we flew to Lukla at 2,900 metres, weaving up the valleys to land on supposedly the shortest airstrip in the world at 527 metres. To make matters worse the airstrip is not flat. It angles up the mountainside at an angle of 20 degrees so when you land you actually taxi uphill.

Here we started our approximately 70 kilometres, 10-day slow trek, acclimatising as we laboured along, up, up, endlessly up to Everest base camp. We wound our way up the magnificent Khumbu Valley through colourful villages, sleeping at tea houses along the route. No words can adequately describe the sense of 'smallness' one feels in the Himalayas when surrounded by such breathtaking grandeur. Everything is special; the views, the local people's hospitality, strength and smiling faces in spite of their hard lives, the graceful yaks carrying their heavy loads, the strangely coloured milky turquoise, fast-flowing streams, the long suspension bridges bedecked by thousands of prayer flags… I could go on and on.

Quite a few in our group succumbed to altitude sickness. The first person to be affected was at 3,450 metres and she had to turn back and go down. Luckily I had no problem and made it to our destination, the Khumbu Glacier on which Everest base camp is precariously spread. The climbers who are hoping to attempt the climb to the summit of Everest select a patch on the ice, where they pitch their tents among and sometimes on stones between the crevasses and listen to the creaking of the glacier as they try to sleep at night. Dangerous living!

I met the courageous icefall doctors whose job it is to affix, attend and maintain the ladders spanning the crevasses and the fixed ropes at dangerous sections which assist the climbers in their ascent of Mount Everest. Theirs must surely rate as one of the most dangerous jobs in the world. As we left base camp with a sense of accomplishment, objective satisfyingly achieved, it started snowing. It took us only four days to make the descent to Lukla.

The complexity of altitude sickness, also known as acute mountain sickness or AMS, absorbed me. It seems as though there are many different schools of thought and controversy regarding this affliction, the most common being whether or not to take a particular drug used to prevent and also treat AMS. Altitude sickness can progress to the potentially fatal high altitude pulmonary oedema, known as HAPE, or high altitude cerebral oedema, known as HACE.

It is commonly accepted that a contributory factor might be dehydration as a result of the higher rate of water vapour lost when breathing the thin, dry air at higher altitudes. This interested me as I observed many of my trekking mates drinking large quantities of water in the hopes of staving off AMS. I asked myself, *How much water is enough?* and I continued drinking only what I deemed sufficient. At one stage, through an unhappy circumstance, I found myself without water at all for a number of hours but luckily remained fit and fine. However, my trekking companion who had consumed six litres of water that morning was not so lucky. She became quite ill and started vomiting, and was sent down.

Interestingly, hyponatraemia, which is caused by consuming excessive quantities of water (over-hydration) and AMS share many of the same symptoms such as lack of appetite, nausea, vomiting, confusion, dizziness, fatigue, weakness and decreased consciousness. I agree that as a commercial hike leader or tour guide the safe option is to send your client down, regardless. However, as a paying client I want my money's worth and I think that it's very important that people are aware of these issues and possibly work out a hydration plan beforehand. Of course this is only one aspect of a complex whole.

Now back to Mount Mulange. The guide and porter arrived early, and even though we felt rather ill-equipped in our combo biking/mountaineering outfits, we got off to an enthusiastic start. Clayton did this entire trek in his surfing board shorts! Nine ("excruciating" said Lara) hours later, after a steady climb, we reached Chisepo Hut. The sun subsided and with it, the temperature. We spent the night with many well-equipped, genuine-looking hikers, in a hut filled with aromatic cedar smoke from the fireplace. Four weeks in the saddle did not prepare us for what this mountain had to offer and we did not have any bona fide mountaineering gear. "But," said Lara "it's an experience we'll never forget."

Mother Earth; a cave en-route to Sapitwa, a most bizarre rock formation!

The following morning Clayton and I set off early on the six-hour, cliff face-climbing, boulder-hopping, icy wind-pummelling expedition to top one of the highest peaks in Central Africa, Sapitwa Peak. Lara declared that this was not one of her objectives. Clayton, our guide, our porter and I achieved the summit victoriously. Clayton reached the goal in style, still in his board shorts, knees blue with cold and right at the top he downed an icy beer with relish. He actually summited twice as he returned to waypoint it on the GPS which I had forgotten to do.

Triumphantly we paced ourselves back to Chisepo Hut and then set off on weary legs to Chambe Hut, four hours away. We arrived at sunset at the cosy wooden mountain hut, which had a huge old stone fireplace. This was Lara's dream come true and fulfilled her objective for the mountain slog. We had a social evening, with the fire roaring, chatting to some Polish people about their wanderings and finally collapsed into bed. Actually we climbed up into our sleeping bags. Strangely enough, these were on top of long tables which doubled as beds as there were no real beds.

These mountain huts are well looked after by caretakers who live on the property. They are clean and fresh water is available for drinking and rinsing your body with. There are no showers but instead a small wooden room in which you soap up and then sluice your body with icy water from a jug provided for you. The caretaker also collects and chops wood for the evening fire. Toilets were clean and a short distance away.

The next morning, with aching knees, we set off down the mountain path which led us on a four-hour, pleasing forest walk with waterfalls. Despite the pain, the scenery was well worth it. We treated ourselves to long, hot showers upon our return.

Happiness was jumping onto a boney for a rough ride on the dirt, off to the nearby town of Mulange to book a table at the pizza restaurant for Clayton's birthday dinner and get necessary supplies – birthday beer! We spent a lovely evening at a super little restaurant having delicious pizza. Happy, happy birthday Clayt!

From Mulange we rode back to Blantyre where we filled up our tanks at a fuel station and this is unfortunately where we had our first encounter with crime. Someone strolled past and casually bent down and picked up Clayton's bag, containing his passport, wallet, cell phone and valuables and tried to walk off. Clayton bellowed loudly and fiercely while running at him and luckily the thoroughly alarmed would-be thief dropped the bag and ran off, terrified.

Using the GPS we followed the road that popped up on its screen, to Zobue, the border post into Mozambique. Oh my! What a mistake. This tar road quickly deteriorated into a pot-holed mess before becoming an unpaved road dog's breakfast. We passed an open air abattoir where the doomed cows had to hear and observe their brethren being slain. The dead cows were being cut up and the earth was stained a deep sickening red. The air was blisteringly hot, tempers flared, I fell over in a ditch and couldn't pick my bike up, there was angry shouting, Lara rode off and left me, I whispered to myself that I would live there forever… until she came back and none too graciously, helped me. I felt that I had let myself down by getting mad at Lara. Eventually we came to a T-junction which led onto the smoothly surfaced, new looking road connecting Blantyre to Zobue. Damn!

Lesson learnt: don't think your GPS knows the best route. Look carefully at road signage for alternative routes and listen to your gut feel. All along I had the feeling that this shocking road with a suspicious lack of traffic couldn't possibly be the main road to Zobue. I was right!

We passed uneventfully through the border post into Mozambique. On we rode, feeling tired and hot, until we made it into Tete, the largest city on the Zambezi and the capital of the Tete Province. There we pitched the tents on the camping ground bordering the banks of the mighty Zambezi River, at that point a sluggish brown force. After revelling in the luxury of a shower, with sundowners in hand, we contentedly gazed at the sun as it retreated over the horizon in a blaze of colour.

All night long the heavy flow of traffic continued across the nearby one kilometre long suspension bridge spanning the Zambezi River. This bridge links the northern and southern parts of the country as well as Zimbabwe and Malawi, so it is a vital link. In the morning we looked across at the bridge and it was still jammed with traffic. We felt lucky to be able to hop onto our little bikes and zoom off, threading our way delicately through the thick traffic. At the toll we took our cue from the local motorcyclists and followed them through the no toll section. For some reason this elicited bellows from the toll collector which we simply ignored. We couldn't turn around anyway.

We were hoping to cover the 400 kilometres from Tete to Chimoio quite quickly. Unfortunately that was not to be the case as the tar road had been replaced by a soft sand road almost all the way, so we didn't make it. We rode in the crazy conditions we had by now become accustomed to. At one point Lara was ridden right off a 20 kilometre sand detour by a speeding truck observing the 'might is right' rule. She careered off the detour, down the embankment and ended up in the ditch below, astoundingly unhurt. A kindly passerby helped her manhandle her laden bike back onto the road.

Even though we had progressed to pot-holed tar, the road deteriorated even further, and we came across large sections where there were more car-swallowing pot-holes than tar. We each rode at our own pace, in our own headspace, catching up with each other periodically and finally completed the tiring trek. We hit upon a surprisingly nice, ZAR 10.00 per person per night (that's almost for free), theme-park looking campsite (the theme escaped us). Tents were erected, showers were taken, food was eaten and as the weather had mercifully cooled down considerably we snuggled into our sleeping bags for a well-deserved rest on this our 35th day on the road.

Not quite at sparrows the next morning we set off in heavy mist which soon chilled and drenched us. We rode through the now familiar Chimoio, Gondola and Inchope. As the morning sun burnt off the mist and warmed us we headed for the coast and Inhassorro, nurturing fantasies of white beaches, a turquoise ocean with wavelets lapping the shore, picturesque campsites on the beach and ice cold beers on arrival. Isn't it funny how people make all the difference to one's perception of a place? When we finally arrived the camp management was too tired to even point us in the direction of the spot where we were to pitch our tents; the barman was of the same ilk. We briefly explored the town we had taken a long detour to visit and lamentably it was a dump and expensive. I suspect that the establishments off the beaten track near Inhassorro are probably quite nice; certainly it wouldn't take much to beat what we saw. We did find an ATM which obligingly spewed out cash after we inserted our debit cards. This was an unexpected bonus.

We were forced to stay the night in Inhassorro by a shortage of time or more accurately, a lack of daylight hours, and ended up sharing the camp with some broadminded German bikers. Clayton and Lara fell over laughing when one of them, the one with the large, soft beer belly, came to the door of the shower to tell me that I could now use it as he had finished showering. He was unashamedly butt naked!

My bike was now losing a worrying amount of oil which was spraying onto the rear tyre and my front suspension was making a loud clacking noise so cornering had become somewhat adrenalin inducing. I could no longer lean into a curve with confidence. I stored a bottle of engine oil in my jacket pocket with funnel at the ready as well as the number 10 spanner I needed to open the nut on the oil-tank cover. Every now and again I would top it up and hope for the best!

An uncommonly early start out of Inhassorro once again had us riding through thick, wet, cold mist. Sixty long kilometres before Massinga, we hit the appalling pot-holes, where once again there was more pot-hole than road. This is where Clayton lost his rear brake completely. The Y-shaped metal part splayed open and to make matters worse his chain came off and jammed in the front sprocket. He found a shady patch under the trees, Lara and I hung around taking photos and 15 minutes later, we were on the road again.

We turned onto the Inhambane Peninsula, heading for Coconut Bay, and that was where my troubles started. I have never really mastered the art of riding in sand and with my suspect front suspension I battled my way every metre of the 16 kilometres there. Being afternoon the sand was churned up and the surface was difficult to read. It was a matter of riding as far as I could and when my strength ebbed and my control slipped I would have to stop, stand up astride my bike, stretch and shake out my hands and arms, take a few deep breaths and plough on again. The sun shone relentlessly, the perspiration saturated my clothing and I could feel the droplets running down my neck, escaping the black, heat-sucking helmet. It seemed to take forever, but eventually we made it and unlike Inhassorro, this was worth it!

The campsite, which we were fortunate enough to have to ourselves, was tucked behind a protective dune in a grove of coconut palms. The ocean here has a reef extending out at an angle from the shore, where whales were frolicking. I felt completely at home and relaxed into the gentle ambience of the place! After unloading the bikes and pitching the tents we collapsed into a short siesta and later ambled along to the charming thatch and grass pub where we sipped our ice cold Dois M's in a contented glow. The setting was picture postcard perfect.

While there we took long beach walks and explored the reef which stretched out for almost a kilometre. Two easygoing days later we had to force ourselves to leave, vowing to come back one day. (We said that quite often on our holiday!)

We had conflicting emotions as we neared the end of our motorcycling odyssey but of course we were looking so forward to getting home to our families and friends. Just a few days to go now… The biggest issue for us was that my youngest son's 15th birthday was coming up and we wanted to be in South Africa in time to celebrate it with him – which we did!

It was 488 kilometres to Maputo! On our small bikes this was a long way. It was a bright idea to set off early as the dew settled the sand, the surface was visible and I had a lovely ride. We knew it was going to be a long, hard, tiring day in the saddle. For once I arrived at the turnoff first. Lara wasn't as lucky as her chain came off and stuck in the front sprocket. But by now Lara and Clayton were both experts at extracting chain from cog and Lara was hastily back on track. We passed through Incoonga, the home of chilli sauce of every description. Bottles of the stuff festoon rough roadside shelves and dangle decoratively from the branches of trees overhanging the road. Later I wished that I had stopped and bought a bottle. Oh well, next time… Then on we rode, through the picturesque Inharrime perched on the shores of unbelievably blue coastal lakes. This area begs further exploration – yes, I will go back there too.

The road for many kilometres before Xai-Xai was an absolute mess with gigantic pot-holes and the dreaded *desvios* (detours) all along the route. Xai-Xai, on the banks of the Limpopo River and the capital of Gaza Province, was a popular tourist destination at one stage but with 'progress' it has lost its allure. It's a busy, grungy town and unfortunately theft is an ongoing problem which helps to keep the tourists away, tourists who would bring in desperately needed revenue to this town.

Some time ago, when we camped here en-route home from Vilanculos after dhow sailing in the Bazaruto Archipelago, the vehicles were broken into when we went for supper in the restaurant no further than 100 metres away. The caretaker on duty swore he had seen and heard nothing and was mystified at how this could have happened! Most tourists now simply pass through, off to somewhere less threatening.

It was uncomfortably hot and humid and the riding required absolute concentration; the usual cars, pedestrians, animals, carts, trucks and bicycles littered the road and not surprisingly tempers became somewhat frayed.

We stopped for a break at a roadside cafe where the owner told us of a shortcut into Maputo. We took his advice and had a most interesting meander, winding through dusty streets and idling along narrow lanes, seeing places we would not have glimpsed otherwise and getting in a little earlier than we had counted on.

Our usual spot, Maputo Backpackers, was full, so no soft beds for us. However, we were able to pitch our tents in the driveway on the hard marble tiles. Oh well, such is life on the road! The agreeable feature about the staff at this particular backpackers is that they are always ready and willing to make a plan to accommodate one. I have stayed at a few backpackers in Maputo and if you are travelling on a budget, they are the way to go. They offer safe, reasonably clean accommodation, acceptable ablution facilities and practical communal areas, the proprietors are often a mine of information and most are conveniently located. The atmosphere is usually quite festive and one has the opportunity of meeting other interesting visitors willing to share their experiences.

Full marks to Lara and Clayton who zoomed off to the fish market and bought a veritable mountain of tiger prawns and crabs as well as our favourite Mozambican beers, Dois M. Although I was fatigued I joined in the big cook-up in the bustling communal kitchen with the proprietress of the establishment slipping us delectable Portuguese spices and recipe suggestions. So with our fresh seafood fiesta, a la Portuguese, we finished the day on a well-deserved high.

We woke up to a cool, blustery morning – perfect for riding – but of course, in my opinion, every day was perfect for riding. We were aiming for Swaziland and had decided, on the advice of the roadside café owner we had met the day before, to try the border post at Goba instead of the bustling Namaacha. What a pleasure. The ride there was scenic, we had the road and then the border post and its entire staff to ourselves and we were through into Swaziland in record time. This has to rate as the number one best kept secret!

Swaziland is a small, landlocked country and has always been a pleasure to visit. Yet the king, who rules as an absolute monarch, the last in Africa, doesn't seem to be too popular. King Mswati III is known for his polygamy; he has 14 wives, in a country with one of the highest Aids rates in the world. An estimated 40 percent of the approximately 1.2 million people are HIV positive. Seventy percent of the population lives below the poverty line while the king throws lavish parties and wallows in a luxurious lifestyle, apparently at the expense of his country.

The good news for the beleaguered citizens is that at least their current king is not nearly as promiscuous as his father, King Sobhuza II, who had a mind boggling total of at least 70 wives, at least 210 children and on his death in 1982, in excess of 1,000 grandchildren! However, King Mswati III is still young. He was born on April 19, 1968, and so he might yet add to his collection of wives. He has 24 children.

As with Mozambique and Malawi the Swazi people are courteous, friendly and hospitable despite their hard lives. The roads, unlike Mozambique, are smoothly tarred and well sign-posted; a biker's dream. After an uneventful, pleasant time we finally arrived at the South African border post. Here I cringed when the person ahead of me was treated with rude disrespect, summarily dismissed and the order "NEXT" was shouted out. We had become accustomed to the politeness of our neighbouring countries.

Anyway we were all thrilled to be in our home country and we found ourselves a wooden cabin with a hot shower and soft beds in the border town of Golela! We toasted each other with celebratory champagne and then got stuck into a feast of treats – all the things we had missed. That very first glass of fine wine with our meal was so special. What a fabulous re-entry into South Africa made possible by our friend and volunteer support vehicle driver who had so thoughtfully selected and brought the champagne and treats!

In the morning of our 41st day on the road, we headed off in the direction of Jozini, with the volunteer who had kindly offered to bring the boxes of condoms in his truck and help with the distribution. This was a route I had been dying to do on my bike as I remembered it from some years ago in a car. However the front suspension which I had become suspicious of in my sand forays (I had blamed myself), now just didn't seem right. The pass heading up to Jozini was scenic but I rode carefully and didn't get to fully appreciate it. Anyway I gingerly rode on and we were directed to a rural clinic by the helpful local police.

There we met the delightful Lindani, the research assistant who was in charge of HIV/Aids education. She told us that men who have paid *lobola* for a woman consider her as theirs to do with as they please – and condoms are definitely not part of the deal. In general, she continued, men are hard-pressed to use condoms.

Lobola is an age-old Zulu custom where a price is paid by the groom-to-be to his fiancée's family, for her hand in marriage. The woman's relations are thus assured that he is financially capable of supporting her and mutual respect between the families is fostered. Traditionally *lobola* was paid in cattle but now most modern urban couples opt for a convenient cash payment.

A local doctor came to join us and concurred with Lindani that he would never consider using a condom! He declared such an idea ludicrous. A nursing sister also joined the conversation and amusingly informed us that she would certainly be trying out all the different flavoured condoms that very night, so her colleagues would not see her at work the next day as she would be far too tired to show up! We did feel that flavoured and coloured condoms have added appeal and are more likely to be used because they are perceived as fun and not just a necessity.

We continued riding on gravel and sand roads, sloshed through a river and on to the next few clinics. At one of them we said we had a donation for the clinic and were told to turn up later as it was their lunch break! Elsewhere the response was generally good and it seems to us that the women genuinely want to try and educate and protect themselves but cultural ways make it difficult for them. We ended off the day at one of my favourite places, a KZN (KwaZulu-Natal) Wildlife hutted camp at False Bay called Dugandhlovu.

We washed the day's dust away, under the stars, in an outdoor shower. A roaring fire added to the magic of the African night. Later we fell asleep in the rustic huts, with night animal and bird noises all around us. In the cool morning we stretched out our limbs on the wooden viewing platform high above the grassy *vlei* below.

From Dugandhlovu we rode to St. Lucia where we booked into 'Sugarloaf', the KZN Campsite. The river there abounds with hippos and crocodiles and the fishermen virtually cast their sinkers onto the hippos' heads. The area that Dugandhlovu and St. Lucia are part of is known as the iSimangaliso Wetland Park.

The park's natural systems range from dune, swamp and coastal forests to grasslands, mangroves, rocky and sandy shores as well as coral reefs. It is the largest protected wetland in southern Africa and is a veritable playground for outdoor enthusiasts, game and bird lovers. I have yet to have the privilege of watching either the turtles laying their eggs or the hatchlings making a run for it, which happens annually here.

Clayton was thrilled to see his parents who motored all the way from Johannesburg just for that one night as they had to leave again the next morning. Later his brother, Warren, friend, Natanya, and my sons, Justin and Thana arrived. I was overjoyed to see my sons whom I had missed while on the road. I couldn't hug them enough!

Clayton's parents very generously treated all of us to a slap-up meal at a restaurant in St. Lucia. Thank you so much Mike and Joy – we all had a fabulous evening! Mellowed by excellent company, delicious food and copious amounts of fine wine I don't think any of us worried about foraging hippos or cared about the hard earth we slept on later at the campsite.

In the early hours of the morning we heard the hippo grunting but luckily they stuck to their side of the river. My diary entry says 'Rugby today – hooray!' It was an impressive game with the Springboks annihilating the All Blacks and lifting the Tri-Nations trophy. We had a festive morning at the Fur Elize Restaurant in St. Lucia, cheering the rugby game on TV and later a nerve-wracking walk past hippos which I guessed were too close. Thana and Justin appeared not to notice them while playing around and trying to perform acrobatics on the beach; luckily the situation appeared mutual.

A sundowner *braai* back at the campsite was the cherry on top. However, some of the group chose to continue the festivities at the Fur Elize, where they watched the Sharks beat the Bulls, but I don't know who was the most trashed, the Bulls or the Car Surfer. I have to elaborate on this because it was so funny. Natanya returned from town in her compact little car and there on top was Warren, gamely surfing the ride. He had his board shorts on and looked the part. He hopped off and carried right on partying with Natanya as if there had been no interruption and is if there was no tomorrow! Right on, dude!

Sadly the final day of our big adventure had arrived. After filling up with petrol it was Durbs, here I come. Lara, Clayton and the others had opted for a Wimpy breakfast, which is not my cup of coffee. Actually, I had already eaten and was raring to go! Apart from the oil leak which I had learnt to manage, my steering became alarmingly unstable. Luckily I made it all the way home in one piece. My dear friend Reinet put on a spectacular, one woman welcoming show at the gate to my house with explosive gizmos shooting streamers all over me and her cheering and jumping up and down. What a fantastic welcome home after 44 days on the road!

It's been hard to knuckle down to work and pick up the pieces of my regular lifestyle. Of course there was so much that I missed at home but hopping on my bike each morning and heading off into the unknown is truly something I would love to do again. A ride like this broadens one's horizons, inspires faith in one's fellow humans, increases one's self confidence and above all it made me realise just how lucky I am to be who I am. There are so many people out there whose lives are a daily struggle but somehow they manage to keep a smile on their faces, treat you with warm hospitality and wouldn't dream of harming you or touching your possessions. I have a lot to learn from them.

Heartfelt thanks to Leatt Brace for their kind donation of two neck braces! I loved my Leatt neck brace. It made me feel safer and I wore this brace all 7,760 kilometres of the ride. We met other motorcycling overlanders and noted that they all wore these neck braces. This is one item of safety gear I wouldn't do without. This, my helmet and my boots were indispensable.

A round of applause to RRT Medcon! The distribution of condoms did not work out as planned as a result of no 4x4 backup all the way, to carry the huge boxes donated by RRT Medcon. However we did distribute these around the Jozini area in South Africa. We were dismayed to hear of the enormous problems facing health care workers when it comes to condom education. It appears that cultural issues have a significant part to play. Thank you so much Clive and his family and staff at RRT Medcon for your generous donation.

A youthful me on the 350 cc Kawasaki Big Horn

On the XT660R crossing the Nungwane River, South Africa

On the Yamaha Enticer in Sauraha, India

The soft sand road to the Quissico campsite, Mozambique

Relaxing at the caretaker's house near the Quissico campsite

Lara had the Quissico beach all to herself

Crossing the Tropic of Capricorn

En-route to Morrungulu

A typical Mozambican dhow in Vilanculos

Roadside repair

About to cross the hippo and crocodile infested Shire River in Mozambique

Mario and friends

Gurue market, Mozambique

Re-enactment of my fall

Fisherman at Cape Maclear, Malawi

Lara and I posing for a pic to make the Booze Den in Cape Maclear proud!

Arriving at the M.V.Ilala

Sightseeing on a Chipoka bicycle taxi in Malawi

Enjoying the sunset while cruising on Lake Malawi on board the M.V.Ilala

Summiting Point Lenana on Mount Kenya

Relaxing at Mount Everest base camp

Clayton and I on Sapitwa Peak, the summit of Mount Mulange, Malawi

Our route from South Africa through Mozambique

From Mozambique into Malawi and back to South Africa

— 4 —

Dhow Sailing

My love of the sea extends to a fascination with dhows and the waters in which they seasonally ply their trade. These large wooden craft are usually built with no plans, no specialised tools and no modern hardware such as nails or screws. They are traditionally 'stitched' together using twine made from coir or hide or flexible wood such as willow branches or roots, and the caulking between the planks is a concoction of coconut fibre rope soaked in a mixture containing resin from a particular mangrove tree, amongst other ingredients. This method of stitching gives them greater flexibility in storms than boats with wooden planks nailed together. Their sails, called lateen sails, are quadrilateral in shape and invariably are stitched together from whatever fragments of fabric are available.

Stupid, crazy, ignorant… I was all that and more when at the age of 19, I had my first, somewhat foolhardy, taste of dhow sailing. A friend and I had set off from Durban in an old VW Beetle bound for Zimbabwe and then Mozambique before returning home. We roamed far and wide and eventually landed up in Vilanculos where we met and instructed a dhow captain in Mozambique to drop us off at an uninhabited island. We floated off at a mild angle of heel into the blue yonder and were dropped off at a deserted island,

who-knows-where. It was gorgeous and exactly what we wanted! As the day heated up we were alarmed at the lack of trees, bushes and consequently, shade. We were dressed in our bathing suits and had brought our mask, snorkel and fins with us so we figured that we'd simply spend the day submerged until the dhow came to fetch us. We had told the captain to come as late as possible.

After about an hour underwater one of us received the first sting from a small floating jellyfish-like creature and shortly thereafter we were both getting stung, to the extent that we exploded out of the water. Now we had a problem; we were getting fried by the relentless sun, we had no sunscreen, we couldn't stay submerged and we had no clothing with which to cover our bodies. We racked our brains to come up with a solution and finally the only idea we could come up with was to roll in the sand and coat our wet bodies with sand. As the day heated up, so did we and we were forced to risk getting stung and briefly dunk ourselves into the tepid, although cooling water before rolling in the sand again... We kept this up all day while miserably scanning the horizon in the hopes that the dhow would arrive earlier than planned. The sand too was dazzling and mercilessly reflected the heat and bright sunlight.

By the time the dhow arrived we were in a mess. Our red-veined eyes were swollen, our scorched skin looked like freshly cooked lobster and large blisters were already appearing. Our misery was compounded by the fresh evening breeze that had sprung up, cooling our burnt skin uncomfortably. We set off for the mainland at a satisfying pace, a pace that soon quickened into an occasional meeting of mast and ocean and while the crew baled, we hung onto the bare ribs of the deckless dhow, wide-eyed, soaking wet and shivering. It got worse! The sky blackened as the storm approached, thunderous claps interspersed with the crackle of intense bolts of lightning which lit up the night sky as well as the turbulent ocean. All too soon our dhow, the captain, crew and ourselves, were immersed in this maelstrom. My friend didn't think that we were going to make it, so handed me the keys for the VW Beetle. As for me, I hung on that much tighter, wondering how the captain knew where the land was as he had no compass or any other navigational aid and there were no lights that I could see on the mainland which had been over the horizon when we set out!

Eventually the storm blew itself out, our dhow righted itself and sailed at a comfortable pace, the stars appeared and we continued on our unhurried, calm way. The captain and crew seemed unfazed by all the action and more than a little proud at the fact that they hadn't dropped the mast and with it the sail – apparently it's considered quite a feat to keep it up in those conditions. We reached land at an ungodly hour, found our way back to the Beetle, dug around for our sleeping bags and slept right there on the beach, relieved and exhausted.

Many, many years later in Mozambique I was able to watch the work of building a large dhow. I watched as the builders chipped laboriously away with adzes to achieve the desired shape. I observed that the strengthening right-angled supports for the deck are chunks of wood that have grown into that shape. I was intrigued and tried to find out as much as possible from the builders but language barriers interfered.

In the old days use was made of the seasonal monsoon winds to facilitate trade between the East African Coast and the coast of Arabia, the Persian Gulf and the west coast of India. From November to April the trading dhows would use the northerly winds to sail down the coast and from May to October they would use the southerly winds, the Trade Winds, to sail back again. I would soon be following for a short distance in their wake.

While surfing the internet I came across a person, Dave, who ran a small dhow charter business out of Vilanculos, taking their customers to the Bazaruto Archipelago. This piqued my interest and I contacted him. Of course it didn't stop there as within a few months I was happily sailing on his crewed dhow into these island-studded waters.

I took 19 fellow hikers from my hiking club along with me and not one of us was disappointed; it was spectacular. Dave had supplied us with two crew members and these talented, well-practised sailors did everything. They cooked in the traditional way, rather alarming for us but normal for them. The 'stove' was an open wooden box at the base of the wooden mast in which they had a wood fire on which they cooked up a seafood fiesta, the envy of any modern restaurant. On one occasion after a fabulous session finning ourselves over a protected coral reef (Two Mile Reef) teeming with a flabbergasting variety of jewel-coloured fish, we emerged thrilled and hungry as horses. We motored back to the shore of the island and the spot where we landed wasn't suitable for lunch but on a nearby, powder-soft, dazzling white sand, island beach was a lunch fit for kings and queens, laid out for us by our crew. After this lip-smacking meal we plopped ourselves into the nearby shallow water and lazed the afternoon away drifting over the breathtaking underwater marine display.

I must mention that snorkelling over coral reefs in Mozambique, is well worth it. The reefs that I have been to have not been too deep, the fish life abundant and varied in spite of the uncontrolled fishing in Mozambican waters, and the water temperature is positively amniotic. Many operators here offer scuba diving tours to exotic, unheard of sites and some of the islands have world class accommodation, many with an upmarket 'Out of Africa' theme. Further north, it is more 'Ali Baba'. Wining and dining is top- notch at these places. The feel is hot, tropical and romantic – I think Mozambique could be the new Caribbean!

However on this holiday we had neither 'Out of Africa' nor 'Ali Baba' but we had acceptable 'Rustic African' round thatched huts almost at the water's edge. The beaches here are glorious; I was captivated by the way the talcum-soft sand squeaked as you walked on it. We based ourselves on an island called Magaruque Island. Our wish was to see a dugong or a whale shark on one of our dhow excursions. We saw lots of other creatures but disappointingly no dugong, and no whale shark!

The Bazaruto Archipelago is well known, relatively close to other major destinations and is a holiday location of note. Quite rightly so and we had the time of our lives.

Ever since my cruising days well over 20 years ago the largely unheard of Querimbas had been a dream destination for me, why I don't know as I knew nothing about this island archipelago. Those little dots on the chart were compelling and were all I needed to fire my enthusiasm. After the dhow jaunt in the Bazaruto Archipelago I understood exactly how this ambition would become a reality. I quickly realised that the Querimbas are not regarded as a tourist destination so there is a dearth of information on this area, little infrastructure to serve tourists and certainly nothing reliable. After many hits and misses via the internet, I made contact with a woman who said she could organise a dhow for me. She would also source a captain. This she did and a fair price was settled on which I immediately accepted. The entire plan was somewhat hazy but as my only option I could and would work with it.

To make it cost effective I needed to share the costs with other people so as a club hike leader I placed a fixture in our club magazine:

1st – 11th July 2007

Dhow Sailing Safari in the Querimba Archipelago. This excursion is definitely only for brave and hardy souls who are willing to take a chance as this is not a packaged arrangement. Tourism is still very much in its infancy in this area and I have never been there before. All information has been gleaned from the internet and all contacts have been made on the internet.

Club hike leaders become leaders voluntarily and do not get paid. Putting interesting expeditions together is gratis and is part of what is required of a Mountain Backpackers Club hike leader.

As a result of the response to this advertisement in our club magazine, 12 hardy adventurers flew in to Pemba which is on the mainland in Northern Mozambique, for what was to be an incredible experience. The town of Pemba is run down, dilapidated and vibrant. We took ourselves off to the rabbit warren of a market and stocked up with supplies. We catered for ourselves and hoped to supplement this with fish we caught along the way. We also had our tents, sleeping bags and backpacks with us. The idea was to sail from island to island and spend the night at specific localities suggested by the woman who had organised the dhow for us. Our accommodation was to be a mixture of beach huts and camping.

Our first two nights camping in Pemba was spent very comfortably at Russell's Campsite, where we enjoyed tasty goat stew for supper, a first for many of us. This campsite served good food, had an excellent pub along with a chilled vibe and we all felt upbeat so it was the perfect place from which to start our journey.

It was love at first sight when I laid eyes on our dhow, Shani Yake, pronounced 'Shunee Yucky', a traditional vessel well suited to the shallow waters of the Querimbas. There she was, in all her glory floating off the beach at Pemba waiting patiently for us to board her. Our sombre-faced captain was from Kenya and he spoke only Swahili, his two crewmen were from Mozambique and they spoke only Portuguese – a motley bunch indeed.

The captain and crew muscled the big lateen sail up and we were off, off on an incomparable adventure. Shani Yake had a small outboard engine for manoeuvring or for use on flat water in windless conditions so the sail was our driving force and we were almost completely reliant on the wind. From Wimbe Beach in Pemba we headed for the island of Quipaco where we planned to spend one night in beach huts. The crossing went well and we dropped anchor in the shallow waters close to the island.

Once ashore we were delighted with our rustic accommodation perched on the sharp rocks overlooking the sea. Fortunately there was still enough time left to go on a long exploratory walk around the island. My son, Justin was wearing brand new, tough beach shoes; by the end of the afternoon they were shredded. The sharp coral and rock formations were formidable and we took numerous photos of their weird and contorted shapes, many embedded with ancient ammonites and fossils.

After a 'chip-in-with-whatever-you-have' type of meal in the communal dining area we all retired to our beach huts, blissfully exhausted after a fabulous first day out on the ocean.

In the morning, the caretaker on Quipaco provided each of us with a bucket of fresh water for our ablutions, strategically placed in a screened off area but open to the sea. I loved that sensation of pouring cold water over myself and then being instantly chilled by the fresh breeze blowing off the sea. It made me feel so alive! After a humble but satisfying breakfast we piled into the dinghy and headed out to Shani Yake, now floating after having been lying comfortably on her side on the sand during the low tide.

We set off on the high tide but as it turned and started draining we could see the sandy bottom get closer and closer until we were bumping along. The captain shrugged his shoulders and indicated that we would be stopping here for a while. This was quite in order as far as the locals were concerned; when the tide receded, you were left high and dry; when the tide came in, you continued with your journey. The captain, crew and very often the passengers would find themselves a reasonably comfy position and take this opportunity to have a siesta. Of course, not us; we tumbled overboard and waded thigh-high in the tepid water to the nearest island, Mefunvo Island, for a few hours of exploring.

There was an enormous baobab tree close to the beach; they are quite common in these areas and I'm sure are used as landmarks in navigation. It was so interesting to see how the islanders ingeniously used the coral and sandstone rock for the construction of their homes. We met the shy but friendly inhabitants and all had a go at communicating with each other, children and dogs squeezing in-between our legs to get a better view of us strangers. It was all rather chaotic but tremendous fun and by the time we left we all had broad smiles on our faces!

With the dhow floating once again we continued our voyage over the flat, protected, turquoise waters with picturesque islands dotted here and there. Our destination was Matemo Island where we planned to camp at the campsite we had been told about. It was dark by the time we arrived and went by dinghy to shore with our gear. My crowd sat on the beach basking in the moonlit evening and celebrating our safe arrival with a few beers.

I set off with the captain to find the campsite but it wasn't long before a voice boomed out an unintelligible phrase in Portuguese and blinded us with a powerful flashlight. We were then herded into an untidy room, clearly the local police station. Shani Yaki's captain, eyes downcast, immediately shrunk behind me and never said a word. The police, in-between swigs of something liquid, took turns at trying to communicate with me, getting louder by the minute. As I gazed around in despair, wondering what on earth I should be doing and worrying about my group on the beach, I heard a strange noise.

Astonishingly it was a four-seater golf cart! The young lady driving rattled off in Portuguese to the police and then said to me, "Good evening Madam, we've been expecting you. Welcome to Matemo Island! Please come with me." I was gob-smacked and although the captain's expression remained neutral, his body language indicated that he was secretly relieved.

I said as cheery a "Good evening" as I could under the circumstances, pushed the captain into the cart, hopped in and said, "Let's go."

We hummed off into the night along manicured pathways, stopping briefly to unload the captain. I hoped he would try to convey the evening's happenings to the others. The driver continued her bubbly chit-chat and then dropped me off at the most luxurious looking building, clearly an upmarket lodge. I felt out of place and stood awkwardly in my sticky, grubby baggies and T-shirt while gemstone-hued chiffon drapes wafted in the cooling night breeze. Satin-pillowed day beds beckoned invitingly and as I looked around for a staff member I noticed the Moorish arches, the dimly lit, coloured glass Moroccan lanterns, the gleaming floors and the potted palms.

Eventually I heard the tell tale tip-tap of a woman's high heels and an elegant woman asked me my name. I saw the confusion on her face as she realised that this was a case of mistaken identity. She insisted that there was no campsite on the island and Matemo Lodge was elite enough that they didn't want a bunch of hiker-sailors wandering around their exclusive turf. Not knowing what to do and being in a quandary she made a few phone calls. The manager was called from her home and she resolved the issue by graciously providing us with accommodation and supper, gratis! This was hospitality over and above our non-existent expectations for which we were truly grateful.

She politely enquired as to whether we would mind eating in the canteen as the dining room was closed. Oh boy, did we mind, what a question? This was a huge stroke of good fortune. After eating our full we retired to our own personal thatched beach cottages which were equipped with sumptuous bathrooms and large fluffy towels, to say nothing of the king-sized beds with fresh, crisp, high thread count linen.

In the morning our caring hostess even arranged breakfast for us. We did a quick round of the old tin mug and managed to hand over quite a tidy tip for the staff. Our hostess also arranged a truck to remove us and our gear from the premises.

The weather was inclement so we had to stay another day; our hostess had taken this into consideration and had arranged for us to be dropped off at the World Wildlife Fund (WWF) compound on the other side of the island, the 'poor' side. On this side the locals could poop on the beach which they weren't allowed to do on the lodge side, evidenced by amusing

'no pooping' signs planted on the beach.

We were hospitably received, handed over our donations for the accommodation and the night at the WWF compound passed uneventfully. Justin and I slept under the eaves of the building in the open and the others put up their tents. In the morning the weather had moderated and we were raring to go despite dire warnings by an 'expert' at Matemo Lodge. He also informed us of the vast numbers of dhows that sank in the area and that we were taking our lives into our hands. We called him Mr Doom and Gloom although he did manage to shake our confidence a little.

The sailing was exhilarating, as exhilarating as a cumbersome dhow can get. Shani Yake felt rock solid, steady and reassuring. We passed over a visible coral reef on which, in retrospect, we should have snorkelled. It was shallow enough to anchor in a nearby sandy patch and I'm sorry we missed the opportunity. The allure of fishing in these fabulous conditions was too much for Julian and he didn't have to wait long after throwing his lure out and trailing it behind us before he hooked into a supper-for-all-of-us sized fish. The captain was lightning-quick with the gaff and almost before we knew what was happening, he had flicked the fish into the cockpit and had walloped it solidly over the head. Within minutes Julian was at it again and this time caught another, slightly smaller fish for the now smiling captain and crew.

Our day ended in Pangane, an isolated village which is renowned for its dhow building. We secured comfy huts for ourselves, right on the beach. With the ease of a practised fisherman, Julian de-scaled and filleted the fish he had caught. When the fire was at just the right temperature he popped the fillets on the grid, while we sat around reminiscing over the day's events.

Justin and I were thrilled at the sea on our doorstep and looked forward to snorkelling and swimming the following morning. We were totally let down in this regard when we noticed that the villagers here also used the intertidal zone as their toilet. This seems to be the way it's done in the Querimbas. We weren't about to slip into that water surrounded by floaters!

Later, in Pemba, when we discussed this floater issue with the 'tourism' lady, she remarked that this custom was damaging to tourism and all attempts at curtailing this practice and introducing 'long drops' were met with strong resistance.

Not to be deterred and hoping to find a poop-free site, we hopped aboard Shani Yake and our captain, on the advice of his crew, took us to the nearby island of Ilha Macabe to engage in a bit of underwater sightseeing. Unfortunately, although the water was clean, it wasn't crystal clear but nonetheless it was most pleasant. Sadly this was to be our last outing on Shani Yake.

While sailing to Pangane I realised that there was no way we would make it in time to catch our flight home if we had to return to Pemba in Shani Yake. She was a dhow, designed to go in one direction in a season, but until the winds changed she would not manage the trip back to Pemba in the time we had left. Clearly we couldn't wait for the winds to change so I had an urgent phone call to make to try and arrange alternative transport but there was no cell phone reception to be had in the area.

Luckily the owner of our thatched huts had a weathered 125cc motorbike with a luggage carrier behind the driver's seat. I immediately hired him to take me to the nearest place in which I could receive a cell phone signal. His wife provided me with a cushion to secure across the carrier and we were off in a cloud of sand and smoke.

We thumped and bounced our way across the landscape with the driver pointing out areas that had been damaged by herds of elephant and places where villagers built look-out huts on stilts so that they could see approaching lion.

At one stage we hit a tree root and we both tumbled head over heels, landing in an untidy heap in the sand. Red faced, we disentangled ourselves and continued our journey. The driver rode through the thick sand as if he was on a national highway and I envied him this ability. I contemplated the 'Sand-master Challenge' back home and knew that this driver could win that challenge, hands down!

A few hours later we arrived at a nondescript location, a slight elevation with a palm tree providing sketchy shade. This was the hallowed spot, the spot where communication with the outside world happened. I phoned our contact in Pemba and requested that she send vehicles to collect us and explained that we could not sail back in time to catch our flight out. To her immense credit she agreed immediately. I was relieved as I had expected resistance and/or the inevitable request for additional cash, neither of which happened.

We had a terrific time in Pangane, exploring the local market, watching the dhow builders at work, playing ball with the kids – even though the substitute ball was a coconut, walking along the beach at high tide, cooking over fires, reading, chatting to all and sundry and generally lazing around. Two days later two vehicles arrived to collect us.

By this time we had formulated a plan, a plan the vehicle drivers astonishingly agreed to, in view of the fact that we hadn't paid extra for this unplanned for portion of the drive. After much discussion we determined that we wanted to see the island of Ibo. This had been part of our original itinerary but wind conditions on the day we were supposed to go there didn't allow for it. The elderly 4x4 vehicles were nursed along by their drivers; one had a steady radiator leak requiring frequent filling and the other one was missing a gear. Motoring by vehicle through the Querimba National Park, a remote area, was exciting. In places the grass on either side of the track was taller than the vehicle. On our numerous stops the driver would climb onto the roof to scout around for the whereabouts of the vehicle we were accompanying.

We stopped in Macomia to stretch our legs and then continued on to Tandanhangue, the closest village on the mainland to Ibo Island. Our drivers dropped us off at Baobab Beach, a down-at-heel place, where we scouted around for a dhow to take us across to Ibo Island. Luckily it was nearing high tide so we didn't have an unduly long wait. We waded out to the dhow and clambered aboard along with a few locals and their chickens. Gear stowed, we selected a place to sit, the patchwork sail was unfurled and we were off on the light breeze, canvas billowing as the hull glided effortlessly through the water. Many of these transport dhows rely solely on wind power as they have no engines.

We passed mangroves, at times threading our way through them while our captain and his helper smoked one fat marijuana 'spliff' after the next. The breeze picked up as the sun was dying and still we couldn't see our destination. The lethargic captain whose bloodshot eyes were by now mere slits, decided that he needed waking up so he challenged the nearby passenger-carrying dhow to a race. We had been cruising neck and neck with this boat the entire way.

The captain sat up, opened his eyes, ordered his helper to haul on a few frayed pieces of rope and the race was on. Both captains demonstrated their impressive nautical skills and at one stage the two boats bumped but neither could pull away from the other. The race came to an end when the final light of day disappeared altogether.

Now we were voyaging in the pitch dark. I think everyone was nervous as there wasn't a sound to be heard, just the whooshing of the water on the hull and the occasional clucking of a fat hen. We were reassured though by the captain and crew who intermittently chatted peacefully amongst themselves. They seemed to have an instinctive knowledge of exactly where to go. Eventually we made out lights on the shore of what we hoped was Ibo Island. As soon as we hit the sand, people bailed over the side and waded in to shore. Luckily for us a young moonlighting schoolboy had appointed himself as the island guide as his school English was pretty good. We put our hiking headlamps on and followed him through the eerily derelict streets to a boarding house.

Ibo was superb, well worth the detour and its history fascinated us. It was once a major slave trade centre and is now home to about 3,500 people, 99 percent of whom are Muslim.

From the decayed grandeur of the buildings lining the dusty streets, the strategically positioned forts with their canons and ramparts, the silversmiths using antiquated methods, the bats hanging in the streets trees, the old run-down Catholic church where we saw a veritable mountain of books documenting the island's rich history, to the dhow builders; we were awed by it all. We felt as though we were stepping back 200 years in time.

The electricity on Ibo is a hit and miss affair with the generator starting up at arbitrary times and running for a few hours only. Most of the residents can hear when it starts up but no one relies on it. When queried if it bothers them they just shrug fondly at the thought of their antiquated generator.

We stayed on the island for two nights and then looked up the French dhow tour operator recommended to us by the 'tourism' lady in Pemba. He agreed to provide breakfast and lunch on board and would navigate us to a sandbar where he said there was a reef close by which was excellent for snorkelling. Later in the afternoon we would sail across the channel to the mainland and he would drop us off at Tandanhangue. He charged in dollars and was pricey but he assured us that what he offered was excellent value for money!

We set off with another South African family of four in what the Frenchman called his racing dhow. He said that it was particularly fast and manoeuvrable. An interesting comment, given that it was the traditional lateen rig. The weather was disagreeable, so much so that it was too rough to eat

the breakfast. After an unpleasant few hours we caught a glimpse of the sandbank in the distance, but Frenchie couldn't point his boat high enough to get there. He then ordered us all overboard and bellowed "Swim!" I suspected it might be too far for me as I am a poor swimmer but everybody including my son was already over the side and on their way, so I jumped in and started swimming. Also as the expedition leader I deemed myself responsible for my group's safety and wellbeing, so I felt obligated to stay with them.

The wind was blowing water into my face so I put my mask and snorkel on and tried to keep up with the others. Every time I looked up to see where I was going a wave would break in my face and I started swallowing water. The sandbank wasn't getting any closer and I was tiring and feeling rather desperate. I thought of my son and knew I had to make it. I could see Clive from our bunch ahead of me and called out to him. Embarrassed, I asked if I could hold his hand and he immediately came to my assistance. I didn't want to endanger him and luckily Lisa, also a strong swimmer, was nearby. She took my other hand and straight away my confidence was restored as we slowly swam in to the sandbank known as Banco de Areia Sao Lourenço, a mere speck in the Indian Ocean.

I collapsed with relief on the sand but this was short-lived as not everyone was in yet. The South African family was desperately scanning the water for their youngest son and for a few heart-stopping moments he was nowhere to be seen. After a relieving head count some of the strong swimmers took off to look for the reef which was nowhere to be found. In the meantime the wind and sea had moderated dramatically; Frenchie had completed a huge circle and had managed to get his racing dhow a little closer to us.

He indicated that we must now swim back to his boat, an easy swim with the wind and waves behind us. Nobody had eaten yet and the youngsters were complaining bitterly so Frenchie finally offered us snacks to eat which were wolfed down in record time. I was so furious with his rotten seamanship and his dangerous attitude that I couldn't even look at him. If anything had happened to any one of us there was absolutely nothing he could have done. We had all made the mistake of thinking that as a recommended tour operator he would naturally observe basic safety measures and his boat would contain all the vital safety paraphernalia.

By this time the wind had all but disappeared, the sea had calmed right down and was a brilliant blue, completely opposite to what it had been like a few hours beforehand. A dhow with an outboard motor arrived with tourists; it drove straight up onto the sand, where the people hopped off with deck chairs and picnic baskets. I fumed all the way back to Tandanhangue.

I was very happy to be back on terra firma where our vehicles were waiting for the roughly 120 pleasant kilometres back to Pemba.

Later, when thinking about our trip, I realised that the Querimba Archipelago is characterised by impoverished but happy people, vibrant markets, magical islands, thick stands of mangroves, coral reefs and dhows of all description going about their daily business.

About a year later Mountin' Man and I sat atop five tons of cargo on a dhow crossing the Pemba Channel from Shimoni on the Kenyan mainland to the Tanzanian island of Pemba, which is to the north of Zanzibar. The dhow was laden, the voyage took forever and we baked in the hot sun but we followed in the wake of a centuries-old tradition. I have a lot of faith in the captains of these dhows; they know what they are doing as they possess knowledge handed down through the

generations. They know their boats and their capabilities intimately and the waters in which they ply their trade are as familiar to them as the back of their hands. In short, they are not Johnny-Come-Lately's. I'm sure that mishaps do occur but even though I scoured the internet I was not able to get any information on this. I would be interested in the statistics; how many dhows go down each year?

— 5 —

The Cruising Scene

All this talk of adventure wafted me back to the happy and memorable time I had spent sailing on Moya with my husband, Rob. A little about Moya: this was the charming pocket-sized, 32-foot (approximately10-metre) 'traditional' cutter we built ourselves over two and a half years in Vancouver, Canada. She had a glowing wooden interior, lit by gimballed kerosene lamps, a gimballed kerosene stove in the tiny, fully functional galley (kitchen), neat heads (toilet) with a small built-in bath tub, a comfy V-berth and practical saloon (lounge) as well as the luxury of a proper navigation area and chart table, which we considered essential.

Our navigational instrument, the sextant, was carefully housed in a solid teak box. These were pre-GPS days! The area under the cockpit, usually utilised by the inboard engine (we didn't have one), provided invaluable storage space for two fold-up bicycles, an assortment of tools, my trusty sewing machine, indispensable fishing gear and all manner of odds and ends.

Our engine was a modest eight horsepower outboard mounted in a well in the cockpit. This was marginally adequate but did the trick in terms of motoring slowly in congested areas. On deck we carried our emergency

Rob sailing the dinghy amongst the Gulf islands in Canada

life raft and hard dinghy which we launched when we were at anchor. This was powered by a two horsepower engine and with the engine mounted was a useful ferry but supplementary to that was the sailing pleasure it afforded us.

We studied the basics of sailing (which we hadn't mastered the first time around), courtesy of the well-stocked Vancouver library and spent a few months drifting amongst the Gulf islands off Vancouver, Canada, getting the hang of it. Rob's area of interest was navigation while I took particular interest in survival at sea and read all I could find on this topic. Stories of survival against all odds by people marooned and adrift for long periods on life rafts were educational and inspiring. We wanted to be bona fide seafarers so we learnt the lingo which was no mean feat, as anybody can attest to who has listened in to sailors chatting with each other. We boned up on the art of tying nautical knots and eventually one glorious spring day we threw off the mooring lines and four of us waved goodbye to our friends, to Vancouver and to the life we had known. (Rob and I had invited my brother, Paul, and his now wife, Pam, to join us for the cruise to Hawaii.)

We had worked so hard towards this day; I even had three jobs at one stage, we had been so focused on our goal and our single-minded determination had finally paid off. A brand new chapter was about to begin!

We crossed the Gulf and leisurely stopped off at a few islands, my favourite being Saltspring Island. On we continued to Victoria on Vancouver Island, the pretty capital of British Columbia. Finally we set off for Hawaii and had absolutely no clue as to the adventures that were to befall us. People frequently asked us if we were ever bored during this period. I'll try to give you a port-light to look through, into snippets of the cruising life (in no particular order), and you be the judge of this.

We left a chilly Victoria with very little blue water knowledge between us but we envisaged learning on the way. Some years before we had had a disastrous attempt at the self-same route we were now following. We had aimed for Hawaii in a 20-foot (approximately six metres) boat best suited to pottering around the harbour. At the time we bought her because that was all we could afford (a recipe for disaster) and we firmly believed in the 'cork' theory. This little Cal 20 was known for its self-righting ability and we figured she would bob along, no matter what. Well, this she certainly did when the granddad of all storms hit us as we were exiting the Straits of Juan De Fuca; it was us who couldn't take the pounding or the freezing cold while being drenched to the bone! We only just managed to limp back into port, sails tattered and torn and our condition bruised and battered. Feeling dispirited, we sold this boat and left Canada to try our hand at living off the land in South Africa. This idea was met with much ridicule and although we were successful at it, it wasn't long before the bug bit again and we returned to Vancouver to build Moya, our dream boat.

Now, as we were sailing down the Straits of Juan De Fuca heading for the North Pacific, the temperature dropped alarmingly and the swells seemed to grow bigger and bigger by the moment until we were flapping in the troughs and being pounded on the crests. The four of us sat shivering in the cockpit bundled up in our foul weather gear, keeping a wary eye on the sea and wind conditions, with Rob and I entertaining Paul and Pam by reminiscing about the last time we tried this. At one point we looked up at the crest coming astern and in it were three killer whales, orca, surfing above us and seemingly looking down at us. Their enormous, glistening, streamlined

bodies were so close. None of us will ever forget that moment of awe with feelings ranging from absolute terror to absolute exhilaration.

Sea conditions deteriorated rapidly after that and we had to face a monster storm on our first night out. Pam and I were violently seasick and in this green, detached state I observed my brother, seasick as well, inserting an anti-seasick suppository into his crying, vomiting girlfriend's rear end. I remember thinking to myself that he must truly love her to do that and today, 30 years later, they are still blissfully married, a loving pigeon pair! I hugged my bucket feeling responsible and guilty for their obvious discomfort. Rob manfully and skilfully skippered Moya through the storm. He had his hands full as we were in the shipping lane and he had to take avoiding action when a ship strayed too close to us.

That crossing from Vancouver to Hawaii was to be our longest ocean crossing at 26 days. It was fabulous, it was terrible; we all flip-flopped between the highest of highs and the lowest of lows. The pitfalls of young, inexperienced sailors, stormy weather, a small boat, limited delicious food, plenty of not-so-delicious food, limited water, heads that packed up a few days into the passage necessitating squatting clumsily off the bowsprit while hanging on for dear life, all combined to make the inter-personal situation somewhat volatile. This was not the romantic ocean getaway our guests had envisioned.

As Vancouver became no more than a dot on our chart the temperature increased, until finally the happy day arrived when we could all bask in the glorious sunshine. The cumbersome but warm heavy weather gear was ditched in favour of bathing suits, fishing lines were rigged and soon we had landed our first catch, a large dorado, spectacularly flashing different colours in his dying throes. Pam's grin stretched from ear to ear and her 'womanly' attributes kicked in as she ran below to fire up the stove. She prepared the fish and served up a meal fit for royalty. On this passage we caught tuna, dorado and barracuda, all for the pot.

We were entertained by the 'flying' abilities of the lovely silvery blue, sometimes silvery green, flying fish. They landed on Moya's decks regularly. I turned one of these hapless flying fish into a frying fish and was pleasantly surprised by the taste. If you enjoy sardine, you'll enjoy this fish. Rob declared that they were bait fish and refused to eat them. He just didn't know what he was missing!

Unfortunately the balmy weather and good fishing didn't make up for the lack of privacy or heal the rifts that had started early on. Unrealistic expectations on both sides had not been met and sadly, in Hawaii we parted company acrimoniously. Paul and Pam set off to explore Hawaii with people they had met while trying to arrange their flight back to South Africa, people who subsequently became their lifelong friends. We continued on. It was to be years before we spoke again and thankfully today we are once again a close and loving family.

The auto helm that Rob designed, built and fitted worked like a charm. He had engaged it after leaving Canada and it was so successful that when we reached Hawaii we found out that our steering abilities weren't what they should have been considering we had just spent 26 days on a major ocean crossing! The auto helm (our silent crewman) had two interchangeable wind vanes; one large vane for fair weather sailing and a smaller storm vane. We learnt that we only needed the fair weather vane and never had to bother changing it, regardless of weather conditions.

As soon as we arrived in Hilo, Hawaii we removed the heads and put them in the dinghy to be rowed ashore the following morning as we planned to visit the yacht shop to buy new heads. Unfortunately one of us didn't secure the dinghy correctly and it floated out to sea that night. We were devastated as replacing the indispensable dinghy would severely dent our limited funds so we cast around for a bargain buy while continuing our daily outings ashore as well as attending to a few chores. About a week later we noticed a fishing boat powering into Hilo, towing a dinghy that looked suspiciously like ours and people were pointing at it and laughing. As it came closer we saw that it was indeed our dinghy with the heads still perched, throne-like, in it. Accompanied by much hilarity and well-intentioned ridicule we gratefully reclaimed the errant dinghy and its contents!

While in Hawaii we were the unlucky recipients of a racist attack and we considered ourselves fortunate to have escaped with only minor cuts and bruises. We were anchored in Keehi Lagoon on the island of Oahu and had decided to visit Pearl Harbour. Four of us went in our friend's dinghy to the shore where we secured it and ambled off on foot. When we came back the dinghy was gone but we soon spotted kids playing in it, a short distance away. We yelled at them to return it which they resentfully did. We climbed in and started rowing towards Moya when one of the boys, about 14 years old, started calling us 'f…ing stupid haoles' (pronounced 'howlies'), in this instance definitely a derogatory word for us 'whites'.

They were joined by a group of huge older men who had been playing baseball nearby, possibly fathers and older brothers. They all started swearing and hollering at us as Rob strained at the oars, trying to put as much distance between us and them as possible. Then they started hurling rocks while some tried to swim after us. Being baseball players they were lobbing with deadly accuracy. It was a heck of a job trying to deflect rocks and keep an eye on the malicious swimmers.

Poor Rob felt as if he was rowing in treacle but we managed to get away by the skin of our teeth. The last threat we heard was, 'we know what your dinghy looks like and tonight we're coming to get you'. We were so scared that we reported the incident to the police and even stretched as far as repainting the dinghy so that they wouldn't recognise it; it metamorphosed from a flamboyant bright orange to a boring white. Then we hauled out the old shotgun and slept with it.

We enjoyed Hawaii. Initially we tried to avoid the constant harassment of the timeshare salesmen who were quick to get their claws into you. Eventually we piggybacked onto their system. We would allow ourselves to be 'caught' and attend their one-hour presentation, the spinoff being all manner of gifts. We earned ourselves delicious meals at fine restaurants, jewellery, a camera and best of all, a rental car. We toured the island in style, visiting Waimea Bay, Sunset Beach and Banzai pipeline and generally did the tourist thing.

At the start of the trip we realised that we would have to budget carefully if we wanted to sail extensively. It was either that or work for a few extra years. Clearly the choice was easy. In reality it was quite effortless remaining within the budget as neither of us were big spenders. Besides we already had everything we wanted.

All good times come to an end and it was time to be on our way again. The night before leaving for our next destination, Fanning Island, one of the Line Islands, we met a yachtie who had recently been to Palmyra Island. He was most impressed with it and suggested we stop off there for a day or two as it was en-route to Fanning Island and also part of the Line Islands. We pored over our charts and set our course for Palmyra. It was a momentous decision.

With 1,200 teabags on board and gear stowed away safely we sailed off into the blue yonder. Paul and Pam would have hated this passage as it was a particularly hard one and if I hadn't been so seasick I would have been terrified.

We had exceptionally high winds and heavy seas for most of the way; in the worst of it we had waves crashing right over the boat. The waves would occasionally land with a loud crack on the deck and we would cringe below, contemplating if it could get any worse. We were so relieved that we had chosen to build Moya sturdily with small bronze port-lights which posed less risk of a port-light blowout in these rough conditions. Thirty nautical miles off Palmyra it got worse, we were caught in a storm and with Kingman Reef in our lee we had to take evasive action. Currents in this area are strong and one cannot rely on dead reckoning so we had to bide our time for two days, waiting for a break in the sky to get a sight. As soon as Rob could shoot a few celestial bodies we were off with the leftover wind from the storm and reached Palmyra at dawn on our 13th day at sea.

What a feeling of relief to see that clump of palm trees on the horizon after being battered around so much. After being seasick every single day of the passage I was desperate for terra firma. The life around us more than made up for it though; sea birds were wheeling above, the air filled with their cries, bright schools of fish could be viewed in the clear waters below us, and porpoises were slicing through our bow wave and were leaping playfully out of the water. Unbelievably the porpoises were virtually horizon to horizon and escorted us to the entrance channel through the reef into Palmyra's protected, welcoming haven of a lagoon. I climbed down from my position high up the mast where my job was to look out for coral heads or shallow patches. We laughed and hugged and I congratulated Rob on his seamanship and navigational skills. I rushed below for a quick wash, dressed myself nicely and finally stood on the bow while we cast around for a suitable spot to position the hook. Happily, wearily, thankfully, we dropped anchor.

Never in our wildest dreams could we have known what was going to happen on Palmyra! There were actually quite a number of incidents; it's a long story so to do it justice and give it the detail it deserves I have dedicated chapters 9 and 10 to 'Life and Death on Palmyra'.

Mal de mer, seasickness – what a horrible malady, a malady that haunted me on almost every passage; I had tried over-the-counter type medications and nothing worked. I tried the awful bum bombs, they didn't work, I tried scopolamine patches behind the ear and my vision became blurred as one pupil dilated while the other one contracted. That didn't seem too healthy to me. I tried home remedies, but they didn't work either. For a time there were those who assumed that it was in the mind – of course, the people who thought that didn't get seasick so they had no room to talk. The only positive was that I had no fear of the storms because quite honestly, my internal storm overshadowed anything nature could throw at us. I persevered because I firmly believed that I had to find my sea legs, sometime or another! My poor husband must have despaired looking at his constantly green-about-the-gills wife although I continued with my night watches and other duties and never let him down. Anyway once we were at our destination I soon perked up and it wasn't too long before I felt fine again. It certainly was a way of staying slim.

Almost five months later we departed Palmyra with heavy hearts and had the wind against us for four uncomfortable days to Fanning Island. The rough seas we encountered put Moya to the test once again and apart from one big scare and my unending seasickness, we coped well and Moya was nothing short of fantastic. What a boat! As soon as Palmyra had disappeared over the horizon I climbed down the companionway ladder for a customary check and was horrified to see the floorboards awash with water. The bilges were already full and the water was sloshing up the bulkheads as we crashed though the waves. I yelled frantically for Rob, thinking that we must have a hole in the hull. While I manned the bilge pump, Rob searched the boat and checked all through-hull fittings but came up empty handed. It was a mystery! Despite pumping the water level wasn't going down and by now we were exceedingly worried and then, finally with breath-exhaling relief, the blissful realisation of where the water was coming from.

We had stayed for such a long time in Palmyra's tranquil lagoon that we had become quite land-lubberly and had neglected to put the stops in the anchor chain-pipes. As a result of constantly burying our bow in the rough seas we had shipped a considerable amount of water through these pipes which led to the chain stowage area beneath the V-berth which in turn had air-flow holes into the rest of the boat, through which the water poured. Whew, what a wake-up call!

Within a day of arrival at Fanning Island we were invited to a feast in the village to celebrate an islander's grandson's first birthday, a very important birthday there. We had anchored Moya securely in the protected lagoon within the atoll, in an area we considered suitable and set out for the pleasant walk, tummies rumbling in anticipation. On our arrival the festivities got underway and we were treated like guests of honour. Young ladies leisurely waved palm fronds over the succulent roasted porker, trying not too successfully to dissuade the hordes of buzzing, hungry flies from settling. Considering that the intertidal zone was the toilet, the fly population was not surprising although most disconcerting.

We all sat around on mats in a circle and to our astonishment were treated to lashings of baby powder poured over and then rubbed into the backs of our necks. Perfume was then splashed over that; we never discovered if there was a reason for that. Perhaps we simply needed to smell fragrant before eating. An enormous cooked pig lay in the middle of a large table loaded with food. Flowers projected from its orifices and where there was no orifice, a flower-laden spike was driven into its hide. There were bowls of sliced pork, curried pork, fried pork and whatever else can be done with pork. There was delicious sweet bread, taro, rice, chicken and coconut milk dyed blue with chunks of banana in it. We were the celebrities and were requested to start the festivities by being the first to help ourselves to food. We enjoyed the food but this was tempered by the knowledge that the people on Fanning were apparently riddled with tuberculosis and intestinal parasites and we worried, not too successfully, about transmission of either of these to us.

After we had eaten our full, there were long speeches and then the guitars were brought out and the party began in earnest. A group of effeminate lady-men played musical instruments (the ukulele was my favourite), and started singing and then to Rob's utter horror he was summoned onto the dance floor by a curvaceous, nubile young lass. His horror might have been more acceptable or understandable had one of the lady-men asked him to dance! Rob had always considered dancing to be a primitive tribal phenomenon that he would never partake in. Conversely I quite fancied dancing. As a guest of honour and as the male, he was required to lead the dancing. He positively blanched and unsteadily got to his feet to roars of approval. He self-consciously jerked his body a little, looking more as if rigor mortis was setting in than dancing. His partner sensuously swivelled her hips in his direction, hoping to encourage him, no doubt. This was altogether too much for Rob and blushing like a schoolgirl, he made a run for his position on the mat in the circle. The crowd erupted into gales of laughter and suggested Rob help himself to a drink instead!

The dancing was extremely suggestive, even crude by our standards. Every now and again between bouts of dancing and singing, below-the-belt songs we gathered, a few long-winded speeches were made. Talcum powder was sprinkled over the guests, liberally and frequently. The people dancing even had powder sprinkled onto their feet. What a feast! What a party!

Towards the end of the afternoon a fierce squall blew over the island. We were forced to abruptly take leave of our generous, kindly hosts and hostesses and make a beeline for Moya. A good thing too as there she was, already in the surf, heading for the beach, snatching at the chain to the anchor which was clearly dragging. Rob got there first and somehow he managed to motor the dinghy to Moya. I wasn't so lucky and had to swim through the surf although in retrospect swimming was probably much easier.

We each knew what to do. Rob chucked the attached chain with spare anchor into the dinghy and did the exhausting rowing run before dropping it off while I cranked away at the windlass. This was repeated a few times and slowly, slowly we crept our way forward and out of danger. It was exhausting work but the only way to do it, considering our little engine was useless in these conditions.

As soon as the wind moderated we relocated Moya to a protected area and then set about the serious business of exploring Fanning Island and leading our typical yachtie lifestyle. While we were anchored in the lagoon the fishing continued but from the dinghy. Mostly we trailed lures, ideally alongside reefs and this proved successful. We never returned empty handed or had a 'bad day'. People have asked me if we ever got tired of fish and the short answer is 'no'. As with pork, beef, chicken and so on, so the different fish tasted very different to us and we never tired of it. We often reflected on how we would ever get used to not having it every day.

A friendly fellow we met on one of our walks, who was researching tropical fish in the lagoon at Fanning, offered to take our mail with him when he flew to Hawaii and post it from there to my mother in South Africa. It is that mail I am now reading to refresh my memory.

The passage from Fanning to Pago Pago Harbour on the island of Tutuila in American Samoa was uneventful. We had been at sea for 15 days; for four of those days we were caught in the doldrums. Pago Pago is the capital of American Samoa and the natural port is quite spectacular with mountains on three sides blanketed in lush vegetation. The protected harbour is known as the finest hurricane hole in the Pacific and here we were able to tie up at the dock. An interesting feature which we noted on our way into the harbour was the cable car way above us, strung across the harbour. This used to take television technicians from sea level, across the harbour, up to the transmitters atop Mount Alava. It is one of the longest single span aerial cable ways in the world. Sadly in 1980 a U.S. navy plane hit the cables and then crashed into the Rainmaker Hotel, killing the six servicemen aboard as well as two tourists visiting the hotel.

While we were sailing, porpoises regularly kept us company by surfing in the bow wave and cavorting in the ocean around Moya. We knew they were around by the friendly clicks and squeaks they emitted. We could hear them through the hull. Also, the sea creatures living and growing on the hull had their own noises. When the anti-fouling paint lost its effectiveness all manner of fauna and flora took up residence and created a mini eco system. This menagerie included diminutive crustaceans, molluscs, regular barnacles and dangly goose barnacles, algae and seaweed which attracted small fish, and marine organisms. Periodically all those familiar noises would suddenly stop and we would imagine that a big predator had arrived on the scene. Often I would find myself being lulled asleep by the comforting sound of the rudderstock rhythmically creaking as we sailed along under auto helm.

Fishing for us was a necessity. We were trying to stretch the finances so had to supplement our stores, which consisted mainly of tinned food, especially peas and big bags of rice, rice that was to become infested with weevils. (Whenever the need arose an afternoon would be pleasantly spent sifting the rice and removing the weevils.) Neither Rob nor I cared too much about food; it was simply a necessary inconvenience, so as a result our food stores were plain but we complemented these with a variety of fresh food. From the start we had strung surgical tubing across the stern to which we tied fishing line with a breaking point of 100 pounds (45.36 kilograms) and trailed an international tuna lure – a white feathered contraption with a chrome head and red eyes. Every day without fail we'd catch our meal – and it would do for supper with leftovers for breakfast, usually with rice or peas.

We had arranged to have money sent to us from Canada to American Samoa, which we had heard was pricey, and when we arrived we were alarmed to find out that it hadn't arrived.

We had used up almost all of our available cash and we needed supplies for the next leg of our journey from Samoa to Tonga. After an hour or two of alarm, calm acceptance set in and we realised we were going to eat nothing but rice and the fish we caught for the next few weeks. As luck would have it several yachties heard of our predicament and kindly donated a few cans of tinned food to our cause which relieved the monotony of fish and rice. Being penniless was liberating because we then understood we could make it, no matter how short the shoestring!

While we were in American Samoa, the chief of a village invited us to a meal at his house. We gladly accepted his cordial invitation and arrived at his house around midday. We sat outside and indulged in fairly stiff small talk. We felt ill at ease for no particular reason and were quite relieved but rather taken aback at his command, "now we sleep". We lay down on outside beds, well positioned in the shade of an enormous tree, closed our eyes and pretended to sleep, wondering what on earth was going on. Chickens flapped their wings in the dust, dogs scratched themselves, children played and birds chirped in the trees. Our host fell into a deep sleep nearby and snored loudly as we slowly relaxed into this strange situation.

On awaking he bellowed for the food. A variety of mouth-watering looking vegetables and seafood was brought out by his women-folk, along with quite a number of expensive, unappetising cans of tinned food. The veggies and seafood were placed on his and his family's side of the table and the tins and a tin opener was brought along to our side of the table. The equivalent of bon appétit was said and the meal began. We tried to share the tinned food with the others but they wouldn't hear of it and eagerly pushed the tins towards us. It turned out that they had observed the yachties buying tinned food so decided that yachties must love it and although expensive, they wanted to treat us to food they assumed we loved! Of course we couldn't disappoint them and ate the food they so thoughtfully provided with fake smiles of enjoyment pasted onto our faces.

While in Samoa a disturbing incident took place. A sailboat with a Dutch father and daughter aboard was moored at the far end of the dock. The story doing the rounds was that the father was searching for his six-year-old daughter who his wife had run off with. Apparently this was the second partner who'd run away from him. We seldom saw them and when we did the father was spouting angry words about one thing or another and the daughter was pale and silent. A boy on another boat took a fancy to her and tried to visit her at the dad's boat. Apparently when he looked through the port-light he was horrified to see her chained to the saloon table. The authorities were alerted but supposedly maintained that a father's words and actions were sacrosanct and one shouldn't interfere in any of his decisions, so on that basis they declined taking action.

The boy's parents were incensed and when we left American Samoa, this was all on the boil. Many years later we heard via the yachtie grapevine that the boy and his family had left American Samoa with this Dutch girl aboard their boat!

Three triumphant days later, after sailing out of American Samoa, we were anchored in the Port of Refuge Harbour off the village of Neiafu on Vava'u Island, Tonga, triumphant because I didn't get seasick once on this short passage! This is one of the largest natural harbours in the South Pacific. The sailing grounds in this area are in protected waters with a myriad of islets and the snorkelling here must rate as one of the best in the world.

In Tonga I bartered with a few items of clothing and donated the rest of my Vancouver working clothes to a gathering of woman I had met. For the remainder of our stay there and until our departure, they would kindly leave fruit, vegetables and useful items like trays made from palm fronds or home-made coconut wood bowls or spoons in the cockpit. We also occasionally helped in 'fish drives' in which the whole village participated. We'd go into the lagoon and by shouting and banging the water, virtually herd the fish in front of us into big nets strung across an opening. The men would grab the fish with their bare hands and bite them in the head to kill them.

Our stay there was pleasurable and memorable as so much happened; meeting many of our old yachtie friends, fish drives, horse riding with no saddles, the underwater cave saga, being given gemstones and the legendary Isaiah's feast. The walks were beautiful and some of the hospitable local people kept drinking nuts in their fridges which they offered to us on these walks. They would lop off the top, put a straw into it and hand it to us with a big smile. There is nothing quite as refreshing as ice cold coconut water on a hot day.

On one of walks we met a horse owner who suggested we go for a trot on his horses. Not being horse riders, Rob and I didn't know what to anticipate but we were game to try. The horses had makeshift bridles, no stirrups and bags of straw thrown over their backs instead of saddles. These horses were small and being tall our feet almost dragged on the grass. We wobbled along precariously with the bag of straw sliding around under our bottoms until we couldn't take it any longer... but it was entertaining trying. Amazingly Rob even galloped, bare feet flying!

The underwater cave saga sticks in my mind as one of my more stupid actions and I feel quite fortunate that I am here and able to tell you about the incident. We had heard the Tongan legend surrounding this cave, which tells of a cruel ruler who ordered a rival family killed. The alluring daughter of the ill-fated clan was saved by an admirer, who hid her in a secret cave, a natural limestone marvel. He visited her daily, bringing food until he was able to rescue his 'mermaid bride' and make the crossing to Fiji.

We were determined to find this cave and received vague directions from a resident person. A band of us yachties sailed over to the island, Nua Papu Island, beneath which the cave, Mariner's Cave, was to be found. It was named after Will Mariner, an early European visitor who noticed that local people spear fishing in front of the cliffs would go down and not reappear for quite a while. Intrigued, he questioned the fishermen who showed him this underwater cave.

Rob and some of the others dived along the cliff face at areas that looked promising. Eventually they found the cave. Rob assured me that even though I'm a poor swimmer, I could do it. He said that our French Canadian friend and he would each hold a hand and guide me straight down for about four or five metres, at which point we would turn and swim horizontally through the underwater tunnel for about 15 metres and then we would kick to the surface inside the cave. Easy!

What they didn't tell me was that it was dark in the tunnel under the cliff or that they would let go of my hands halfway along. I jumped off the boat into the tepid water, resolute in my decision to see this legendary cave. They held my hands, I took a big breath of air and down we finned, from bright and sunny into the darkness. When they let go of my hands I assumed that we had arrived so I shot upwards and straight into the roof of the tunnel. I was stunned and it took everything I had to keep my wits about me and hang on to my remaining air. I kicked my hardest and kept going, my head throbbing painfully and my chest bursting. Eventually I saw a silvery glimmer and knew I could make it and then I felt hands grabbing me and mercifully hauling me to the surface.

My first reaction was to suck in huge lungfuls of air, almost sobbing with relief at the same time. My second reaction was one of concern as I was convinced that the bash on my head had affected my senses. I couldn't see properly, I seemed to be swathed in fog and I couldn't hear properly, my ears felt odd, as though they had cotton wool stuffed into them, and people talking and even the sound of splashing sounded odd, not like it was supposed to sound. Suddenly it all cleared, my vision was crystal clear and my hearing sharp. What was going on?

As I paddled breathlessly to keep my face above water (there was no place to stand), I looked around and found myself in a wonderland. Lacy looking deposits adorned the walls of the cave, stalactites hung above us and sea snakes lay on ledges. Best of all was the dim, ghostly quality of the pale turquoise light that flooded the cavern.

Suddenly my ears underwent the sensation of being pressurised, the cavern was again engulfed in fog, and I was now convinced that the bang on my head had possibly left me damaged. I found out later that everybody else endured the same thing which was caused by the swells breaking against the cliff face outside which forced water through the tunnel, thus creating a change in pressure which in turn condensed the air and caused the fog to form. As the water receded so did the fog, and this goes on in a continuous cycle of clear, fog, clear, fog!

The worst though was yet to come; how was I going to get out of this underwater cavern? I was too scared to do the return swim through the tunnel. Rob and our friend, who was now keeping me afloat, couldn't paddle and support me forever in this cavern. One by one the other yachties went back to their boats as did Rob and our friend. I was left alone to ponder my situation; there was no way out other than the way I had come in. I needed to dredge up courage in a hurry. It was definitely a case of 'do or die', so I propelled myself down, this time solo, into the tunnel and mercifully I had a point to aim for as I could see the brilliant blue, sunshine rich water at the other end of the tunnel as well as the legs of the others. It was so much easier this way round and also, knowing what to expect was half the battle won.

I emerged feeling victorious and well satisfied. I might not have looked like the mermaid bride of legend but I had done it and this never-to-be-repeated experience had been worth it (despite the painful lump on my head)!

Rob and I had sailed across to Mariner's Cave in our dinghy, and on the way back to the anchorage where Moya was securely anchored, we visited Swallows' Cave. One can only get to Swallows' Cave by boat. A few days before, around sunset, we had noticed bats pouring out of this cave and we were keen on a closer inspection. We doused our sail and fired up the two horsepower Suzuki motor and slowly put-putted our way in. The vaulted roof of the cave was thick with bats hanging overhead; all of them eyeing us inquisitively while below us lay a multi-coloured coral garden alive with both hard and soft corals, foraging crustaceans and bright, darting fish of all sizes. It was another extraordinary cave.

The coral, fish and sea life in Tonga is worth mentioning and worth making a special visit to, as the snorkelling is exquisite. Daily I would don my mask, snorkel and fins and spend hours pottering around the reefs. I would force myself out of the water for lunch and then get back in as soon as possible to continue my underwater exploration. On one particular occasion I identified an impressive lionfish and decided to observe it for a while. Next to me was a rock covered in what looked like a soft coral, mustard in colour. I leaned my bikini-clad buttocks against it and was instantly in agony. I had received horrible 'burns' from this coral, known as fire coral. I had automatically, wrongly assumed fire coral to be red.

In the mornings we regularly spotted sea snakes coiled in the engine well which we simply ignored. We had been told that although poisonous their tiny mouths were unable to nip a human. Whether this was true or not we simply adopted our usual 'don't mess with snakes' policy. The beaches were awash with gorgeous shells, the finest we had come across anywhere.

While we were at anchor there, we attended one of Isaiah's famous feasts on the beach where my long dormant taste buds were shocked into life. Isaiah was a local resident whose culinary talents were acknowledged far and wide. This enormous seafood feast was prepared in an 'oven' under the beach sand and the end result was succulent, juicy food, all wrapped individually in banana leaves like small gifts. Each wrapped gift had a delicious and unexpected delicacy within; for instance octopus was cooked inside coconuts with chunks of papaya (paw-paw), no doubt being tenderised by the papain enzyme in the papaya.

One day a 65-foot long (approximately 20 metres) Luderitz trawler from Namibia, known as South West Africa then, powered into the anchorage. We were gobsmacked! It had been converted a little and it boasted a stubby mast and forestay. Later we were to discover that they had gutted and rebuilt the interior of the boat to a luxurious standard. The owners, a delightful couple and their two children, had originally lived in Windhoek and had given up their life goals there as a result of political turmoil. We became good friends and shared many a fine bottle of South African wine with them. Their last port of call had been in New Zealand and they were en-route to the U.S. They told us a dreadful story of how, after leaving New Zealand, they had weathered an almighty storm, a storm in which close friends of theirs had apparently disappeared and now their confidence was severely compromised. Eventually they had to leave Tonga and we sadly took leave of our new friends, but one and a half days later they pitched up again, their confidence shattered.

Rob offered to make the passage to Pago Pago with them, an offer they gratefully accepted. They knew that I would be left alone on Moya in the anchorage but of course I didn't mind at all. They showered me with gifts before they left, despite my protests; spending money, a cinnamon tourmaline, eight moonstones, a 4.7 carat yellow tourmaline, a garnet and silver necklace as well as medical supplies, a fishing rod and reel and several books on Australia and New Zealand. Their generosity was boundless and while on their boat Rob lived like a king. They flew him back to Neiafu on a small plane so he had the added enjoyment of seeing the islands from above.

While he was gone I took the opportunity to sand and varnish our saloon table as we were particular about keeping our woodwork looking good. We always kept Moya shipshape and maintained her well in the years that we sailed her and she nearly always looked stunning.

After leaving Tonga we had awful weather for almost all of the six days it took for us to get to Fiji; blustery winds, rain, heavy cloud cover and rough seas as well as submerged reefs, rocky outcrops and new, uncharted islands to keep an eye out for. Earlier in the year, new islands had been born as a result of undersea eruptions. Rob battled to get sun, moon or star sights and worked ceaselessly on our dead reckoning. We were in the tail end of a hurricane with dangerous obstacles in our path. It was a nightmarish passage with both of us on the go around the clock, snatching brief power naps when we could. At a crucial point a gap opened up briefly in the cloud cover and Rob was able to get the sight he so desperately needed to get us safely through the worst of the obstacles. As usual I magnanimously fed the fish daily.

By the time we arrived in Suva, Fiji at sunset, Rob was stressed to the max and completely exhausted. That first night there we both slept the sleep of the dead. After clearing customs the following morning, then half an hour later immigration and later still, obtaining visas, we gave up on the inspection by the agricultural department as we were tired of waiting and headed straight for the post office. Collection of mail was one of our constant joys and that was always given precedence. The second thing we did was go to a restaurant and order big, fat juicy steaks! Thin, juicy steaks arrived but boy, were they delicious!

Suva was exciting and the culture vibrant. The many Indian traders – "special price for you" – reminded us fondly of home and we loved the Fijians large, frizzy hairstyles. Every day we passed through the Royal Suva Yacht Club where beers were sold at giveaway prices. This is where I perfected the fine art of drinking beer and so we whiled away many a genial afternoon with friends. It was here we discovered that two of our friends' boats ended up on the rocks as a result of their anchors dragging during the hellish storm we had weathered. Luckily they were in a protected anchorage when this happened and they were both able to winch themselves off without incurring too much damage. A third boat had put down two anchors which both dragged and it narrowly missed the rocks.

— 6 —

Australia And Beyond

Rob and I both suffered with the scare we had had on the passage to Fiji. On top of that we were exceedingly homesick, we missed our friends and particularly our families and to crown it all I had missed my period. Within four days of arrival in Fiji, Rob had struck a deal with an Australian to swap Moya for the Australian's smallholding in Willunga, near Adelaide, South Australia. We were on the verge of becoming farmers! The smallholding had a modern three-bedroomed house, a hangar-sized shed in which there was a tractor, a highly modified 820cc motorbike as well as a creek running through the garden. Included in the deal was a car, a Morris Minor Utility vehicle which was waiting for us in Sydney. Two weeks later the Australian was the proud owner of our beloved 'Moya' and we were airborne, winging our way to Sydney, Australia.

We collected our funny little car and had a whirlwind two days in Sydney before driving to Willunga. Our mini road spree took three days and we marvelled at the flocks of parrots and the many kangaroos that hopped across our path. The smallholding was exactly as the owner had described and we were thrilled with it and the new life ahead of us. What he hadn't described was quite how cold it gets there in winter; we were freezing! Luckily the house had a fireplace which kept us toasty.

This swap was fortuitous as our suspicions were confirmed after a visit to the doctor; we were having a baby! This was monumental news and we were ecstatic. Living on a smallholding and learning basic farming skills seemed nicer than night watches, shimmying up the mast to scan the ocean, the sticky, salty atmosphere, the perpetual motion and the chronic lack of fresh fruit and vegetables. We settled in to our new home where we embraced life on land with enthusiasm.

Rob found a good job in the electronics industry in Adelaide while I embraced the spirit of being a farmer. I acquired 18 egg laying hens, one rooster who found himself in rooster heaven, three goats, one of them a striking, silky haired creature, four calves and a baby galah (common Australian parrot type bird) called Smurfy. I loved my farmyard animals; the hens scrabbled amongst themselves to sit in my lap, and I shampooed, conditioned and blow dried the goats. The little bulls, Teddy, a Black Angus, Bobby, a Murray Grey, Ben and Sam, both brown beef cattle, wore collars and I trained them to walk on leashes. They all became pets. Rob had concluded that his job in electronics was preferable to bottle feeding calves, mucking out the shed and planting seeds with the tractor. I could not yet drive a car so I had to go for my antenatal check-ups on the motorbike with my growing tummy resting comfortably on the tank. I suppose this was really Lara's first motorcycling experience!

Time passed gloriously slowly. Our farming neighbours taught me how

to put in a crop of oats using the tractor and how to look after and feed the animals correctly. I also learnt how to drive the 'Ute' on the district roads of Willunga, my favourite goat, the silky Suzie, sitting on the seat next to me as we chugged to a nearby farm to collect hay for the animals.

Life was idyllic for me and I was happy living on the smallholding, but Rob was having second thoughts – he had for quite some time been depressed over his impulsive swap and all he wanted was to have our yacht, Moya, back. He longed for Moya and knew he had made a mistake and that he had relinquished her before giving it enough consideration. He was tired of commuting to Adelaide every day where he was employed as an electronics consultant. As yet no paperwork had been affected regarding change of ownership of both the smallholding and the boat, so when John, the owner of the smallholding phoned and stunned us by declaring that he was reneging on the deal, Rob couldn't have been happier. John's rather desperate phone call had come through in the early hours one morning and we gathered that he had lost his nerve completely after sailing through the end of a hurricane. He too had suffered the nightmare we had had when crossing from Tonga to Fiji and he never wanted to sail again. He wanted his house back immediately. That was music to Rob's ears and without a moment's hesitation he swung on to the motorbike and rode off to claim Moya, 2,700 kilometres away in Bundaberg.

As soon as the swap-back had been affected, Rob hurriedly came back to Willunga to help me and after finding homes for my adored animals, apart from the galah, I sadly packed up my gear, said goodbye to all that I had come to love and bade a teary farewell to the neighbours who had become my firm friends. With my now significantly larger tummy I climbed into the car, galah perched on my shoulder, and we left Willunga for good. We passed through the fascinating Australian countryside stopping only to refuel. Our beautiful baby daughter, Lara, was destined to be born in Bundaberg, famous for its rum.

The first two weeks back on the boat were difficult for me. I was terribly unhappy and I missed my animals, friends, home, garden and to add to it,

I had to find Smurfy a new home as well. He had taken a shine to the boat's woodwork and was attempting to turn Moya's immaculate woodwork into matchwood, much to Rob's horror; he would dig his beak into a join and twist and tear off splinters of wood. We arranged for the local zookeeper to have him and slowly introduce him to other galahs in a massive aviary. While cycling leisurely to the zoo (I was too pregnant to go any faster) with Smurfy perched on the handlebars I hit a bump and he fluttered off in alarm. His wing had been clipped but he managed to lopsidedly stay aloft and I lost him. Two days later there was a knock on Moya's hull and there was Smurfy! Some people had found him sitting on a pole nearby and recognised him as belonging to us. It was heartbreaking parting with him all over again.

Adding to Rob's and my unhappiness was that in the few months we had been away from Moya the 'new owner' had done a considerable amount of damage to her, damage that would dent our limited resources. This was concerning, especially now that our baby was only three months away from being born. We resolved to stay moored in the river in Bundaberg and repair her there. We had fold-up bicycles on board and the hospital was within easy cycling distance from Moya. It wasn't too long before we had completed the repairs and got used to life in the slow lane once again. Our excitement, along with my stomach, was growing, as our baby's birth loomed closer.

I must tell you that up until now I had never, ever, even so much as held a baby in my arms, nor had Rob. Even though this baby was planned and wanted I still regarded babies in general as foreign, squalling, pooping and demanding little creatures. I knew nothing about them but this was speedily rectified at the efficient, countrified hospital in Bundaberg. They gave us the tools for survival at the classes we attended there.

The one thing everyone lied about was in answer to my question, "How sore is giving birth?"

Answers ranged from "Uncomfortable" and "If you breathe correctly it's not too bad" to "You'll cope, don't worry". Thinking that I could now make an informed decision, I opted for a natural birth, no painkillers or any other medication. Nine weeks to go!

The weather was stifling, my ankles swelled, I was corpulently uncomfortable, food disagreed with me, the baby never stopped kicking, I read endlessly, I waddled around; the days dragged… would this never end? Before I was terrified to have the baby, now I was terrified it would never arrive.

In the meantime Rob went to Adelaide for a few days to attend to the final bits and pieces as well as collect one or two items of jewellery I had left behind. While he was gone the rain pelted down torrentially and the river flooded. I had, in the meantime been admitted to hospital for observation. Poor Rob arrived back at midnight to a flooding river and he yelled for me from the bank to collect him in the dinghy. It was a while before he noticed that the dinghy was not with Moya and his first thought was that he had missed the birth he was so looking forward to attending. He came running wildly into the hospital, dripping wet, with anxiety written all over his face. The next morning I was fine again and still pregnant, returned to Moya.

Two weeks later, at my check-up, I begged the doctor to not admit me into the hospital for the mild toxaemia that had set in. After much persuasion he reluctantly allowed me to remain on Moya, insisting on bed rest, broken only by ablutions. "If this baby doesn't manage to kick its way out of my stomach sooner, it's only three weeks and four days to go to the due date!"

By now we had wiped out all traces of the previous 'owner' and with the new curtains I had sewn up, Moya was looking grand, perfect for baby's arrival. Another check-up for me and apart from the information that the baby's head had engaged, the diagnosis was the same, so back to bed it was. Interestingly I had developed an alarmingly dark, almost pitch-black line heading downwards from my naval. This is quite normal and happens in about three quarters of all pregnancies. The nurses had gathered around and had all agreed that this was the darkest 'linea nigra' they had ever seen but assured me that this would disappear soon after the birth. I hoped so!

Two weeks and one day to go, woo hoo! Excitement as well as my girth was beginning to reach mammoth proportions in the light of the forthcoming attraction. All systems were ready to roll with Braxton Hicks contractions giving me a taste of what was to come. Baby clothing – sorted, hospital gear – sorted, boat – sorted, nothing left to do but be patient. Oh, we can't wait for this baby to arrive!

Inevitably the long-awaited day finally did arrive. The contractions appeared with a vengeance and I had to carefully time these contractions with the rocking of Moya and the bouncing of the dinghy that I was trying to climb down into for the row ashore. Halfway down, while clinging onto the rigging, I had to stop and perform my Lamaze breathing exercises before continuing. Rob radioed our friend on 'Shalmar', who was on standby and she took us to the hospital. This was at about 6:30 am. All went well for the next four to five hours with the labour progressing as it should. Rob helped me with the correct breathing technique and coached me through each contraction until the time came to move from the pre-delivery room to the delivery room. It was all downhill from there. The final contractions were unexpectedly, flipping painful and this scared me. My usual calm handling of any situation was beginning to slip and spiral out of control. With Rob's help I managed to rein myself in and focus on breathing correctly.

Just as I thought I was probably going to burst, the doctor informed me that it was time to push. Push and push I did, intense eyeball-popping pushes and I can categorically state that the birth of this baby was the most painful, shrieking, body-cleaving event I could imagine. I sensed a gush of body soaking fluid and was convinced that this was my life blood and I had split in two. At this point the doctor, the two nurses and Rob yelled in unison, "Give it another push!" I did and out came the rest of the baby. Everybody was smiling. It was a girl. My husband looked positively radiant, congratulations were being extended and all I could hazily mull over was, why were they smiling? Why weren't they sewing me together again?

We had a daughter, a healthy, beautiful baby with an Apgar rating of nine out of 10! She was tiny, alert and hungry. Our work had started! We had a small scare in the hospital as it took a few days for my milk to come in and our tiny scrap was exhausted by the shortage of 'food', the hot weather and constant handling by nurses and friends. A feeding tube was inserted into her nose the next night and by the following morning my boobs had doubled in size and Lara had more milk than she could drink at any one 'meal'.

The other yachties were fantastic; they were so supportive and sent cards, gifts and flowers, cooked meals for Rob while I was in the hospital, offered to do the washing for me, kept me supplied with magazines and visited us regularly.

Less than a month later I wrote to my mother, "My goodness a baby is a lot of work – demands all your time," and then later in my letter I went on to say, "Rob has this problem – he can't stop kissing Lara. Actually he's a super father. He has Lara lying on his chest and they both take a snooze. The first time Lara lay on his chest she had no nappy on and you can guess what happened. Not only did she wee on him but she did a poop at the same time. A yellow, runny one! Ha, ha."

As soon as Lara had had her six week check-up we set off for Lady Musgrave Island, an uninhabited coral cay (a small, low-elevation, sandy island formed on the surface of a coral reef) in the Great Barrier Reef and a World Heritage Listed Marine Park. While writing this chapter I 'revisited' Lady Musgrave courtesy Google Earth and it's hard to believe that I was ever in this incredible place. It boasts an abundant variety of sea life in and around its azure lagoons and of course is an underwater paradise.

Lara loved the rocking motion of the boat at sea and she was no problem; she was obviously a born sailor. I was the problem and once again battled sea sickness; it was often bucket on one side, with Lara on the breast on the other side. Lady Musgrave was marvellous and while there Rob used his homemade 'Hawaiian sling' with deadly accuracy and speared a few delicious eating fish.

Our next port of call was Gladstone where we booked Moya for a haul-out; she needed to have her hull scraped as the growing appendages were now slowing us down considerably and she needed a fresh coat of anti-fouling paint. The last one had been at the tidal slip in Suva, Fiji. The detail that sticks in my mind about Gladstone is the 'no-see-ums'. In the evenings the air was thick with these tiny bloodsucking biters and from Gladstone on we were plagued by these insects. I had to make sure that Lara was constantly protected by fine mesh netting but that made it hot for her.

Disappointingly, this is as far as my letters go. I suspect that over time the rest were lost, so from here on I will simply give a brief narration and hope that my memory serves me correctly. The letters have been so useful in reminding me of incidents that were buried in the recesses of my mind but anyway, I find that the more I think about it, the more the cobwebs disperse.

We continued cruising amongst the islands of the Great Barrier Reef as well as visiting Rockhampton, Mackay, Townsville and finally Cairns on the mainland. We loved Queensland but we agreed that the Great Barrier Reef was somewhat over-rated. Safe anchorages were few and far between and we had a repeat episode of the Fanning situation where Moya was nearly washed ashore by the fierce wind and waves. Often the water was brownish and visibility poor so the snorkelling wasn't ideal. We preferred the islands of the South Pacific for snorkelling.

With Lara on board bad weather became problematic and the worst was when I was working on deck and she was desperately crying below for her feed. This happened quite often; Rob would need me urgently to help navigate or work on deck and Lara would be either left alone or rapidly pulled off the boob, mid-feed, so that I could rush up and do the necessary. Of course I still had to do my night watches. I felt that I wasn't mothering Lara properly, I was exhausted, often seasick and I couldn't continue at that rate much longer.

We both concluded that this was not the way to go, so Rob's sister, Jenny, joined him in Cairns for the passage across the Indian Ocean. I hopped on a plane back to South Africa with Lara where she was spoilt by loving grandparents.

Rob continued on, heading for the Indian Ocean and South Africa, stopping off at Christmas Island, famous for its annual red crab migration, Cocos (Keeling) Islands which consist of 27 coral islands, the mountainous Rodrigues Island and Mauritius before arriving triumphant, in Durban, our hometown. I was overjoyed to see him and of course Lara and I rapidly moved on board but not for long as we realised that this was the time for a major interior refit. We rented a house in a quiet suburb and enjoyed life on land while working on Moya.

About 10 or 11 months later the authorities informed us that if we stayed any longer we would have to pay import duties. This was out of the question so we set off for Reunion Island. I was violently seasick (as usual) and Lara decided now was the time to try to start walking!

Lara stunned us with her adaptation to this rough passage. Rob had his hands full above decks and I hardly mothered her as I was so green-about-the-gills but this didn't worry her one iota. She discovered the galley cupboard with our food supplies and when hungry wedged herself into the galley and munched on whatever she could lay her hands on.

She used the motion of the boat to get into a standing position and with feet spread wide apart she actually managed to take her first steps.

By the time we arrived in fragrant Reunion, which we could smell long before it appeared on the horizon, I was wan and stick-thin and Lara was healthy, happy and walking. Initially her style of walking was so funny; typical drunken sailor but it didn't take her long to start walking normally. Reunion, the island of sweet-smelling flowers used in the perfume industry, is a blend of French, African, Indian, and Chinese cultures. Its population of roughly 700,000 inhabitants speaks mostly French or Creole. This scenic island was well worth visiting with its pretty beaches, jagged peaks and lush forests.

Then it was on to Mauritius where we stayed for a number of months. We met up with old friends we had last met in the South Pacific, we snorkelled and swam daily, we shifted to different anchorages and we bussed around the island, explored the market in Port Louis and ate the delicious, freshly prepared food from roadside vendors. Lara was now almost a year and a half old when I visited a doctor, specimen bottle in hand. A test quickly revealed that I was pregnant with our second (planned) child. I was issued with a stern warning not to continue sailing as I was considered 'high risk'. So Lara and I flew back to South Africa while Rob went on a crayfishing (spiny lobster) spree.

While cruising we always kept our ears and eyes open for opportunities to make supplementary cash. In Mauritius we found out that selling crayfish to the local hotels was lucrative so after I left for South Africa, Rob hired a deep freeze which he strapped to the foredeck of Moya. Rob and a local guy, whom he had befriended, navigated to a nearby island where crayfish was abundant. They filled up the deep freeze and the catch was subsequently sold to the local fellow's hotel connections. A few weeks later Rob voyaged the 1,580 nautical miles to Durban. We had big decisions to make!

As I should have presumed, decisions were made and the sailing life was the order of the day. After a lengthy stop enjoying parents, relatives and friends, Rob set off for Cape Town without me. The intention was to join him in the Dutch Antilles where we hoped our second baby would be born. I was most astounded then to receive a phone call from him when he arrived in Cape Town, telling me to leave Durban with Lara and catch the soonest possible train there. He said he had booked a berth for us on the RMS St. Helena!

On our arrival he whisked us off to this ship bound for England via St. Helena. My sea sickness returned with a vengeance and the doctor on board insisted I accept an injection of Phenergan.

The Phenergan, which is actually an anti-histamine although it does have anti-motion effects, exceeded all my expectations and from that moment on seasickness on the long ocean passages was a thing of the past, the only side-effect being drowsiness which was infinitely preferable to being seasick. I didn't use it when we were moored or at anchor because the drowsiness would then have been an irritation.

A young couple with two small children befriended me on this idyllic 1,697 nautical mile passage to St. Helena and in exchange for au pair duties, Lara and I were given accommodation in Jamestown, the main town on

Looking down at the anchorage in St. Helena from Jacob's ladder

this island, a speck of land of volcanic origin in the South Atlantic Ocean.

Napoleon, Dinizulu kaCetshwayo and about 5,000 Boer prisoners were exiled from South Africa to St. Helena by the British. I found Longwood House Museum to be fascinating; this was Napoleon's home before his death. His autopsy was apparently carried out here on a table which bears a small rust-coloured stain, said to be his blood!

A pleasant week later Rob arrived and Lara and I joined him once again on board Moya.

The anchorage was exceptionally uncomfortable and Moya rolled from side to side, necessitating my frequent sprints to the rail to feed the fishes. Unbeknown to me this had been observed by some kindly ex-pats living there. They insisted that we spend the remainder of our stay in their stone cottage in the interior of the island. Rob baulked at this suggestion but I gladly took them up on their offer and Lara and I moved in for a relaxing, peaceful, if short-lived, stay.

We walked many kilometres exploring and admiring the beauty of St. Helena. We also walked to the local hospital to arrange the impending baby's birth there. But no such luck; the hospital was exorbitantly priced and they suggested we continue on as they could not assist us. Our next stop was the library, where we took out books on delivering babies so in the event of this happening at sea Rob would know what to do. In retrospect we must have been crazy!

Rob had taken on a crewman in Cape Town for the passage to Brazil, so when Lara and I re-embarked I didn't have to work very hard at all. We became quite fond of this guy but years later we heard that he had been tragically lost at sea while crewing on a yacht from Brazil to the Caribbean.

Thankfully the trip to Natal in Brazil was uneventful, with no alarming signs of the baby arriving! Before departing South Africa, Rob bought a few cases of whisky because we had heard that it could be sold for a profit in Brazil. This he sold on arrival in Natal.

We didn't have too long to wait before the baby made his decision to arrive. Our thrilled toddler was bundled off to a friend's boat to await our return the following morning. This time, at the first sign of a twinge Rob hurried me off the boat and into a waiting taxi, a vehicle packed with passengers who needed to be dropped off at various places along the pot-holed dirt road en-route to the hospital. I thought this baby was going to arrive in the car! By the time we arrived at the hospital my baby had started his journey into the world and I could no longer walk with dignity.

The diminutive doctor we had entrusted with delivering our baby swooped into the room wearing a long white lab coat, white pants and black boots with raised square heels. He couldn't speak a word of English but that didn't bother anybody. He chirruped away in Portuguese and reminding me of an Indian Mynah bird, busied himself with the tools of his trade. We became the objects of tittering fascination as the staff had never seen a man accompany his wife into the birthing room. This was customarily 'women's business'.

The doctor's chirps rose in pitch and I gathered from his miming actions that I should now push. I burst out laughing and battled to concentrate despite the pain of labour, that is, until I saw him brandishing a pair of scissors! I shrieked "No!"

Rob yelled, "The doctor knows what he's doing!" and our interpreter chose this moment to walk in, the moment the doctor decided to cut. She turned a paler shade of white and staggered out again and my son was born into this crazy scenario.

Our beautiful boy, our longed-for son – we couldn't have been happier! Rob stayed on mosquito watch all night as there was no glass in the windows. Mom and baby slept soundly, ready to face the yachting world once again the following day. We collected an excited little Lara and introduced her to our latest bundle of joy, her new brother, Thana. Our family was complete; life wouldn't get better than this.

Apart from whisky, outboard engines also sold well in Brazil and a week after the birth of our son, Rob skippered a boat to Rio carrying a friend's outboards, which he sold. He had a fabulous time as this luxury yacht had a bevy of scantily clad models aboard. The party continued for another few

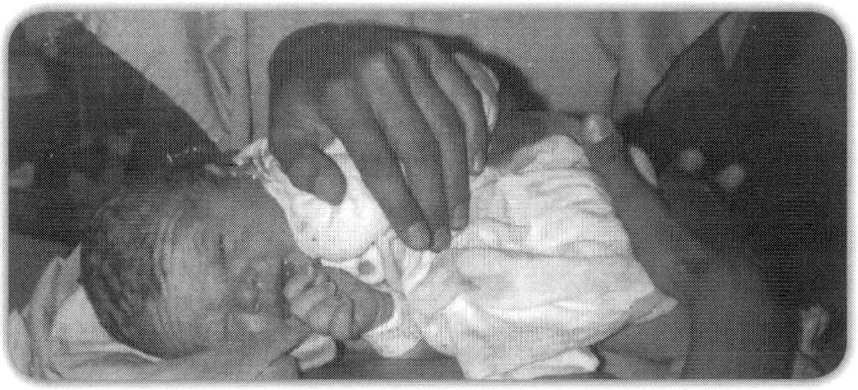

weeks in Rio while I was left to fend for myself with a newborn, a toddler and a dinghy with no oars. Well luckily I believe that adversity is character strengthening!

Our flawless baby developed horrible sores while we were still anchored off the yacht club in Natal, sores which coincidentally are known as 'Natal sores' in South Africa. This is a common problem there but with the correct medication they clear up quite quickly. As soon as baby's sores healed, Rob negotiated a lucrative charter which involved transporting a cameraman and a diver to the Brazilian island of Fernando do Noronha to film porpoises.

Babies aren't supposed to get seasick, or so we were told. Thana was very seasick on this excursion to Fernando do Noronha. It was heartbreaking.

The Brazilian cameraman and diver were amiable guys but had no idea about water conservation on a small boat and ultimately, to our red-faced embarrassment, Rob had to put out an emergency call requesting water because our tanks were dry. I was breastfeeding both children and this situation was a huge wake-up call and utterly intolerable for me. I issued my spouse with an ultimatum, "Your family or the boat".

My babies and I moved ashore in Fortaleza, into a boarding house with no plan as to the future. I only wanted my babies to be safe. Rob continued on with another charter, into the Caribbean. There in Fortaleza we lived a strange and lonely life, in an alien country with an alien language where no one spoke English. However Fortaleza was quite charming. The people in the boarding house pretended to understand me and with patience and good humour put up with my dismal attempts at speaking Portuguese. My toddler, Lara, also learnt the lingo and spoke Portuguese (probably a whole lot better than I did).

One day I received the anticipated but dreaded phone call from the authorities, telling me that my stay in Brazil was now over and I must leave the country. I was aghast but my money had almost run out and I didn't have a clue as to what to do. Synchronicity works in weird ways as that very afternoon I received a surprise call from Rob in the Caribbean. He was missing us and had come to the conclusion that we were his main priority.

He immediately booked tickets for us to fly to South Africa.

Leaving all my gear behind in boxes at an acquaintance's house, my Australian-born toddler, my Brazilian-born son and I flew home. I took up electronics and assembled printed circuit boards for a company in the entertainment industry. My little ones were no longer comfortable sleeping in a regular bed, so I had to have hooks affixed to the walls of our tiny apartment for their hammocks.

Many moons later, Rob sold Moya. It was the end of a pretty wild, but certainly exciting era. Things would never be the same again. Rob returned to South Africa, where we bought a house and set up an electronics business, producing amplifiers for vehicles, which we ran from home. It was successful, the children were happy and I took pleasure in the home and garden. Eventually though, the daily grind wore Rob down and his thoughts turned to sailing again.

He couldn't resist the tempting allure of this lifestyle and so he bought a ready-built hull and deck. Over the next couple of years he completed the boat, a Lavranos design 'Vickers 41'. I named her 'Energy', and part two of the saga began. By this time Lara was five years old and was in Grade One at school, while Thana was three years old and still enjoying his 'toddler time' at home with Rob and me.

Once again I had life-changing decisions to make. The children were older but would that change anything? I had one of two options; save my marriage by sailing with my husband or call it quits and deprive our children of a father and face hardship and heartbreak.

The answer was clear; we boarded Energy and shortly thereafter left Durban bound for Mossel Bay. We had a crewman on board who happened to be an old friend; this was helpful in many ways but we faced the difficulties of all living together in close quarters which ultimately proved to be a hindrance.

The sail to Mossel Bay was rough and tough on us but we persevered. From there it was on to Hout Bay and once again the Atlantic crossing to St. Helena Island, the speck in the ocean worth stopping at. I enjoyed visiting people I had met the previous time who were flabbergasted at the news that I was doing it again, this time with two children!

Energy was light and fast as well as being fairly spacious at 41 feet long (roughly 14 metres). The children enjoyed the sail across the Atlantic and kept themselves busy; Lara wrote in her diary or worked on her cross stitch picture and five days a week I tutored her with Grade One lessons. We would net sea creatures for Thana to examine in a bucket and draw – these enthralled him and together the children would often play and splash in the dinghy, which we filled with sea water. They both enjoyed colouring-in books and being read stories was their favourite. Rob had installed netting all around the boat, an additional safety feature for the children.

We decided to call in (again) at Fernando Do Noronho, declared a Marine National Park in 1988, en-route to Natal and Fortaleza, roughly 350 kilometres distant. What a disaster!

We dropped anchor at Fernando and we all piled into the dinghy to motor ashore. A heavy swell was running but by this time Rob was an expert at powering the dinghy through the surf. The children were wearing flotation devices on their upper arms and were very excited to plant their little feet on solid soil. We idled slowly on the ridge of a swell, Rob and our crewman watching intently, waiting for the right moment to open the throttle and surge forwards with the wave. The moment arrived, Rob twisted the hand

The navigation area on board Energy

grip opening up the throttle and we were off, off on a thrilling propulsion towards the shore… but it all went horribly wrong, almost tragically so!

The huge swell we were riding started breaking and break it did, with us in it. We shot forwards, the dinghy overturned and mayhem prevailed. Lara disappeared, Thana was torn from my arms, I was pushed down under the surf and Rob and our crewman were somewhere in the broiling surf. I surfaced, desperately scanning for the children and heard a person screaming. The screaming went on and on until I finally realised that I was the one doing the screaming. My focus was on finding my children but being a poor swimmer I was battling myself. Next to me our crewman, John, surfaced with Lara. She had been trapped under the upturned dinghy. Where was Thana? He immediately dove down and to my immense relief returned almost immediately with Thana who had been rolling along in the surf. We managed to struggle to the shore where we lay panting like stranded fish.

Rob and John went straight back into the surf to salvage whatever they could, while we waited on the shore. While they searched for the outboard engine, the snorkelling apparatus and all the personal possessions we had lost from the dinghy (which luckily was equipped with flotation chambers in the bow and stern), I searched for coconuts so that I could give my children food and liquid. This done, we set about relaxing until the guys came to fetch us. A lizard approached. Transfixed, we stared as it came closer. Suddenly it darted forward and tried to bite Lara. We shooed it off but another two darted in, then another three or four, until we were surrounded by aggressive lizards trying to bite us. We tried to distract them with morsels of coconut but they remained interested in us.

We spent our time fielding lizards while hollering in vain for John and Rob to come and fetch us. They were busy trying to fix the motor they had luckily recovered, along with quite a few of our other possessions but we also lost a lot of invaluable stuff like fishing and snorkelling gear. Eventually they gave up on the motor and swam in to shore, body-surfing in the breakers, to collect us. It was dusk and a bad time to attempt the dangerous swim through the breakers to the boat but we had to do it. My courageous children bit the bullet, the little one, tearfully so. Assisted by Rob and John they managed the pulverising swim back to Energy. My confidence was badly shaken; this wasn't right.

We were relieved to be on our way to Natal, where we spent a leisurely four days soaking up all the social and gastronomic luxuries the Natal Yacht Club had to offer. It was a short hop to Fortaleza where we had planned to collect all the goods I had previously left behind in storage. Astonishingly, (for us having come from a city where the goods most likely would have been 'lost') everything was still there, unopened. The kids couldn't contain themselves; they knew that long forgotten toys and books were in those boxes so to relieve the tedium of ocean sailing we allowed them to open one box a day and take pleasure in the items of interest they found in them. It turned out to be pleasurable for us as well; little gifts I had forgotten about, like fresh clothing, some of it new, unread books and so on.

Our first port of call in the Caribbean was Martinique, followed by Dominica, Guadeloupe, Montserrat and Nevis. Then it was on to St.

Thomas and Virgin Gorda in the British Virgin Islands. Cruising in these areas, as with the Bahamas, was tremendous; the welcoming turquoise waters were clear and the snorkelling top notch, the island scenery was spectacular and the people we met along the way, affable. We continued our lazy way into the Bahamas visiting Mayaguyana, Plana Cays, Crooked Island, Long Island, Say Island, Adderly Cay, Staniel Cay and Hawksbill Cay with New Providence Island being the last island stop before our arrival in Fort Lauderdale.

Three of these places stand out in my memories:

Virgin Gorda because of The Baths, where massive boulders provide a jungle of rock pools and secret beaches, so secret a couple decided they could copulate without fear of being caught. As we crested a rise, the children scampering along the path in front of us, we nearly stumbled over them. They didn't know where to hide their faces or indeed, their other bits.

Staniel Cay, home of Thunderball Cave. This was where the James Bond movies, 'Thunderball' was filmed in the '70s as well as 'Never Say Never Again'. 'Splash' and 'Into the Blue' were also filmed here. No wonder movies were made in this location; the scenery is unique as you are swimming inside a hollowed-out rock, no fishing is allowed and consequently the multitude of fishes are tame and the encounter with them quite extraordinary as the fish shoal around one, begging for food! There are below water as well as above water entrances and when we visited, there was even a sunken treasure chest, spilling its 'treasure', a grand reminder of the movies made here. The beams of light that make their way into this grotto light up the water with breathtaking effect. Happily, Thunderball Cave is protected by the Bahamas National Trust.

Hawksbill Cay was where my little one sliced his big toe to the bone. While Rob pottered around on Energy, Lara, Thana and I had wandered off together, slowly following a meandering water course upstream. It was a perfect sunny day with a few puffy clouds and a gentle breeze keeping us cool. The children were enjoying themselves immensely, examining shells, noticing little crabs and brightly coloured fish when all of a sudden they caught sight of a massive shell. Thana accelerated as fast as his small legs would allow, reached it first and excitedly picked it up and turned it over. An appropriately massive hermit crab popped its head out and gave Thana the fright of his young life. He immediately dropped it but unluckily it landed sharp side down and gashed his big toe badly. Blood squirted, he screamed and I scooped him up and started running back to Energy. Lara couldn't keep up so I scooped her up onto my other hip and continued my now ungainly run to get help.

Once on board, we lay our sobbing patient down with his foot up and started cleaning out the fragments of shell and granules of sand that were embedded deep in the wound. We administered a paediatric syrup painkiller which eventually helped to soothe him while I cleansed and bathed his toe in an antiseptic solution before closing the wound with steri-strips, a good alternative for stitches in such injuries. We were most anxious as we couldn't be sure that the wound was completely clean, the weather was hot, we had no antibiotics and infection was a strong possibility. We hauled our anchor up and set sail for Fort Lauderdale, anchoring off New Providence en-route.

Well, needless to say, our fears were realised and after initially looking quite good, Thana's foot swelled up as infection took hold. By the time we reached Fort Lauderdale four days later the steri-strips had burst open and the cut was suppurating. Most worrying was the insidious scarlet stripe creeping up the inside of his leg. We rushed him to the nearest hospital where

Energy in Fort Lauderdale

his now gruesome-looking toe was treated and he was put onto a course of antibiotics. Yet another wake-up call – how many more did I need?

As I write this, I feel so forlorn as this was effectively the end of my cruising days as well as my marriage. To cut a long story short, the children and I fled back to the safety and security of a home on land in South Africa where we suffered the heartbreak and hardship I had anticipated. However we did have the support system of loving grandparents. Rob pursued his sailing dream, on and off, for another 20 years or so. The children missed out as they never had the opportunity to get to know their father as they grew up and Rob missed out on being a dad to them, an unrecoverable loss. As for me, I was faced with the responsibility of single-handedly providing for and rearing my two children, so for the time being, all thoughts of life on the ocean were on hold.

Many years later, long after Rob and I had parted company and gone on our separate ways, I was stunned (happily so) by a generous offer from him. He had chartered a boat for a cruise in the Caribbean with a couple I knew and liked but unfortunately for him, fortunately for me, his girlfriend at the time couldn't make it. There was a space going begging so would I like to join them? Would I indeed – my bags were almost packed!

Off I flew, immensely thrilled. My dear friend, Reinet, had extended her motherly wing to include my children while I was away. Both our sets of children got on well together so it was a fun time for them as well. It was splendid to see Rob and meet with my old friends again; we boarded the immaculate charter sailboat, 'E.Z. Concepts', in St. Thomas and started our leisurely, luxury cruise amongst the Virgin Islands. In between snorkelling, fine dining, long walks, browning our bodies in the sun, and gentle sailing we sipped Margaritas and generally lived the high life for a moment in time. At the end of the trip they all went their respective ways, but I had one remaining day in paradise and finished off my surreal holiday at a charming boutique hotel before flying home and facing reality once again.

— 7 —

My Diary – A Solo Ride Of Exploration From Durban To Cape Town

Part 1

I mulled over the idea of a solo ride and found that the thought didn't faze me at all. Well-wishers had tried to dissuade me with all manner of stories of misfortune and the foolishness of going alone but nothing could shake my desire to at least give it a shot. My preparations were exactly the same as they had been on my trip to Malawi with Lara and Clayton – thorough. My motorcycle was in fair condition and I had all the necessary tools and spares. Being an eternal optimist I didn't dwell on mechanical failures, punctures, falling off, medical emergencies or any of the myriad of maybes. It was just as well as pondering the negatives or 'what might happen' has a way of stopping adventure in its tracks. I felt that the first night out would put to rest any last vestiges of doubt and in that I was correct.

August 27, 2010

After a rushed, stressful week I finally managed to jam all my gear higgledy,

piggledy into the biking bags. I left Durban at 10:00 in the morning feeling totally disorganised, without a proper route plan and no idea as to where I'd be spending my first night on the road. I figured that I would sort everything out properly at my first overnight stop. My odometer read 11,868 kilometres.

The moment I hit the tar I knew I'd made the right decision. Initially I had idly given consideration to riding to Cape Town to see the famous spring flowers but a phone call from my sister-in-law inviting me to her 50th birthday bash in Cape Town cemented this idea. The day was sunny and clear and warm along the coast. At Port Shepstone I stopped for fuel and to have air put into my tyres. After wondering why the pump attendant was taking so long and not successfully putting air into the rear tyre I hopped off my bike and had a look. She was gamely trying to put air into the tyre lock valve!

From Port Shepstone I headed inland and the temperature seemed to drop with each kilometre gained. The scenery along this route is lovely.

Initially one follows the Mzulkulwana Valley with Oribi Gorge on the right, passing villages tucked in amongst the rolling hills. Along the way I caught glimpses of the old narrow gauge railway tracks which run between Port Shepstone and Harding. The train transported sugar cane in bygone days. This reminded me of stories from my youth because my brother used to go to a boarding school in Harding – to get there from Port Shepstone he was welcomed by the train driver and sat up front in the locomotive with the driver. If the proliferation of weeds growing over the tracks is anything to go by, it might no longer be in use. By the time I passed Harding I was shivering with cold despite my new triple-layer winter touring jacket.

Thankfully the temperature picked up again the further away I rode from Harding. Through Kokstad I went and on to Matatiele where I left behind a plethora of Bed and Breakfasts – this little town must survive on them. Exiting Matatiele was illuminating, as there in front of me, dramatically framed by the afternoon sun, were the southern Drakensberg Mountains!

The grubby little town of Mount Fletcher made me feel like I should keep going although I was tired by this stage after many unaccustomed hours in the saddle. My rear end was slowly but painfully reshaping itself from office chair shape to motorcycle saddle shape. The road ahead continued winding its way through now rocky, dry hills with evidence of sugar cane and grass fires, some still raging. At one point the road in front of me was obscured by thick smoke; I took a deep breath, held it and hoped for fresh air soon as I rode through.

Eventually, just when I was beginning to regret not overnighting in Matatiele, Maclear came into view and what a sweet little town. A most helpful man at the local tourist office insisted I take a brochure with phone numbers of local B and B's. I tried a few and was rather taken aback at their tariffs which seemed quite high considering that what was on offer was fairly basic. I selected Tortoni's and rode on towards Ugie for another six kilometres before reaching the turnoff to this delightfully rustic farmhouse.

While on the road a taxi came up behind me and started hooting so I pulled over to allow him to pass but he didn't. I turned off and he also turned off, still hooting. He was fully loaded with passengers and when I stopped, he did too. I couldn't believe it – I had dropped my notebook, he had picked it up and was desperately trying to return it to me. There are some first-rate people in this world of ours! I am ashamed to admit that I was secretly quite scared when I initially noticed this vehicle 'following' me.

At Tortoni's I was welcomed by the owner and shown to a homely, comfortable room which was perfect for my first night. I drank what seemed like a few gallons of tea, fully hydrating myself, and then sank into a comfy armchair armed with hospitality map and GPS. This was the life. The hospitality map was the best I could conjure up as I had accidentally left my detailed, indispensible map book at home. Damn!

August 28, 2010

The next morning all notions of an early getaway were banished on seeing the frost-covered landscape and my frost-covered motorbike. At 7:30 am the temperature was minus two degrees Celsius. The owner of the farmhouse prepared a large breakfast for me, enough to fill me for the day and I put the last rasher of uneaten bacon in my pocket for *padkos* (a snack) in case I felt peckish later. By 9:30 am it was suitably warm and I set off with a hand-drawn map that the owner had penned for me. The Garmin GPS in my pocket was of little use as it was impossible to stop all the time, take off my helmet and gloves, look for my glasses and then finally examine the GPS. It needed a mounting bracket on the handlebars, so I'd certainly have to attend to this for future trips.

On I tootled past Ugie and Elliot with the strong side-wind increasing in intensity. By the time I passed Cala I was riding at an uncomfortable angle as I was being buffeted by the wind. I was now having difficulty appreciating the beauty around me, the Maluti Mountains on the right and farmlands on the left. On I crabbed past Lady Frere and into Queenstown – the only poorly signposted town on my trip. At the petrol station I met the first biker and he complained bitterly about the wind that he too had battled on his ride from Tjarkastad. After a few wrong turns but without too much of a problem I found my way out of Queenstown and headed for Fort Beaufort.

Although the day was sunny and clear, the wind was now pumping and I was riding at an alarming angle. As soon as I rode into a forested area the wind disappeared and the going was easy but for most of the day I took quite a pummelling.

I had hoped to try an alternative route to Fort Beaufort which involved lots of dirt and two winding passes. The biker I had met in Queenstown warned me against doing this as he said that there were a number of wash-aways on the way there, it was very isolated and indeed might not even exist anymore. I elected to give it a shot anyway. I turned off onto a narrow unpaved road in poor condition and rattled my way along, going past villages and homesteads but nothing remotely pass-like. Eventually I had to admit defeat and retrace my route to the main road.

Just before I arrived in Fort Beaufort, hungry and thirsty, I came across a delightful farm stall where I had tea and cake in the fragrant flower-filled garden. I enquired as to where I could find accommodation for the night and the amiable lady managing the stall suggested that I come and stay at her place on a nearby farm. She lived in a small cottage with her children (who were spending the weekend with their dad in Port Elizabeth) and six dogs that at one stage or another she had rescued. Her yard was open veld with kudu and all sorts of game that she chanced upon regularly when she took her dogs for a walk.

We had lots in common and got on exceptionally well. She treated me to a delicious meal which we washed down with wine and whisky and had a marvellous evening lounging on her comfy couches, dogs all over the place. Her lifestyle intrigued me; it was so different to mine. In her younger days she had been a ballerina, which was still evident in her poised gait. She rarely bothered with locking her doors and she enjoyed the isolation. She had carved a niche for herself in the small local community and was kept busy with a variety of jobs. In that one evening we forged what I think will be a long-term friendship.

August 29, 2010

The ride to Grahamstown was scenically magnificent with the road snaking through hills and valleys but I froze all the way there and shivered and shook on to Port Elizabeth, despite adding another layer of clothing at the fuel stop in Grahamstown. From Port Elizabeth I headed for Hankey, but was horrified when my bike started spluttering on the freeway. I immediately swung the fuel lever onto reserve. The engine caught and I continued but now I was worried as this happened at 160 kilometres instead of 180 kilometres. I knew that I only had 20 kilometres of fuel left in the tank and urgently needed a fuel station. A worrying 10 kilometres later there was still no sign of one so I hauled out the GPS, clicked on POI (points of interest) 'fuel' and hey presto, there was fuel at Thornhill six kilometres ahead. So with the GPS guiding me I found my way to the modest fuel station, which was closed! The reason for this poor mileage was the dreadful headwind which simply ruined my petrol consumption.

A passer-by told me to bang on the door of the service station building, which I did, but disappointingly, the proprietor who opened up told me that the fuel tanks were empty but would be refilled the following day. I was now marooned but at my suggestion of erecting my tent next to his fuel pump for the night the proprietor hastily offered to go across to the hotel opposite and try and find fuel for me. As luck would have it he found a man with a stash of petrol which he used for his generator in the frequent power outages. He was generous with it, almost filling my tank to the brim and refusing to take a penny for it. So a big thank you to my kind and generous saviour in Thornhill.

While I was waiting for the saviour with the petrol my tummy grumbled; I needed a snack. The day before I had searched for the bacon I had stashed in one of the numerous pockets of the touring jacket before leaving Tortoni's, with no luck. I was getting worried as it might go off and start to smell so this time I searched properly and found it. It was absolutely fine; it actually smelt delicious and so I ate it with relish! It is disturbing what one eats when hungry.

With a feeling of relief now that my bike was tanked up, I continued riding to the Patensie turnoff. The road to Patensie via Hankey was very scenic so I idled along, enjoying the ride, especially since it was marginally warmer so I felt a lot more comfortable. Once again I stopped at a *padstal* (farm stall) for tea and a sandwich and thoroughly enjoyed the break, sitting in rustic surrounds, playing with my GPS and generally absorbing the homely ambience.

After Thornhill I seemed to enter into Afrikaner territory. English was no longer spoken and I had to dredge my memory for a smattering of long-forgotten school Afrikaans. I tried hard to speak it to the Afrikaans-speaking people I met along the way but invariably the person I was trying to hold a conversation with would gently suggest we revert to English. I suppose this was testament to the quality of my verbal endeavours.

With the lengthening of the afternoon shadows I had to start looking for accommodation. I saw a road sign indicating a campsite so I followed it along a narrow, rough track into the bush. It wound its way into the mountains and became steadily rougher. After about 10 interesting kilometres with no campsite in view I decided that it was never going to materialise, so I executed a U-turn, retraced my route, continued along the main road for another few kilometres and ended up at the delightful De Mist Cottage, perfectly positioned for my start into the Baviaanskloof Wilderness.

August 30, 2010

Once again the day dawned clear and sunny and I idly watched the domestic helper feed a breakfast bottle of milk to the baby duiker which had been wandering around the cottage. Sadly the mother had been caught and eaten, so the baby was handed over to the owners of the cottage for hand rearing. The helper showed me 10 new tortoises, each the size of a matchbox, whose mother was roaming around their garden and informed me that their other tortoise had 16 babies. The ducks were happily quacking

in a mini ornamental pool – they looked like ornaments themselves and just to remind me that this was indeed ordinary life here, the farmer working within earshot started to loudly berate his workers. It was time to leave.

The scenery was spectacular and in my haste to pull over onto the shoulder, stop, haul the camera out, twist and shoot I lost my balance and the bike went crashing over. I felt so clumsy; dropping the bike on a perfectly flat section and this before even starting the rough stuff. I tried to pick it up but it wouldn't budge so it was either unpack my gear, pick

the bike up and then repack everything, which would have delayed me by about an hour, or wait for a passing car instead, which might be the quicker option. I smelt fuel so scrabbled under the bike, found the fuel lever and switched it off, refreshed my lipstick and settled in for the wait.

Luckily I didn't have to wait for more than about 15 minutes to wave down a farm truck trundling along. When the driver got out my heart sank. He was white-haired and bent with age but gamely insisted on giving it a shot. Together we counted to three, huffed and puffed and up she came. Five minutes later I was on my way, thinking that this was a timely lesson for me to remember not to lose concentration. If I were to fall over while attempting to ford a river in a lonely area I might not be so lucky.

Shortly after leaving De Mist cottage the road turned to dirt as it meandered into the Baviaanskloof Wilderness Reserve. The weather was comfortably warm so I was able to shed all excess gear at the gate to the reserve. I was comfortable, happy and in my element. No words can really do justice to this magnificent nature reserve.

The going was challenging in sections and I battled to maintain concentration as the scenery was so spectacular. The road itself is a marvel of engineering. I was thankful not to be doing this route in a 4x4 as the road occasionally narrowed with vertiginous drop-offs. Scaredy cat that I am, I hugged the side furthest from the edge and tried not to glance over the verge. I wound my way up hairpin bends until finally I was on top. The wind was blowing hard enough to be unpleasant on the long flat section that followed but as I wound down the other side the wind dropped and I entered a quiet wonderland, with the road twisting between imposing mountains on either side.

A little about the road, or more accurately, the track; for the most part it is gravel, some sections have loose stones on the surface, and some sections have concrete patches as well as concrete strips in the worst parts. These strips are quite difficult for a bike as they are fairly narrow and one has to be careful not to fall off the strips. There are lots of corrugations, a few wash-aways and very little sand and depending on the time of year, lots of river crossings, with the boulder beds being the nastiest. I considered myself fortunate as the area was experiencing a drought so I only had 13 river crossings, the deepest being the height of the top of my riding boots.

While moseying slowly through a treed section alongside the river I was rewarded with a herd of buck (kudu) leaping across the track in front of me. Later on a troop of baboons (I always think of them as hairy men of the mountains) ambled across my path and tortoises seemed to be all over the place. I took a photo of one entering a pond and cooling off in the shallows. This was when I had stopped for a break and splashed some cooling water over myself. I caught sight of buck frequently as well as vervet monkeys and an assortment of birds.

This was one ride I didn't want to end but even after I exited the official reserve it continued to be enthralling. I pulled in for fuel at a miniscule *dorpie* (village) called Klein Poort. Klein (small) it definitely was – it consisted of a trading store, post office and bottle store all under one roof and on the other side of the large, sandy square a petrol and a diesel pump.

The man who managed it all complained that he was 44 years old and still living with his mother in the same family home he had lived in all his life. He said that tourism had in the past supplied most of their income but this had dwindled drastically in the last few years. He had a flock of sheep and had posted a big sign on the trading store frontage, warning people not to touch the Anatolian sheepdog. I queried this and he said that they have a tendency to transfer their attention to humans and then aren't very good with the flock of sheep they are tasked to look after; more about that later.

After a not so cold Coke I went on my merry way, looking out for a place shown on the map as Studkis as I knew that my destination for the day was just after Studkis. I never did see it – maybe I was concentrating too hard on the road or, if Klein Poort was anything to go by, I could have missed it in the blink of an eye. I was then happily surprised to come across my turnoff to Makkedaat Cave sooner than I had anticipated.

At the check-in where I paid for my cave stay, the incredibly gracious and hospitable hostess who owned the farm on which the cave was situated sold me a tasty kudu pie with a crunchy sweet and sour green salad. What a taste sensation! I bought a beer from a farm 2.5 kilometres away where the farmer pointed out a large dog and told me that it was an Anatolian Sheepdog and advised me not to touch it. He said that it frequently wandered over from the farm where Makkedaat Cave was situated and it was best to ignore this dog.

Makkedaat Cave is actually a most unusual cave-cottage set far away from farmhouses or other signs of civilisation, so you are all alone in this glorious wilderness area. The hot water of the outdoor bush and geranium covered stone shower washed all the dust and fatigue away until I felt clean and relaxed. A cunningly camouflaged gas cylinder heated the water. Later I sat outside, my back safely against my bike as I had been told that there were leopard roaming around. I lounged there until long after the sun had gone down, savouring my ice cold beer. I witnessed the first stars come out and listened to the orchestra of night sounds. Eventually I retired to my cosy cave where I read by solar light until my eyes drooped heavily and I knew that it was time for a cup of ginger tea and bed. My bed was a mattress on a stone ledge, the sides made comfortable by numerous soft cushions. On the mattress lay my toasty down-filled sleeping bag, almost beckoning me!

August 31, 2010

In the morning when I went to the farmhouse to check out I noticed a medium-sized dog with dreadful injuries. It looked as though it had been caught in a snare which had cut deeply through skin and muscle in at least two places. I asked what had happened and was told that this dog had wandered too close to the sheep and the Anatolian Sheepdog attacked it; it was simply doing its job of protecting its flock. Apparently it will try to kill any animal it sees in the vicinity of the sheep, including buck. It would appear that there are positives but also quite a number of negatives to consider when getting this breed to look after your sheep.

The mountainous vistas stayed with me all day. I passed citrus groves, herds of Angora goats, flocks of Merino sheep, cows, donkeys, horses and ostrich. The donkey drawn cart is alive and well in this part of the country and I saw one being pulled by two donkeys doing 25 kilometres per hour! The young lads driving it waved merrily as I passed by and continued on my way.

I explored the little town of De Rust which has a quaint, arty feel to it with its brightly painted facades and colourful pots of flowers decorating many of the cottages and shops in the main street. After leaving De Rust I rode up the stunning Meyringspoort Pass which I did slowly so that I could enjoy the scenery. I stopped often to take photographs and simply gaze at the mountains surrounding me.

All too soon I reached Prince Albert, clearly a prime tourist destination, as there seem to be more B and B's, little coffee shops, restaurants and art galleries than anything else.

Five kilometres outside Prince Albert and close to the Swartberg Pass I found accommodation for the night at Bushman Valley. There was a choice; I was offered a room, a cottage, a caravan without standing headroom or a rather curious hut, which the receptionist told me is called a *boesman's* (bushman's) hut but quite fitting I imagined, so I booked it. I took myself on a walk and was very quickly tucked in amongst the mountains. It was easy to imagine the San people (Bushmen) living in this area. The reception area sold all items to do with the San – books, paintings, bone and clay necklaces and an assortment of odd looking artefacts.

My boots and socks, wet from river crossings, dried nicely in the hot afternoon sun. I even washed soiled clothing. The moment the sun dropped below the mountains the chill set in and as had become my habit on this trip, I basked in the hot water of the shower. Then I relaxed in my hut, had a cup of tea and a bite to eat and finally hauled out my little netpad. As I typed this a suspiciously large 'mouse' ran around. I imagined he was looking for a morsel to eat. I immediately hung my food from a hook in the beam of the thatched roof. A small bat flitted about my head; maybe it was curious? Where did he come from in that enclosed space?

I slept heavily and dreamt Bushman-like dreams. 'A finely woven grass cowl shaped net is hanging from a rock face. I climb into it and immediately become weightless and float in a foetal position. The cowl closes around me and becomes a womb. My life plays through my mind, wrongs are righted, hurts are soothed away, bad decisions are changed into good decisions, all the negatives are turned into positives and I awake feeling light and refreshed, ready for my rebirth into the world. The cowl opens and I step out'. Wow, if life could be like that…

September 1, 2010

The next morning the wind was cold and blustery so I took my time getting ready and noted the temperature slowly creep up. By 8:45 am I was ready to roll and headed for the gravel Swartberg Pass. It was difficult to keep a straight line as my head was swivelling from side to side in awe. This part of the world has spectacular scenery and I don't think that I ever fully realised that.

With this realisation came a new thought. I didn't think that I wanted to go through Namibia and Botswana too soon and so I made a decision to put my planned visit to these countries on hold. My choice for the future is to first explore many areas of the Cape instead, especially the distant coastal areas of the Northern Cape. It would be a shame to go further afield and forego all this beauty on my own doorstep. People I met along the way told me about interesting places which I won't be missing on my next journey.

All too soon I came across the Gamkaskloof (The Hell) turnoff with its attendant dire warnings as to the dangerous conditions of the dirt road. As far as condition goes it was similar to the Baviaanskloof road with possibly a tad more sandy drifts over the road. In total I crossed the river four times here. This fertile valley is isolated and peaceful. Apart from the caretakers and the Cape Conservation people, no one lives here anymore. Its very isolation contributed to the mass exodus of its inhabitants. The history of the area and the people who lived here is riveting and is told in picture form in the offices of Cape Conservation and on story boards outside the original homes. I unloaded my bike and now feeling a lot lighter, went on a joyride, visiting the original homes and one of the families' graveyards.

My accommodation in Gamkaskloof was a roomy caravan with a rustic stone ablution block close by. An outdoor table and chairs added to my comfort as did the marinated kudu steak and salad which I had ordered on my arrival. This was prepared by Mrs Joubert, the owner of much of the land and caretaker who ran the camping area, restaurant and office. (She was an original occupant and a Mostert before her marriage.) This delicious meal was delivered to me by friendly nearby campers on whose fire I later *brauied* the meat. Talk about home comforts!

September 2, 2010

The day dawned cold and there were a few dark, heavy looking clouds hanging around. I put on as much clothing as I could in anticipation of a freezing stretch. On with the thermal underwear, layered with Cordura riding pants, overlaid with rain pants and on top, two long-sleeved shirts, my triple-layered touring jacket and then finally a rain jacket over the lot. Once the boots, gloves, scarf, Leatt Brace and crash helmet were added, I looked ridiculous and I could hardly move… but I was warm.

After paying my bill and waving goodbye to the delightful and hospitable Mrs Joubert I left, wishing I could stay a few days longer. As I wound my way up the pass out of The Hell those saturated clouds opened up – not too much though, and it rained. I had to take my goggles off in order to see but ended up having a splendid ride out and then down the other side of the Swartberg Pass. I took the dirt road to Calitzdorp, passing memorable scenes of mountains, farmsteads, tortured rock cliff faces and calming isolation.

Seweweekspoort Pass had been recommended so I took the turnoff and meandered my way through eye-catching scenery, this time with the massive rocky ramparts towering above me on both sides of the road. Crystal streams flowed and little bridges crossed them – luckily no river crossings were necessary because the water levels were so low. I continued on through the Karoo taking unpaved roads all the way to Montague. That day I laid eyes on only three cars and I was in the saddle from 8:15 am to 5:00 pm – I was so saddle sore at the end of the day!

The Karoo is such a special place; it has a wildness about it that is found nowhere else that I have been to. The biggest scare of the journey happened on this section. I passed a substantial looking, two metre long, bright green snake, way too close for comfort. It was negotiating the road and its head was raised above the ground. As I whipped past I lifted my legs to handle bar height, hoping that I had missed it. Apart from that nothing frightening happened on the whole trip. Of course there were no fuel stations in the area I rode through and my longest stop of the day was when I had to unpack the fuel container in order to refuel.

I had plenty of time to think about anything and everything and a funny thought popped into my mind. I mulled it around for an hour or two and now firmly believe that we all have an internal compass. The needle is still swinging around a little crazily but I think that if I work on 'connecting' with it, my navigational skills will improve. Before you think I got lost, let me tell you that I NEVER did, not even once. I'm rather proud of that considering my GPS remained in my pocket for most of the time with flat batteries, I had forgotten my map book at home and when I asked for directions they were mostly given in Afrikaans and mine is dismal. However, our sign-posting in South Africa is top notch and that had a lot to do with it too.

Eventually I reached Montague and then followed a tiring 15 kilometres to a wine-farm B and B owned by my brother's friends, where I was treated to a sociable evening with good company, tasty food and fine wine. The following day, sadly my last day on the road, was warm and sunny. My brother, Paul, left Cape Town and drove to Worcester where we met. He came in his latest toy, a dinky car, a 25-year-old Suzuki 4x4 which he had recently restored. He chose to take me on an interesting route into Cape Town – with a bit of gravel thrown in, in case I hadn't done enough.

We had been told that Bainskloof Pass was closed but we took our chances anyway. Luckily, although they were still working on the pass, they let us go through. We stopped at the convict graves; the convicts who had helped build the remarkable Bainskloof Pass. We then looped around using the less common route and entered Blouberg from the Melkbosstrand side and were welcomed in by a glorious multi-coloured display of flowers all along the roadside.

I was thrilled to see Table Mountain, sad that my journey was over, warm and fuzzy at the thought of seeing my family at the birthday bash the following day and relieved that I had come this far with no mishap or serious problems.

Riding alone had been rewarding. People seemed so much more eager to chat to me, to look after me and to offer accommodation. As a result it wasn't a lonely or frightening experience at all and one that I was eager to repeat.

I left my bike in Cape Town, knowing that my loving brother would fuss over it and generally fine tune it for my return. I was not to be disappointed.

Lara and I at Ponta Dundo on Bazaruto Island, Mozambique

Our Captain aboard Shani Yake – fishing while helming with his foot

With Justin in front of the enormous Baobab tree on Mefunvo Island in the Querimba Archipelago

Off to the 'spot' for the cell phone signal in a remote area of Mozambique

Racing another dhow on our way to Ibo Island

Dhow builders in Mozambique

Derelict building on Ibo Island

Banco de Areia Sao Lourenço in the Querimbas

Moya – from the companionway ladder looking for'ard

Our sailor-baby, Lara, surrounded by cuddly toys and diapers in the V-berth

Baviaanskloof Wilderness Reserve, South Africa

The only road in Gamkaskloof

The winding descent into The Hell

Made it! Table Mountain (Cape Town) in the distance

Chatting to Dave with his famous Chilli Pepper, in the Karoo

Waiting for the ferry at Sendlingsdrift on the Namibian/South African border

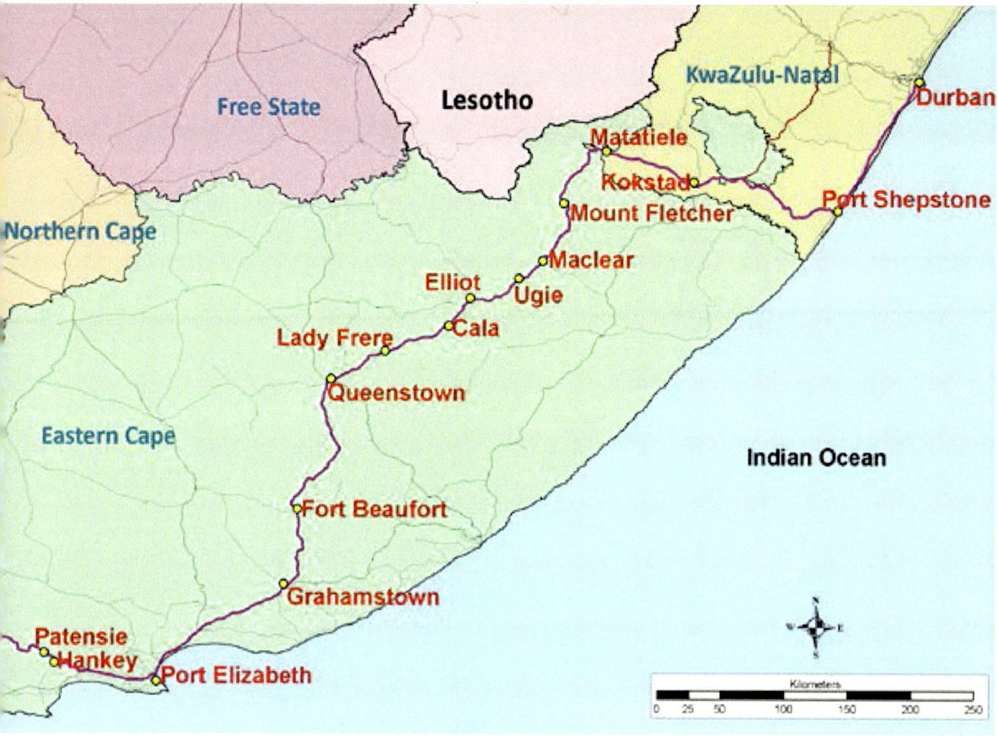

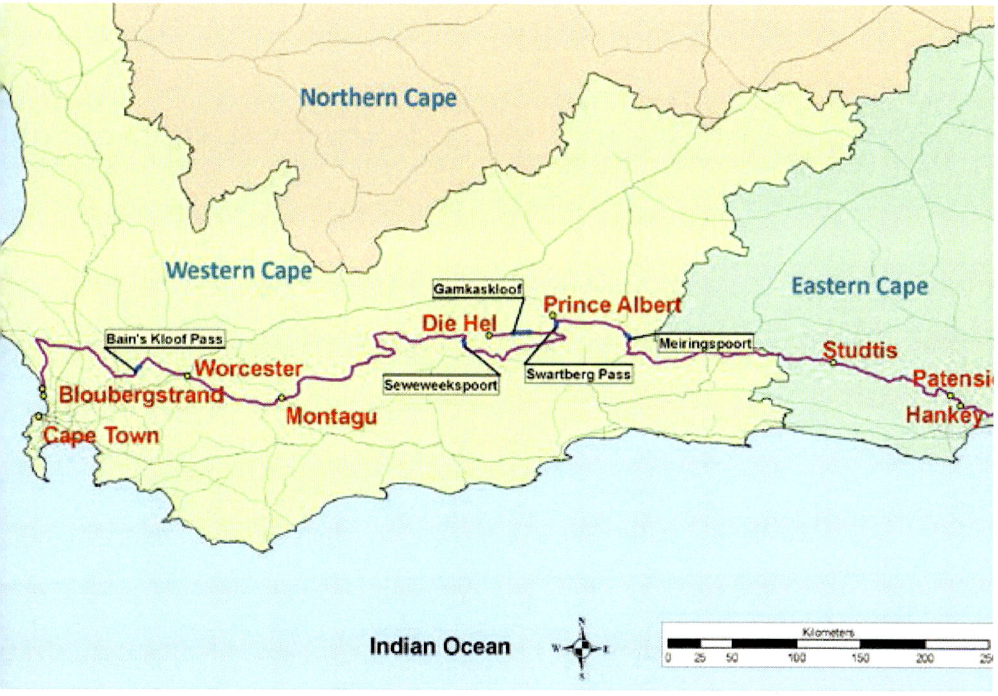

The route from Durban to Cape Town

Continuing the ride from Cape Town to Namibia and back

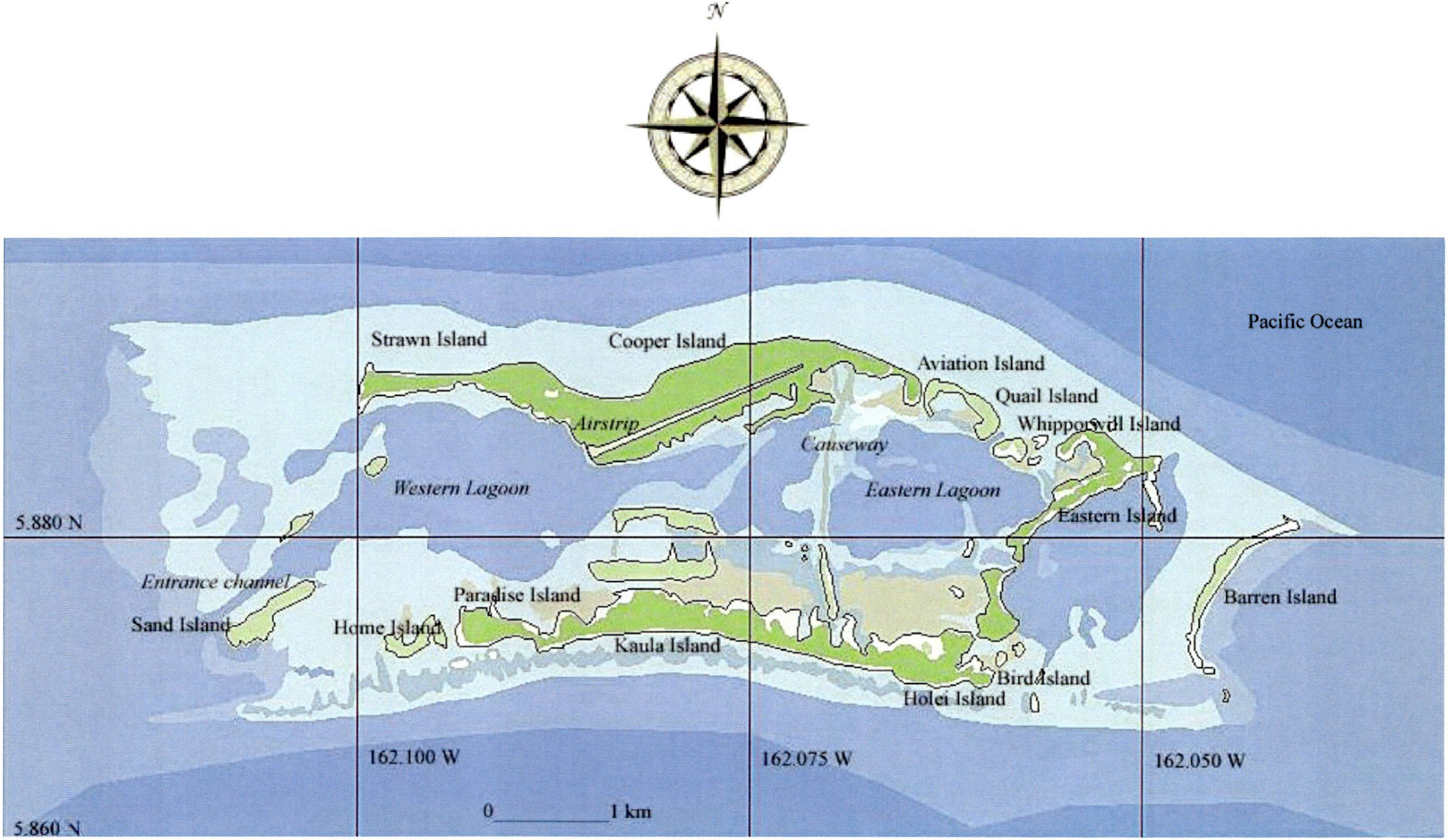

Palmyra Atoll

— 8 —

On To The Northern Cape, A Taste Of Namibia And Crossing The Western Cape

Part 2

A month later I flew back to Cape Town for part two of my solo motorcycling jaunt. While in Durban I had attended to pressing work issues, caught up on all the chores at home and I was ready for whatever lay ahead. My kind and talented brother, Paul, had done so much work on my bike; it was now more prepared than ever to hit the dirt. As was I!

After a wonderful weekend in Cape Town socialising with my family I finally settled myself in front of the computer on the Sunday evening and began the time-consuming process of route planning. I am not too fussy about this but do need a general idea as to where the out-of-the-ordinary places are, so that I can at least plan the skeleton of an interesting route. Paul wanted to help with this and before long we were both raring to go. The start of the route looked so inviting and he became so enthusiastic that he decided that he wanted to do it too, and that's as far as I got with my route planning.

So early the next morning we hopped into Paul's sturdy little 4x4 and off we went. We left Blouberg in dismal weather, the clouds above promising worse to come. I was secretly happy that today I was in Paul's vehicle and not drowning on my bike. We sloshed past Atlantis and Mamre and then off the tar and onto a secondary road. A bit later we slid onto the railway line service road and had the unusual experience of driving right alongside a noisy diesel train transporting coal. We popped out in Darling, at Evita se Perron, a well-known restaurant, but unfortunately it was closed so we then turned onto another dirt road leading to Mareesburg. The cloudbursts were frequent and intense but we didn't care one iota. The giant pot-holes we splashed through rewarded us by finding every nook and cranny to seep into and drip over us. Our feet were soaking wet and Paul's foot-well had become a muddy puddle, so much so he had to roll up his trousers.

From Mareesburg we took the N7 (tar for about 40 kilometres) to Citrusdal, then onto the dirt road to the Algeria crossroads. We bumped and bounced our way alongside the scenic Clanwilliam Dam past Lebanon Campsite and turned onto the road to Cedarberg which went past the Algeria Campsite. The deterioration in this unpaved road coincided with the deterioration in the already dreadful weather and the going was painfully slow. Into the Cedarberg mountains we went, up, up we laboured, up the Uitkyk Pass and then down the other side to just past Driehoek. It was at about this point that we realised that we weren't going to make our destination which was Wuppertal and still be home by dark. So, with a slight sense of disappointment we turned around. However we were rewarded with the sun breaking through the clouds as we reached the top of the pass so we were able to drink in the stunning view. We took the shortcut to Algeria and then onto the N7.

On the way home we stopped off at De Tol on the Piekenierskloof Pass, a roadside cafe/restaurant, to quench our thirst and pacify the ravenous appetites we had built up. We were both shivering with cold so the hot chocolate that we ordered really hit the spot. While eating our juicy fat bacon, egg and cheese toasted *sarmies* (sandwiches) the proprietor's daughter told us an absorbing tale.

She explained that the house we were sitting in was built in about 1853 and was originally a toll house where tolls were collected from the citrus farmers who brought their citrus in donkey carts from Citrusdal up to this point. They overnighted here and the following morning continued on to the train at Eindekuil to load their produce for the delivery to Cape Town.

Then the house became a Red Cross first aid station and for the past 10 years has been a restaurant. "BUT…" she emphasised, "there is a spook that haunts this house." She and her mother had personally coped with the spook's actions on at least three occasions. She went on to tell us how she and her mother were alone late at night in the house painting the main room when a clock which hadn't worked for years started chiming. On another occasion the pockets of oranges in the shop area had been opened during the night and were found the next morning in places where it was impossible for them to have rolled to. Leaving the most eyebrow-raising yarn to last, she told us how a relative had sworn while working in the room with them and suddenly a teacup had been flung at him. It hit him on the head and he accused them of throwing it, which of course they denied, as it had been the work of the spook!

After the stop at De Tol we continued on past Citrusdal, Piketburg, then took the turnoff to Veldrift, drove past Saldanha Bay, Langebaan and Melkbos, and finally home.

Despite arriving wet, cold and tired we had thoroughly enjoyed the drive of 560 kilometres which took us 8.5 hours.

My first day on the road, Blouberg to the Karoo

October 14, 2010. Wednesday

It seemed as though I had too much to organise and ended up getting off to a late start. The weather was cool and blustery but this is what I expected at this time of the year. Unknowingly I forgot my route plan as well as my map.

You'd think I would have learnt by now!

I took the coastal road to Melkbos then the Slentpad past the wind turbines. The dairy farms with the strong smell of manure attracted insects which splattered and dried on my visor. I rode on past wine farms and the small towns of Klipheuwel, Malmesbury, Riebeek-Kasteel and Gouda. Gouda was a fortuitous stop as I was able to talk on my cell phone to David Moore, creator and producer of the 'Couch Trip' and the brilliant 'Going Nowhere Slowly' series, a South African travel television series. In 'Going Nowhere Slowly' a variety of characters drive around South Africa and neighbouring countries in a splendid old, red Chevrolet Impala dubbed The Chilli Pepper, meeting and filming 'salt-of-the-earth' people along the way.

As it turned out he was en-route to his farm in the Karoo and suggested I spend the night there. So from Gouda I made my way to Ceres, then straight out the other side of the town and continued on the dirt road to the farm.

Shortly after my arrival there I went for a leg-stretching, long walk into the *veld* – after being in the saddle this was just what I needed. We had a friendly evening *braaing* on the indoor fire, drinking red wine, telling stories and catching up on all the news since the 'Couch Trip', a reality show that I was a contestant in, which Dave had produced a few years ago. Dave, eleven other contestants, a presenter, two cameramen and a soundman had all travelled together in the western Cape in an overland vehicle for about three weeks visiting and filming out-of-the-way places where physical and mental challenges were conducted. I had become friends with Dave on this trip and was lucky enough to be a finalist however I lost in the final game of chance!

Dave's pal, George, kindly gave me a map book and together they helped me re-plan my route, which I think was similar to the first plan Paul had helped me with. They also gave me a bottle of red wine for my sundowner when visiting Augrabies National Park. Thank you Dave and George!

To Brandvlei

October 15, 2010

Thursday morning dawned chilly and overcast with fat grey clouds hanging low in the sky. We had an impromptu photo shoot at the gate of Dave's farm – my bike posing with Dave's famous Chilli Pepper, an honour for me. The road was wet with patchy puddles that were slippery and saw me doing the fandango quite a few times.

I took the turnoff to the Tankwa Karoo National Park and the road conditions deteriorated even further. In places the road seemed to have sunk below the water level. I met a Canadian RTW (Round-the-world) traveller who had given up on his efforts to reach the Tankwa Karoo National Park and suggested I turn back as well because the river was flooding across the road. I said that I was keen to have a look. He left but a short distance later did a U-turn and kindly drove to the river with me and stood by as I attempted the crossing. The water was swirling and muddy but not too deep so I manoeuvred slowly and carefully… and made it to the other side safely. I waved goodbye to the kindly Canadian and spent the next few hours enjoying the stark beauty, wide open spaces and sheer loneliness of the Tankwa Karoo while trying to negotiate the difficult road conditions.

It was a good thing that I was carrying fuel as I had to use it – the next fuel station was 275 km distant at Middlepos; the previous fuel stop had been in Ceres. This was way too big a distance for my little bike's tiny tank!

Then it was up, up, up, the exceedingly slippery Gannaga Pass and the distance to Middlepos seemed insurmountable as I fishtailed along in the thick mud, shoulders and arms cramping from the strain of trying to keep the bike upright and moving forward.

Finally the road conditions eased but the wind was freezing cold so I had to stop and put additional clothing on. It was such a relief to eventually pull in to Middlepos where I met a fellow biker, Koos. He was doing a round trip from Paarl and generously insisted I accept a 1:250 000 map of Namaqualand. We chatted for awhile and then he set off for Sutherland, home of South Africa's largest telescope and me for Calvinia, home of South Africa's largest post box, where I had a soft landing at a local guest house.

In the morning my room was still toasty from the oil heater I had on all night and my boots and washing were crispy dry. A late start from Calvinia meant a warm start and I was tired of freezing, so this was much better. I took the tar road through flat and featureless terrain to Nieuwoudtville although occasionally mountains could be viewed in the distance. I went into the little *dorpie*, took photos and then continued on to Loeriesfontein.

A few kilometres after the turnoff to Loeriesfontein, the scenery and vegetation changed dramatically to mountains, gorges, trees and abundant greenery but after the Nieuwoudt Falls, a worthwhile stop, it reverted to 'Karoo normal'. While at the falls and ambling to another viewpoint I noticed that a big transport truck had stopped opposite the entrance gates of the falls. Then I saw another one stop. The two drivers walked across to my laden bike and examined it. I, in the meantime, being a woman alone in this isolated setting, in a country where rape tops the crime list, quickly put my crash helmet on in the hopes that they would think I was a man. Of course I must have looked ridiculous wandering around the bush with a crash helmet on. They came up to me and politely greeted me and looked amazed when I greeted them in return – a woman's voice emanating from the depths of the crash helmet. The game was up – I took it off. They then asked me if I was alone. "No, of course not," I lied, "I'm with a gang of bikers; I simply left Nieuwoudtville a few minutes before they did. They'll be here any minute." I got onto my bike with a feeling of relief and then discovered that in my nervousness I had lost a glove, a very serious loss given the cold temperatures I had been riding in. The two truckers immediately started searching for my glove. We had an amiable chat while searching and I felt mortified that I had thought they were anything but nice. Eventually one of them found the errant glove and off I rode to my next turnoff which was to the quiver tree forest.

I rode along this well-maintained dirt road for about three kilometres until I discerned the eye-catching silhouette of the quiver tree, also known as a kokerboom (Aloe dichotoma), on the hill in front of me. This sight is typical of the Northern Cape landscape. Here the forest begins and continues for about three kilometres. The San used the branches of this tree to make quivers for their arrows, hence its name.

By the time I reached Loeriesfontein I was starving, so I stopped at the Boesmanland Pub and Grill for a toasted egg and bacon sandwich. I

met some locals and one kindly gave me contact details for his friend in Alexander Bay, a place he assured me was delightful despite what I had heard. Then off I went to the Fred Turner Museum and adjoining Windmill Museum. This Windmill Museum is one of only two in the world and no two windmills here are the same. In Afrikaans it is called a *wind-pomp*, pronounced 'vindt-pomp'. The historian who showed me around was informative and I found the tour interesting. At the Fred Turner museum I laughed at the timeworn hawker's wagon; it had been lovingly restored and fittingly, a special garage was built for it, the only problem being, it didn't fit! As they say in Afrikaans '*'n Boer maak 'n plan*', (a farmer makes a plan) so a plan was made; detach the tyres, now it fits!

Initially I had planned to spend the night in Loeriesfontein but couldn't find a place that grabbed me so I decided to continue on to Brandvlei, on a dirt road in excellent condition. This little *dorpie* had dismal accommodation and quite by chance I ended up staying over at the local police captain's house. She and her husband had friends over that evening and they invited me to join them for their *braai*. They were incredibly hospitable and went to great lengths to make me feel at home. Even though I was the only English speaking person there and they were all Afrikaans speaking, they kindly spoke English instead.

Brandvlei to Augrabies National Park

October 16, 2010

A late start saw me on the road heading for Augrabies National Park. I passed the turnoff to the famous Verneukpan, a dry salt pan approximately 50 kilometres long and 11 kilometres wide. '*Verneuk*' is the Afrikaans word meaning to trick, mislead or swindle. The mirages there contributed to this name, which translates into 'Pan of Deception'. It is famous for the attempts made there to smash the world land speed record.

This record is currently held by Andy Green who visited Verneukpan in 2008 to check the surface for possible use by the Bloodhound Supersonic Car in late 2011 or 2012. The hope is that this vehicle, still being developed and built, will break the land speed record by the largest ever margin.

On June 27, 2006, the South African land speed record holder Johan Jacobs, a popular person in South Africa's racing fraternity, attempted to break the 24-second world record for the standing mile. During a practice run, his jet car, Castrol Edge, went out of control and it seems that the vehicle turned sideways at a speed of about 500 kilometres per hour and rolled three times. Although Johan Jacobs was given medical attention by paramedics, tragically he died about 45 minutes after the accident.

In 1929 Sir Malcolm Campbell came to South Africa with his Napier-Campbell Blue Bird, but failed to break the land speed record as a result of tyre damage. Interestingly though, the track that he compacted is still visible today. He broke the record on his next attempt but not at Verneukpan.

Vic Proctor crashed his Vincent HRD Black Lightning motorcycle at around 160 kilometres per hour when attempting the land speed record in the late 1920s at Verneukpan.

I'm so disappointed that I didn't take the detour to visit Verneukpan. At the time it seemed a long way off the beaten track to go and have a look at a flat, barren expanse. Now that I know a little about the history of this pan it makes it so much more interesting. Apparently the mirages can be quite spectacular and I have since discovered that there is even a rustic campsite there.

My friend, Dave, had told me that a sundowner on the rock at Ararat in Augrabies National Park was something I shouldn't miss and it was a suggestion I looked forward to putting into practice. It was quite a long haul to Kenhardt from Brandvlei, especially as the wind was blowing straight at me and so I battled to get 80 kilometres per hour out of my bike. It also reduced my petrol consumption by about 20 litres to the tank. Kenhardt was surprisingly busy and I stopped off here for fuel and a leg-stretching visit to a bustling *padstal*. This farm stall had mini Mount Everest loads of junk creatively displayed and all of it for sale!

The landscape around Kenhardt was arid and brown with wide open spaces and only the occasional rocky outcrops to break the monotony. Most of this area is characterised by this type of scenery.

After Kenhardt I started to see the huge nests of the sociable weaver hanging, impossibly suspended from the tops of the electricity poles.

And then there was Keimoes, an oasis of lush green in a sea of dusty brown, neat vineyards, irrigation canals with big water wheels and a vibrant community. The reason for this is the Orange River – my first glimpse of this mighty force. I arrived there on a Saturday morning and pulled over to the side of the busy road where I contentedly absorbed the bubbly atmosphere. Across the road a shop had positioned huge speakers on the pavement outside. Music with a catchy beat blasted out and a group of people started dancing in a way I had never witnessed before. It seemed to be a cross between breakdancing and an ostrich mating dance. I sat on my saddle utterly charmed, wishing that I too could dance like that.

From Keimoes the scenery was lovely, lush green interspersed with dry brown. I stopped off at a *padstal* (these are my favourite places), and in its imaginative, artistic surroundings I ate a delicious, inexpensive lunch. As I walked in a Scottish Terrier dog ran up to me and tried to sink its teeth into my rock-hard biking boot and then ran off, it's owner sheepishly apologising.

The temperature here was considerably warmer than anything I had felt thus far, so the clothes shedding began, layer by layer. From here to Kakamas, then it was a hop, skip and a jump to Augrabies National Park where I set up my tent in the delightful campsite and luxuriated in the hot, dust-rinsing shower. The Extreme Challenge was starting the next day, a week-long running race across the Kalahari Desert. I chatted to the runners, many from different countries, and bade them well on their extreme undertaking. I reflected on how the fair-skinned people from Northern climes would find the searing desert temperatures.

I went exploring and viewed the spectacular Augrabies Falls from a well-placed viewing platform (of which there are many) as they thundered 56 metres onto the rocks below. The San people called it 'Aukoerebis' which translates into 'Place of Great Noise'. On the rocks around the viewing platform brilliant orange and blue coloured lizards and well-camouflaged *dassies* (Rock Hyrax) were lounging around. They are also known as rock rabbits and unbelievably are the African elephant's closest living relative. Apparently, despite the massive size difference, this is because there are similarities in the structure of the feet and teeth.

At about sundowner time I went to reception to find out where Ararat was and was told that motorbikes were not allowed to go there as it was inside the game park. To make it worse, there was no way for me to get there as it was too far to walk. I found the staff in the reception area rude and disinterested and I have since met other people who also found them rude. This is a shame, especially for our overseas visitors! I was so disappointed but enjoyed my sundowner anyway in the quiet, cool greenery of the campsite, which I had the pleasure of having all to myself, with not another camper in sight. Thanks Dave and George for that tasty bottle of wine!

I slept soundly until a strange clicking noise woke me up. I lay there silently, listening intently, wondering if someone was walking around my tent. I suddenly felt terribly alone and now wished that I wasn't the only camper in the campsite. Then whatever it was it came even closer and suddenly the clicking stopped. I stiffened up, feeling really scared and exposed as my tent door was wide open. My body went into fight or flight mode and the perspiration welled up. I started over-heating in my down sleeping bag! Click, click and then it stopped right at the door of my tent. I silently shot upright, still in my sleeping bag... to be confronted by a set of four legs silhouetted at the tent door! I exhaled a great lungful of air. Animal legs! My first thought was "a giraffe", but the proportions weren't right and finally I made out a set of imposing long horns, a dangly thing that looked like a dewlap and a large buck-shaped body. There were two of them contentedly grazing around my tent. With feelings of relief mixed with pleasure I drifted off into a peaceful sleep.

Namibia and the Orange River

October 17, 2010

"Here I am, lucky me, sitting on the bank of the Orange River in Namibia after an enjoyable 456 kilometre ride. It's 6:40 pm and the sun is setting downstream of me. Opposite me on the South African side is a glowing golden cliff face where the rock has set in waves."

After leaving Augrabies I headed towards Pofadder, a town seemingly in the middle of nowhere and known by some as South Africa's Timbuktu. It is situated at the edge of Namaqualand and falls within the spring flower region. After good rains around September, the area is ablaze with colour as a result of the carpet of flowers covering the landscape. At the moment though, the landscape was uniformly arid, brown and barren relieved only by the occasional rocky outcrop. The further I rode, the hotter it became, until just over a ridge the pleasant town of Springbok appeared, set amongst rocky hills and huge rock domes. This is the largest town in Namaqualand and was originally a copper mining settlement.

I stopped off in the town for an icy Grapetiser (sparkling grape juice), got out my maps and strategised. I was planning to sleep here but I was relishing the day and it was still early so I decided to continue. My destination was the river rafting camp in Namibia called Felix Unite. So on I rode.

About 10 kilometres from the border the road started descending and it wound its way through barren rocky areas, the rocks now being house-sized boulders. The hot blast which hit me was eyeball frying and I felt as if I were descending into hell itself. Never have I suffered such heat. I worried about my tyres – would they cope, in fact would my bike cope or would it overheat? I certainly wasn't coping and I was definitely overheating. So off with the gloves, I unzipped the jacket liner and pulled it out, I opened the helmet vents as well as all the jacket vents but nothing helped.

Eventually the border post of Vioolsdrift came into view and I crossed into Namibia with the minimum of fuss. I found my way to Felix Unite on the banks of the Orange River but sadly they had had a fire in the morning and were not in a position to accommodate any new guests. They suggested I go further along to Abiqua River Camp, now called Amanzi Trails. I did and wasn't disappointed as the campsite was actually nicer than the one at Felix Unite. I relaxed, downed an ice cold cider, then booked in and ordered a canoe for the following day. After pitching my tent with a commanding view of the Orange River, I finally washed my grubby clothes and tired, dusty body.

The next day dawned sunny, windless and warm. The owner of Amanzi, Daryn, transported the double canoe and me to the start upstream, collecting the guide, Jaco, en-route. We set off in perfect conditions paddling easily with little help from the current as the river was so broad (at that point). The scenery was varied with long grasses interspersed with bushes and trees as well as rocks and cliffs. The birdlife was prolific with herons, cormorants, kingfishers, ibises, Egyptian geese and swallows. We also caught a glimpse of quite a few water monitors in the rocky areas. And then the wind hit us. It came from exactly where we were headed so we had to dig in and paddle like hell. The tendonitis in my right elbow, which had been plaguing me the entire time, was killing me, as was the damaged ligament in my left thumb which had never quite healed. But paddle I did, with Jaco in the seat behind matching me stroke for stroke. We came down the final weir and a wave washed over the bow, drenching us, but it was most exhilarating. We made it back to the campsite in good time, both in high spirits; I had had a most enjoyable time on the river with the capable and efficient young guide, Jaco.

The latter part of the afternoon was spent quite lazily, listening to music, recharging my cell phone, my GPS, computer and MP3 player batteries. What a pleasure it was doing these simple things in such stunning surroundings, with the mighty Orange River flowing past. My right arm was very painful so a quiet afternoon was just what the doctor ordered.

Note: There is a road on the South African side of the river which is not shown on my GPS or my map. Apparently this goes all the way to Sendlingsdrift but I gather one needs a 4x4 to do the section closest to Sendlingsdrift. There is also a road linking Kuboes to Eksteenfontein but this too is not shown on the map.

Back to South Africa

October 18, 2010

It was a shame to leave such a desirable setting but with a cheery wave to Daryn I was off into the Richtersveld and the Ais-Ais Richtersveld Transfrontier Park. The white, sugar-crunchy road meandered alongside the Orange River on my left. The river, bordered by thick greenery, cut a brown swathe through the stark mountainous backdrop, which was totally devoid of visible vegetation. Now and again I came across huge mine dumps, jarring in this wilderness. Occasionally I saw a lonely caravan or shack in the middle of nowhere with signs that read "Private area – keep out". Apparently these are individuals seeking their fortunes with diamond diggings. A lonely life!

I passed the confluence with the dry Fish River, the longest interior river in Namibia and reflected on the boulder-hopping, toe-destroying hike I had done a few years ago, further upstream in the Fish River Canyon. This has the distinction of being the second largest canyon in the world at around 160 kilometres long, 27 kilometres wide at its widest point and in places almost 550 metres deep.

Eventually I reached Sendlingsdrift where I waited and waited for the ferry based on the South African side of the Orange River, but the place seemed deserted. I contemplated the road I had travelled that day, the one I had been warned not to do alone and I felt chuffed with myself. I had been told that I would never make it without numerous punctures and it was simply not the place for a lone person let alone a woman (!) to venture because if I had a puncture or breakdown of any sort that I couldn't fix, it could be many long days before help came along. (There is no cell phone coverage here.) Clearly my extra heavy duty tubes had done their job, along with a liberal dose of luck! It was extremely hot and with all the biking gear on it was as though I was being slowly baked.

I tried hooting but the hooter didn't seem to be working; it warbled pitifully instead. My brand-new massive truck hooter of which I was so proud had let me down. One blast from this oversized piece of equipment was enough to send the biggest of trucks into a panic! So I whistled and finally two men ambled down the road on the other side, leisurely climbed aboard the ferry, started its engines and slowly made their way over.

I tried to start the bike but to my alarm it was totally dead; nothing worked. I pushed it onto the ferry. I figured that the problem would be one of two things – the main fuse had blown or the battery terminal had come off. When we reached the other side, the ferry operators came over to have a look and one of them, Chris, insisted on doing the dirty work and wouldn't even let me try. We took all the luggage off, I got out the tools and then he undid the bolts under the mud-encrusted rear mudguard in order to loosen the seat. We carefully slid the seat out from under the luggage carrier and checked the main fuse – it was blown. We replaced it with a new fuse I had amongst my assorted spares and problem solved! Of course I didn't think the problem was finally solved as I was aware that there was a reason for the fuse to blow, but what? For the time being though I had power.

I completed the fast and efficient immigration formalities as well as a payment of ZAR 100.00 for the ferry and finally I was able to continue my journey to Alexander Bay. The gravel road had hard, sharp, stony drifts and I had to concentrate on my riding. Many kilometres later I came to a lonely looking office with a boom across the road. A man came out and demanded proof of payment for the ferry. This was his job and he needed the receipt. It seemed silly and a waste of money to have this manned office simply checking one's ferry payment! As I rode along I sensed the temperature steadily dropping until I was riding into the teeth of the icy wind blowing across the frigid Atlantic Ocean.

I had a look at the Alexander Bay/Namibia border post just because I was curious, then later on had to stop at a boom before going into the town of Alexander Bay. I was asked a few questions as to where I was going and so on, my identity book was scrutinised, and something was noted on the computer. I queried the person as to why she was doing this and she said that it was a security regulation because of the diamond mining. Anyway my planned overnight stop there didn't work out. The town was ugly, desolate and decaying so I continued on to Port Nolloth, a delightful little village, although many don't agree with me. This is the only coast in the world where gem quality diamonds can be manually dredged from the sea bed by divers.

On the way I repeatedly saw green net 'fences' with what looked like plants in between the fences. I found out later that these are dune rehabilitation programmes carried out by the mining company after the area has been mined.

Port Nolloth is postcard pretty with fisherman type cottages, white sandy beaches interspersed with rocky areas and fynbos, seagulls squawking… All I needed now was a cosy little spot next to the beach.

As I rode along I saw a signpost for a backpacker's hostel. I couldn't find it so I asked a person in front of a picturesque little beach house for directions. He couldn't help me but instead kindly suggested I stay the night at the beach house where he, Francois, and his work colleague, Sydney, were staying. He elaborated by saying that they were contract workers from Gauteng and would be leaving Port Nolloth early the next morning. I knew it was a chance but my sixth sense told me that the offer was genuine so I accepted. What hospitable people and what a pleasure it was. After unpacking my bike I walked along the beach, enjoying the sunset and later the good company and a delicious *braai.* A roaring fire ensured that the cottage remained cosy throughout the cold night.

Off to Garies and the HOGS

October 19, 2010

After a healthy breakfast we all left the cottage together. I tried to give Francois and Sydney a final hoot goodbye; I felt the bike gurgle gutlessly before catching again and noted that the hooter didn't work. I immediately understood that the fuse had gone again and that the next time I switched the bike off it wouldn't start. I drove to the petrol station, filled up, disconnected the hooter and put in a new fuse. This was most annoying.

The day was cool and I hit the dirt for 'The Diamond Route'. The first stop was Kleinzee. Although a pretty place it seemed like a ghost town with not a soul to be seen – I guessed they were all at work but I guessed wrong. It seems as though many of these De Beers mining houses are empty as a result of the cutback in mining operations.

There was a welcome stretch of tar linking Kleinzee to Koiingnaas then dirt again to Hondeklipbaai, another postcard pretty *dorpie.* I met two guys out on a jaunt in their Landrover and we had lunch together in a small restaurant overlooking the boats in the harbour; delicious ocean fresh fish. They were full of adventurous tales and bright ideas and suggested I join them to see the Spoeg Caves and the seals. While savouring our lunch a young fellow who had been flying his model aeroplane outside came into the restaurant and asked to borrow an Allen key from the guys I was chatting to. They didn't have one but I did – in my top pocket, a handy place to keep it for the frequent fuse changes. They all had a hearty laugh at this with one of them commenting that he would have expected me to pull out a tube of lipstick, not an Allen key!

I agreed to join them on their excursion to the Spoeg Caves and followed them on the road leading out of Hondeklipbaai. Unfortunately the side road they turned onto consisted of talcum-soft, powdery sand and with my heavily laden motorcycle I would have struggled and probably slowed them down. So I waved goodbye, made a mental note to explore this area at a later stage and continued on to Garies.

The road took me inland, away from the coast and I had it to myself all the way to Garies where I pulled into the fuel station. While I was filling up a large group of testosterone-enriched Harley Davidson riders came into the station with a lot of loud revving, chrome, bling, denim and leather jackets adorned with badges and emblems and flapping leather tassels. Apart from one woman in the group who I spoke to, who said they were all from Johannesburg, they didn't seem friendly – not at all like other bikers I had met in Durban and on my travels. Well, on the positive side at least the weather had warmed up nicely and off I went, Vredendal in my sights.

About eight kilometres out of Garies I heard this horrible, loud whining noise emanating from the front end of my bike. I stopped and examined the bike. The front disc was hot so I thought that possibly the brakes had locked onto the disc. The engine oil window showed no oil and although potentially very serious that's not where the noise was coming from. The noise was so bad that I was convinced that I would damage my bike irreparably if I drove it any further so started pushing it back to Garies. Puffing and panting I pushed and pushed and pushed, up the hill, down the other side and on up the next hill… it seemed to take forever. It was exhausting work and I was pouring with perspiration. As I was hanging over my handlebars trying to catch my breath and calm my racing heart, I was relieved to see the Harley Davidson riders I had seen an hour and a half to two hours before appear on the crest of the next hill. My relief was short-lived as they came roaring right past me in enviable formation, machines gleaming, tassels streaming, seemingly not seeing me at all. I was gobsmacked; the entire convoy appeared not to see me! I guess the acronym, HOGS (Harley Owners Group), they use for themselves really suits them!

Luckily the vehicle behind them (not with them) stopped and the driver, shaking his head at the attitude of the Harley bunch, thoughtfully offered to try and get transport for my bike to Garies. He drove off and I wondered if I would see him again but half an hour later he was back. True to his word he had managed to find a trailer and a helper and we loaded the bike up. I requested he drop me off at the local campsite. This Good Samaritan took the time and effort to help find the problem and fix my bike. Later he even returned with cold drinks, chocolate, chips and brake fluid. (In the fixing process I had lost all my brake fluid.)

Fun in the campsite

Garies Campsite was truly uninspiring; windswept, dry and not a soul in sight. I felt nervous about the obvious lack of security and so decided to camp on the verandah of the ablution block so that I could lock the gates with my bike chain. Just as it was getting dark I started worrying that I

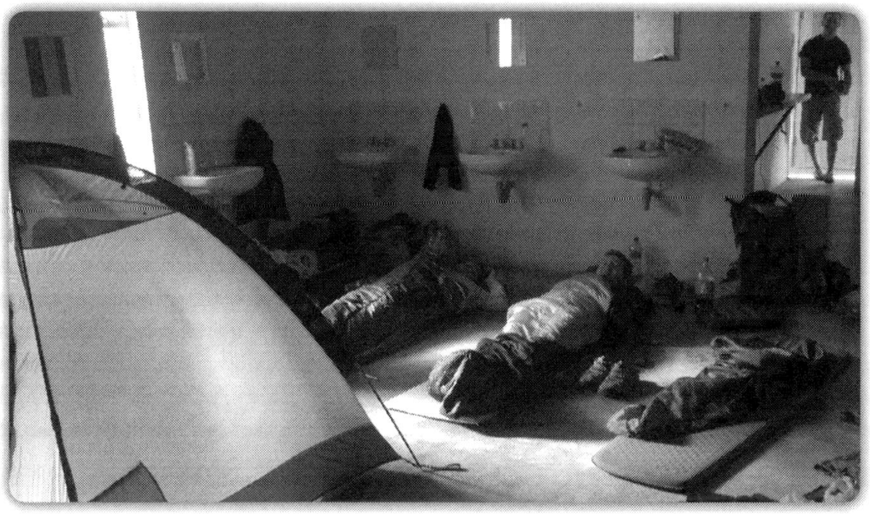

had made the wrong decision. I felt anxious about being alone in this large (clean but spooky) building. Luckily a quintet of Polish bicyclists arrived and loved the idea of spending the night in this unlikely spot. One of the team, a bubbly girl, decided that she wanted a spin on my bike so I took her on a tour of Garies. I think we looked rather comical as she had perched herself cheerfully on top of my luggage carrier with both her arms wrapped around me. Later bicycles and motorbike were carried into the ablution block, hot showers were had, sleeping mats rolled out, gates closed and chained, food and drinks appeared and the party started. What a fabulous bunch, bicycling for a National Geographic article in memory of a famous Polish bicyclist/ explorer. Despite language difficulties, we had a splendid evening swapping stories and their funny descriptions had me in fits of laughter.

Garies to Dwarskerbos

A sunny warm day dawned and I set off in high spirits, minus front brakes and odometer. I headed for Lamberts Bay via Lutzville and Vredendal. The weather had cooled down considerably and I went through patches of light rain which made the roads slippery and speckled me with mud. I stopped on the railway bridge just before Lamberts Bay and watched mesmerised as the unending train clicketty clacked its way into the distance. This is the incredibly long train transporting iron ore from Sichen to Saldanha, 861 kilometres away. It was made famous in the Guinness Book of records over 20 years ago as the longest goods train in the world at 7.303 kilometres, comprising 660 loaded wagons, pulled and pushed by 16 locomotives, nine electric and seven diesel. The gross mass was 71,210 tons and it averaged a speed of 38.04 kilometres per hour with a staggering maximum speed of 80 kilometres per hour! I took a photo of this train. I didn't realise it then but this was to be my last photo as my camera had finally succumbed to the rough conditions. Later, at the small harbour in Lamberts Bay, I was disappointed to discover that my camera had packed up so no more photos, a valid motivation for returning to Lamberts Bay.

Just after Lamberts Bay (which had run out of petrol) I stopped off at a delightful farm stall restaurant where a friendly, older group touring in a bus, fascinated by encountering a lone woman on a motorbike, requested I join them for lunch and tell them my story. From there it was on to Elands Bay where I filled up with petrol.

The tendonitis in my right arm was getting worse and what with no front brakes, no odometer, no camera and a faulty arm I decided to start looking for a place to stop. I continued hugging the coast and finally found a little guesthouse in Dwarskerbos. This is the town that time forgot; it still lives in the 'old' South Africa. I was told that a curfew is imposed here and as a result criminals stay away and the crime rate is minimal. If anyone suspicious is spotted hanging about after the start of the evening curfew, a certain number is phoned and the person subsequently escorted to outside the town limits.

The cherry on top was when I opened my (new when I left home) netpad and discovered that the vibration of riding on the unpaved roads had damaged the screen. Luckily I was nearing the end of my trip!

Friday and back to Cape Town

After refreshing my spirits with an early night in the comfort of the guesthouse I packed my luggage onto my bike and hopped on, pushed the start button and… dead! Dead as a doornail. "Oh crap, not again and look at the bad weather moving in!"

So off I hopped, dug in my top pockets for the Allen key and new fuse, opened the side cover, pulled out the fuse box, disconnected the blown fuse and replaced it with the new one. I was getting proficient at this.

I pressed the start button again and with a roar (I liked to think of the soft burble as a roar – it sounds more impressive) I zoomed off into the cold, grey, overcast day. I rode on past Velddrif where I bought a handful of fuses, on past Laaiplek, then I explored pretty Port Owen, viewed the scenery of St. Helena Bay, enjoyed the character-filled Stompneus Bay, popped in to Britannia Bay and finally in the now pouring rain, visited the exquisite little village of Paternoster. To do it justice in this weather was impossible. It was at this point that I decided to give up on the coastal sightseeing jaunt as I was cold and wet and I didn't feel like changing fuses in these conditions. It seemed a shame to turn back when the interestingly named Tittiesbaai was so close. So I headed for Vredenburg where I changed the fuse yet again and then onto the West Coast Road (R27) to Blouberg. Sadly, my journey was almost over, a quiet ending to my glorious, solo exploit. On arrival in Blouberg my sweet sister-in-law warmed me up with steaming coffee and shooed me into a hot shower as I was soaking wet, blue-lipped and shivering with cold. The weather in Blouberg was mild and dry as a bone!

On reflection I knew that this experience had been so enriching and rewarding. So much so that I am going to go back and ride sections again as well as incorporate a whole bunch of other places I didn't have the opportunity to get to. I have discovered that there are many more challenging dirt routes as well as scenic hikes, pirate caves and eccentric lighthouse keepers out there just waiting for me to come along.

My right arm, which I could hardly use by the time I got to Blouberg, was exceedingly painful. When I arrived in Durban, my home city, I had an ultrasound scan which confirmed a torn tendon. The orthopaedic surgeon tried a cortisone injection and said that hopefully the pain would subside but he strongly suspected that he would have to operate to re-attach the tendon to its spot near the elbow.

Well, as it turned out my luck didn't hold and I had the 're-attachment' operation. Apart from the pain the worst was the recuperation – boring, boring, boring – there is nobody quite as bored as a right-handed person with a right arm out of action. At least I was able to put time into writing this book although I had to tap away frustratingly slowly on my keyboard with my left hand. The physiotherapist said that I should count on a healing period of at least a year and the surgeon advised against riding altogether, saying that the strenuous, long distance riding in the dirt caused the overuse injury in the first place.

Note: The fuse problems I had from Sendlingsdrift all the way to Blouberg turned out to be as a result of the massive hooter filling up with water as well as a faulty switch cluster (supplied by M. Motorcycles) on the left handlebar which shorted out the works; that's why disconnecting the hooter didn't solve the problem.

— 9 —

Life On Palmyra Beautiful, Tropical, Pristine Palmyra; Paradise On Earth

The next two chapters are about my five-month stay on the most beautiful atoll imaginable. It's about life in the slow lane, life at its most exquisite, where all the senses are tuned to an excruciatingly fine pitch, where the trappings of civilisation are but a memory. It's about an experience that in retrospect seems impossible, ethereal, never to be repeated.

Palmyra, in the Line Islands Archipelago, is one of the last uninhabited atolls in the Pacific and it has been called the remotest place on earth. An atoll is formed by the growth of coral around the rim of an ancient oceanic volcano, which generally has the classic circular or horseshoe shape and has sunk below the surface of the sea. This unique island, which lies well off the major shipping lanes, is almost in the centre of the Pacific Ocean, more or less between Hawaii and American Samoa, and is six degrees north of the equator. It is a mere speck on the chart at approximately 2.4 kilometres in length by 0.8 kilometres wide with an elevation of about 2.8 metres. It is made up of roughly 50 islets or motus, many of which are connected, sand flats, lagoons and coral reefs. There is a narrow channel from the sea, which enters the west lagoon for vessels with a draft of four metres or less.

This smidgen of land was occupied by up to 6,000 American servicemen during World War 2. Long-range air patrols and submarine missions against Japan used the Palmyra Atoll Naval Air Station primarily as a convenient refuelling station. It saw action on December 24, 1941 when the island was attacked by a Japanese submarine which surfaced offshore. It began shelling but was driven off by a gun battery on the island. When the servicemen eventually left the island, they left much behind; Quonset huts, hundreds of gallons of fuel in drums, gun emplacements, ammunition, shell and grenade casings, bomb shelters, a variety of military relics and war equipment, a workshop where amazingly, there were still tools, a massive rainwater collection tank, roads, an airstrip – we were constantly bowled over by what we found abandoned by the military.

During World War 2 a construction battalion, the Seabees, dredged the channel for ships to enter the protected lagoon. They used the coral for building the airstrip so that the supply planes could land and be refuelled. Not unexpectedly, after the war, the military were reluctant to lose this

The old rain water tank on Palmyra

strategically placed depot but after years of fighting, title was restored in 1947 by the U.S. Supreme Court to its rightful owners, the Fullard-Leos.

We were fortunate to have the opportunity to anchor in one of her protected lagoons and to spend many idyllic months exploring her secrets. This deserted island, actually atoll, was ours for a fleeting moment in time. Time I wish I could have again. I connected solidly with this atoll and explored every cove, I marvelled at her forests of gigantic trees (apparently Palmyra atoll has one of the best remaining examples of Pisonia grandis forest found in the Pacific region), I delved into the thick undergrowth and discovered exquisite beauty and rank decay.

I swam in her teeming lagoons, I waded across the artificial causeways, built during World War 2 which connected many of the motus, I snorkelled around her exquisite coral reefs boasting gigantic coral heads, I eyeballed sleek, glistening game fish with massive eyes, so curious and close that they drove me out of the water in a game of chicken I was forever losing. On my lucky days I would come face to face with turtles, some of them enormous. They seemed to have no fear of man and would simply continue on in their calm way.

The well-fed sharks and the ones I called the big greys, hung around cautiously keeping their distance but as with the game fish when they came too close I chickened out. The black-tipped reef sharks had a disconcerting habit of zooming in close and then zooming off again. They gave me the jitters. When gazing across the water one could see the black tips of these reef sharks as they foraged around like the scavengers they were.

The birdlife was profuse and mesmerising; the antics of the birds could keep me entertained for hours. The frigate birds, also known as man-of-war birds with their testicular looking red throat pouches, were masters at aerial acrobatics in their attempts to force other birds to disgorge their meals and in mid-air the victorious frigate would scoop up the food. The harassed bird, usually a booby, would try all sorts of tactics to throw the frigates off their tails but were seldom successful.

This island paradise had birds nesting everywhere. The huge colonies of breeding birds were a busy sight with parent birds coming and going with food for their young, jostling with birds incubating their eggs. At around sunset the cacophony set up by the birds was unbelievably loud. My favourite, the pure white Fairy terns, were particularly enchanting, as they had a tendency to circle curiously just above one's head. The birds on Palmyra were completely unafraid of man. It was distinctly odd being able to walk right up to one and then look at it while it looked at you. Now and again one would squawk as if to say 'don't mess with me', but on the whole they were quite tame.

The human population of the island varied while we were there. When we arrived there were three Gilbertese islanders and a handful of visiting yachtsmen. The islanders left for their homes on the Gilbert Islands shortly after our arrival but neglected to take their animals with them. A visiting yachtsman decided to take two of these dogs out to sea and shoot them. Unfortunately we only found out about this after the deed had been done. He was of the opinion that the only female needed to be put out of her misery as she had a skin infection and would in all likelihood continue breeding and the dominant male dog might as well go too. We heard that he threw them overboard and as the female thrashed in the water and tried to get back into the dinghy he took aim and fired. Apparently the male then turned and frantically tried to swim away from the dinghy but it was hopeless. He was shot as well. This act really upset me and I found it impossible to understand.

Generally (and to our delight) the yachts didn't stay long and most of the time we'd be privileged to have the island to ourselves. We took the opportunity of refreshing our reading matter by swapping sack-loads of books with the visiting yachties.

For the most part Rob was content to lie in his hammock reading our endless supply of books. Often an island dog called Navy would join me on my meandering walks, eating coconut with me when I opened one. Occasionally Rob would come along and we'd explore companionably together. On one of these occasions we walked to the far end of the island

and being low tide we took the opportunity to cross to a motu we hadn't yet explored. Time ran away with us and on our return the channel was flooding. We had observed the fins of sharks regularly in these channels when the tide came in and we assumed that they must be feeding. Now we had to cross the channel!

My brave husband decided to try the waters first and he made it across the approximately 10 metres in record time. The deepest section was probably about chest deep but the strong current and the coral underfoot made the going tough. With Rob shouting encouragement from the opposite side I strode in and promptly lost my footing. I clumsily regained it and tried to cross as speedily as possible. My feet, encased in 'jelly baby' sandals to protect them from the cutting coral, were slipping in and getting wedged between the chunks of coral as I struggled against the incoming tide. When I was about half way across Rob screamed, "There's a shark behind you! Get out, quickly!" Time slowed right down and I felt as though I was moving through treacle. I turned to see a swirl and a large dark shape. The next moment I was hit from the side with tremendous force and my legs were completely knocked out from under me. I struggled momentarily but fear gave me new-found balance and strength. This was the impetus I needed and I virtually shot across the remaining stretch… minus one of my jelly baby sandals!

Rob and I both shakily crumpled in a heap on the sand, staring at my legs, relieved that there were still two of them. Rob was convinced that it was a shark as he was sure he had glimpsed a shark's fin. I disagreed as I was positive that I would have lost more than my shoe if it was a shark. I surmised that it was a large game fish, much like the ones I'd come across while snorkelling, which had seen the flashing silver buckle on the sandal. I believed that this had acted as a lure and that's what it had gone for, successfully. My leg was marginally grazed and we felt so very fortunate that that was the only damage.

Our diet consisted mostly of fish, rice, coconut and the occasional 'runway' salad, being an edible green collected off the old landing strip.

Initially eating the fish we caught in the lagoon gave us cause for concern as ciguatera, a food-borne illness, is usually associated with fish caught in tropical waters. The ciguatoxin producing organisms adhere to coral, algae and seaweed which are grazed on by herbivorous fish which store the ciguatoxin and are then eaten by carnivorous fish in which the toxin accumulates. We read that the species of fish we commonly ate were the most likely to cause ciguatera poisoning which is heat resistant and cannot be destroyed by cooking. This toxin does not affect the taste of the fish nor can it be smelt or detected in the fish.

The symptoms of ciguatera are extremely unpleasant and can include nausea, vomiting, and diarrhoea, headaches, muscle aches, numbness, a burning sensation on contact with cold and even hallucinations. Surprisingly it seems that the toxin may be sexually transmitted as well as transmitted through breast milk. Worst of all is that these symptoms can last from weeks up to as much as 20 years in severe circumstances. Just when you think you've recovered you can trigger a relapse by eating, drinking or doing the wrong thing.

Second to ciguatera as the most common type of seafood poisoning was scombroid food poisoning. This results from eating spoiled fish and resembles an allergic reaction as one of the toxic agents is histamine, a chemical released by the body which causes the symtoms of allergies as it acts on a person's eyes, nose, throat, lungs, skin, or gastrointestinal tract. Histamine is not destroyed by cooking, freezing, canning, smoking or curing. Again the species of fish we commonly ate were implicated and this type of poisoning results from inadequate refrigeration or preservation or inappropriate handling of the fish during processing.

The symptoms are nowhere near as bad as ciguatera and rarely exceed two days. You can expect to feel flushed, dizzy and nauseous, have palpitations, maybe wheezing, an unpleasant peppery taste in the mouth and the mother of all headaches. Fortunately this should be all over in about six hours unless you are truly unlucky.

Now that I've put you off eating fish for ever let me hasten to say that

Rob and I ate fish of every description all over the Pacific and we were never once sick. Touch wood! (We had no refrigeration facilities on Moya either.) I have since read that many people avoided eating fish on Palmyra for fear of ciguatera poisoning. We caught and ate fish abundantly there. I have a feeling that this was either an 'urban legend' or simply an over-rated tale. Maybe we were just lucky!

The worst thing that happened as a result of eating fish happened in the civilised surroundings of Durban, South Africa. I had bought a delectable looking fillet of barracuda as I knew this was Rob's favourite. While he was relishing each mouthful at supper, an unseen bone lodged in his throat causing him to gasp, croak and battle for air! I rushed him to hospital where he was given an emergency general anaesthetic. The offending bone was removed by a surgeon (with a sense of humour I suspect), put into a bottle and taped onto Rob's arm so that when he woke up he could see the size of the bone that had caused all the problems; an unusual keepsake.

Our diet was reasonably varied with tinned food, mostly tinned peas, from our stores, birds that we shot with our trusty old shotgun, octopus, palm heart, terns' eggs, shellfish and a variety of crabs - land crabs, sea crabs, hermit crabs and coconut crabs.

Interestingly enough the terns' eggs made pinky orange coloured omelettes. Occasionally other yachties approached us with offers of swapping food, offers we generally accepted as it helped liven up our diet a little. But for the most part, we lived off the land in enviable style.

Coconut is, without doubt, the most remarkable food of the Pacific and elsewhere, I'm sure. The coconut palm (Cocos nucifera) is used extensively. Apart from the edible palm heart, the wood, roots, fronds, frond spines, shell and husks are used in a variety of ways. No wonder this palm is called the 'The Tree of Life'.

Coconut palms offer so much. Apart from being food and drink in its own container with an impressive shelf life, uses include oil for the skin, beauty products and soap, as a fuel in lamps, shelter, jewellery, ornamental beauty, clothing and so on. We always had chunks of coconut available for snacking on. I regularly grated coconut, poured a small amount of boiling hot water into the gratings and then squeezed them out to extract the milk, which was useful for cooking with. This milk was very rich so I'd let it stand until it separated and I was able to decant the oil portion. I'd dry the extracted gratings in the sun, roast them gently with brown sugar and add them to our precious supplies of breakfast cereal or I'd use them, sans sugar, to coat the fish we grilled, fried or baked. Occasionally a storm would down a few palms and we'd be able to cut the palm 'heart' out and put it into a bucket of water to keep it fresh. We'd then slice it finely and eat it like a salad or cook it like mushrooms. This 'heart' is actually the base of the fresh young leaves within the trunk, found at the top of the palm trunk.

When I left Moya in the mornings for a day's outing on an island I would arm myself with my machete and with time this became an extension of my right arm. Coconuts were bountiful and they provided food and drink. If you've ever tried to open a coconut you'll know that until you get the hang of it, it's nearly impossible to get through the fibrous outer husk to the nut inside. Eventually I was able to swing the machete with deadly accuracy and lop the top off, drink the delicious, cool liquid and then with a clean slice, halve the coconut. This refreshing fluid provides an isotonic electrolyte balance, and is a highly nutritious food source as well as being a natural, gentle laxative.

The hard shell of the coconut is used for the production of charcoal and the fibrous husk has many uses. Coir is made from this material and is used in the manufacture of sacking, upholstery padding, fishing nets, brushes, cordage, floor mats, mattresses, insulation and packaging. It is used as a substrate to grow mushrooms, it repels snails, is great for barbecuing on and even repels mosquitoes. It doesn't break down like many other fibres do and it is resistant to salt water.

The young green drinking nuts which can contain up to a litre of liquid, have soft flesh called 'meat', that is more akin to soft-boiled egg and this can be spooned out. As the coconut gets older so the volume of liquid decreases and the consistency and volume of meat increases. When it's much older a spongy substance develops inside sustained by the surrounding diminishing liquid and meat, like a baby in a uterus surrounded by the placenta. This spongy substance is also edible and can be eaten raw or cooked. I have since read that at some stage of the development of this sponge ball it becomes poisonous. Whew! I never knew that and ate lots of it. When this coconut is exposed to the right conditions a green shoot erupts, roots are sent down and a new palm is born.

Water wasn't a problem either. Afternoon squalls were the norm; they were short and fierce and we collected the rainwater for Moya's tanks. We would take the opportunity to strip off and rinse all the salt off our sun-browned bodies and if we were quick enough, rinse a few items of clothing as well. Not that we wore much, most often on Palmyra and while sailing we dispensed with clothing altogether.

My forays on Palmyra always yielded 'treasure' of one sort or another but not the Inca gold from the Esperanza, reputed to be under a tree, speculated to be Home Island. This Spanish pirate ship had plundered the temples in Peru of their gold and silver but in 1816 came under attack. Surviving crew members wrecked on a nearby reef supposedly transferred the treasure to Palmyra where they buried it and a year later set off in rafts they had constructed. The single survivor rescued by an American whaling ship soon died, and with him the true story of the whereabouts of the treasure.

However, as you will see in the next chapter, I did eventually find gold but in the most upsetting scenario. Palmyra is situated at a point where the southern and northern currents meet so consequently its beaches are littered abundantly with all manner of flotsam and jetsam such as bottles, mooring buoys and plastic slip-on sandals as well as a variety of assorted junk. You would never need to buy sandals on Palmyra. Robinson Crusoe would have done very well here! Beachcombing was a pleasure and I tried to beachcomb as many different areas of the atoll as possible. Now and again I would come across the king of all finds, a glass float! Over time I found glass floats in all colours and in all sizes until Rob insisted I give a couple away as we didn't have too much storage space on Moya. (She was a mere 10 metres long.) My home today contains many reminders found on the beaches of Palmyra.

Humans weren't the only ones to herd fish as we had done in Tonga. On Palmyra Island we saw dogs behaving in a similar fashion. These dogs had been left behind by the Gilbertese Islanders who had lived on Palmyra in the hopes of manning a working copra station. This was a failure as apparently the atmosphere was too humid and the copra grew mouldy and became unsuitable. The dogs would 'prance' in the water looking for the tell-tale black tips on the fins of the black-tipped reef shark. Once they had spotted a give-away moving black tip they would all rush towards it, splashing and barking and then patiently herd it onto the beach where they would attack it. The downside of this was that these dogs had teeth that were worn down to stubs as sharks' skin is extremely abrasive. Luckily they were also adept at making a small opening in a bird's egg and then carefully licking the nourishing contents out. Being scavengers they ate anything and particularly enjoyed coconut. One of these dogs, the most lovable one, was called Navy. His brother was Army. Anyway, Navy enjoyed our company and followed us wherever we went on Palmyra Island.

Not a day went by without catching fish for the pan. Eventually I was making the lures myself out of scraps of tin can, hooks from our supply and feathers from the two ducks that had been left behind by the islanders. They also left two hens, who between them supplied an egg a day, a rooster and six dogs. When we arrived there were four ducks but other yachties on the island yearning for a change in their diet killed and ate two of them. The tin in my home-made lures rusted very quickly but not before they had paid for themselves; the fish loved them! The only fish I didn't eat were the surgeonfish.

One of the yachties had shown me his foolproof way of catching fish. He would pump his heads (flush the toilet) and these fish would crowd the head outlet. He would then drop a hook down into this melee of fish and haul them out with ease. It made my stomach churn and I avoided them like the plague. I didn't like handling these fish either as they have a hidden 'scalpel' which they use with deadly efficiency. I have been sliced many times by these appropriately named surgeonfish while trying to get them off my hook and the 'scalpel' leaves a deposit of anti-coagulant so the cut bleeds profusely.

If I used bait it certainly wasn't the contents of the head (toilet). I would carefully break one pincer off a hermit crab and use that for bait. It was sustainable as hermit crabs regenerate their pincers so I didn't have to kill them.

The fishing was terrific close to islands but the downside was the boobies. They would dive onto the lure from above and invariably get it hooked in

their beaks. We would then have to bring an indignant, screeching bird on board and try to get the hook out of its razor-sharp, slashing beak. (The name 'booby' comes from a corruption of the Spanish *bobo*, which means 'clown' or 'fool.') These comical looking birds would entertain us when taking off into the air from their colony. They would invariably get up a lopsided looking run, jump off the edge of the island which was about a metre above the water, and then while squawking and flapping they would paddle the surface of the water before finally achieving lift-off. Of course, the predatory sharks knew all about the booby's lift-off tactics and could be seen moving up and down, biding their time, waiting for just the right moment. The end came swiftly and with a tremendous swirl and splash the booby would disappear from sight.

On one such occasion we noticed a large, fluffy baby booby bird obviously lost, falling and flapping ungainly near the water's edge. These babies are so fluffy that they appear larger than their parents. We rescued him (or her) and took him to the boat with us where to our dismay we discovered that he had a voracious appetite. After feeding him for two weeks we had had enough and decided that it was time for him to go home. We took him back to his colony where we removed an egg from a nest and replaced it with 'our' baby. When the parent returned there was a great deal of squabbling and general confusion and then everything calmed down and seemed okay. Today I know that this is not done, but in those days I was quite uneducated in the ways of the wild.

There were always interesting happenings on Palmyra. One day a small plane arrived with four pilots aboard. They had been liaising with Ray, who I'll talk about later in this chapter, and brought us the 10 gallons (37.85 litres) of kerosene we badly needed for our stove, as well as fresh greens and meat. Apparently the crashed Lockheed Loadstar lying on the runway had been crashed by one of them and they had come to salvage as much as they possibly could. Another guy owned a small flying transport company and flew to all sorts of unusual and strange places in the South Pacific. They were a thoroughly entertaining bunch and we listened to their jaw-dropping stories with amazement and just a touch of salt. They kindly offered to take our mail with them to Hawaii where they posted it to our parents in South Africa. That they did, as I am now using those letters to refresh my memory and assist me in the accuracy of my recollections.

When this little plane arrived and when it departed it created devastating carnage amongst the nesting birds. Wings and legs were chopped off, bodies sliced, heads decapitated and hundreds lay injured and dying amongst the already dead. Rob spent quite a few unpleasant hours putting these poor birds out of their misery. Nature's garbage collectors, the crabs, angled in and feasted.

One of the characters we met while living on Palmyra or more accurately, while living on board Moya in the lagoon at Palmyra, was Ray Landrum. He had arrived there on a small ship, the Lahaina Turkey, (which he had apparently salvaged) with his wife or girlfriend, Patti, her dog and crew he claimed to have picked up in the local pub in Hawaii. They then couldn't find Palmyra, had engine problems, weather problems and gear problems. Eventually they made it in to Palmyra, where the crew, having had enough, jumped ship. They all hitched lifts off Palmyra with visiting yachts. This left Ray and Patti in a quandary, but being resourceful, Ray set about building an attractive, comfortable cabin around a palm tree in a secluded spot with views across the lagoon. Life continued with Ray and Patti out of sight, a fair distance away from us. We kept to ourselves and we all felt that this idyllic island was ours alone.

Our Christmas feast was one of the many highlights of our stay on Palmyra. At that time friends (French Canadians) from Vancouver were visiting. We had built our yacht alongside theirs in a boatyard in Vancouver. Every morning was glorious on Palmyra and Christmas morning was no exception; we awoke to the gentle rustling of the wind in the palm trees, the sparkling lagoon with the occasional splash of a fish breaching and the all-encompassing warmth and tropical smell of the island.

Two weeks before Christmas we had started preparing our alcoholic brew – our very own version of coconut beer! (Unfortunately I didn't keep the recipe but I did keep brief notes, so you might not want to try this as I might have left out an important ingredient.) We had husked loads of coconuts and poured the coconut water into large containers to which we added yeast. We floated the yeast on a piece of the coconut husk which slowly wicked up the liquid which in turn dissolved the yeast as this was supposed to stop the brew from being cloudy. A few days later we bottled this liquid, adding half a teaspoon of sugar to each bottle. A few bottles burst their lids but we had a reasonable supply of 'fizzy beer' by Christmas.

If I remember correctly the taste of this 'beer' didn't inspire any additional attempts.

On Christmas morning we all set about carrying out our allocated task in preparation for Christmas lunch. Rob and I took our trusty old shotgun out and went hunting a particular bird that didn't have a fishy taste, apparently the nicest eating although I could never bring myself to even try one of these birds. Rob managed to bag six birds which we dressed. They would do as an acceptable replacement of the traditional Christmas turkey. We caught a few big land crabs and collected a number of terns' eggs which we used for the angel food cake. Our French Canadian friends, the island gourmets, produced delicacies fit for a king while Ray and Patti did a sterling job of preparing the cabin and making it a suitable venue for the feast to top all feasts.

Dress was casual; brightly coloured sarongs for the ladies and shorts for the guys. The weather remained postcard perfect, the food on the groaning table looked fabulous, was filling and delicious and the atmosphere mellow and contented. The coconut beer induced a mild buzz and a vague feeling of heaviness in the temples. It was late afternoon by the time we all drifted off to our yachts for a well-deserved siesta.

We used to go fishing every evening in the dinghy, trolling in the lagoon alongside the edge of the reef. My usual seat was in the bow, trailing a lure and looking over the edge and signalling Rob. He would have his rod and line out the other side, and would man the engine to go either port or starboard. These outings would take place around sunset and it was a special time of togetherness at the end of the day. Invariably Navy would join us and take a keen interest in the sea life beneath us.

The sea life on Palmyra is astounding, so much so that it is now a marine preserve and rightly so. In December 2000, most of the atoll was purchased by The Nature Conservancy for the purposes of coral reef conservation and research and in January 2001 the U.S. Fish and Wildlife Service designated it a National Wildlife Refuge.

On one memorable occasion we disturbed an exceptionally large manta ray on the surface. Its reaction was to soar out of the water and glide over the dinghy. It clipped my head as I tried to duck, the dog barked madly and it was all over in seconds, leaving the dinghy rocking and us shaken and amazed. The mantas of Palmyra were huge and plentiful and we saw them regularly in the lagoon gracing the water with their languid presence.

Sadly a massive manta entangled itself in the French Canadians' anchor chain where it died. We helped disentangle it and towed it to the seaplane

ramp to examine it. I noticed a little tail protruding from the hole on the underside of the manta. I pulled and a dead baby manta came out. It was so upsetting and in case there were any live ones in there that I could save I pushed my hand in and felt around. There were more babies; I pulled them out but they were all dead. Their fate made me feel quite heart-sore.

Rather than let the manta go to waste we cut off the choicest morsels to cook for the dogs, the wings in particular. While we were cutting the tide was coming in and the blood and entrails in the water started attracting the sharks. We stopped what we were doing and sat spellbound, captivated by the spectacle. The water at this stage had not quite reached the manta, however this did not deter the sharks. They would swim in as close as possible in a zigzagging motion, then actually propel themselves out of

Looking towards the seaplane ramp and Quonset hut on Palmyra

the water, tear off a chunk of meat and wriggle back into the water. It was astounding and made me think of a pack of dogs. The biggest of these black-tipped reef sharks was only about a metre long. They feasted royally but as the water level rose, so the menacing big greys circled warily and started savaging the manta. This manta was so big that they couldn't eat it all in one tide. We were stunned at the ferocity of their attack and made a mental note not to swim over or around the sea plane ramp as was our habit, at least for a while. We decided that it was not a wise idea to leave the manta's remains there so we towed what was left into the middle of the lagoon but the sharks continued nosing around, scrounging for scraps.

That night we invited Ray and Patti aboard Moya and opened our last precious bottle of sherry. We had a garrulous evening chatting in the cockpit with the full moon shining brightly and for once the trade winds had all but stopped. The lagoon shimmered in the moonlight, we could hear the occasional splash as a fish broke the surface and every now and again our lulled senses would be jarred by the raucous screech of a booby.

Eventually it was time for Ray and Patti to leave and make their way to their cabin. I offered to dinghy them the short distance from Moya to the seaplane ramp. By this time the moon had disappeared and heavy clouds obscured the stars so it was pitch-black. I have never before or since been in blackness like the all-engulfing velvety blackness of Palmyra.

The kerosene lamp which hung from the boom cast a weak yellow glow over the cockpit but wasn't enough to light our way. We climbed down into the dinghy and pushed off. I dipped the oars in cursorily and coasted in to the side of the seaplane ramp. Feeling slightly light-headed and wobbly I stood up to secure the dinghy to enable Ray and Patti to step off but instead the dinghy skidded away from the ramp. For one abdominal-crunching instant I was suspended horizontally between the ramp and the dinghy, bowed out over the water, imagining sharks snapping at my midriff. My muscles screamed in protest and I fell with a yell and a splash. For one horrified moment I visualised the attack on the manta and then I galvanised myself into action. How I got out of the water as quickly as I did that night, I'll never know. The next morning while we were drinking coffee on the foredeck of Moya we saw a number of fins darting around the ramp and in the very area I had fallen into!

On one of our usual fishing outings Rob manned the little two horsepower motor, we had a line with a lure trailing behind us and I was hanging over the bow peering into the water. This was our customary way of fishing for supper. I would indicate port or starboard and Rob would steer accordingly so that we could follow the reef where the fishing was best. Suddenly I saw the clear lines of a sunken boat approximately 25 feet (7.6 metres) below us and within sight of the seaplane ramp. We couldn't believe our eyes – what an incredible find!

We immediately enlisted the help of another couple on a visiting yacht as well as Ray and using the hookah gear, which pumped air through a hose, we displaced the water out of these drums which then floated the salvaged boat up to the surface. Everybody threw themselves into the salvage operation which consisted of floating empty 44 gallon drums (166.56 litres) out to the submerged boat, filling them up with water to sink them and then tying the many water-filled drums to this boat. (The island was littered with 44 gallon drums, many empty and many still full of fuel.) This necessitated diving up and down over and over, exhausting work. Using the hookah gear we pumped the water out of these drums which then floated the salvaged boat up to the surface. We rigged a line to the shore at the ramp and using this we dragged the whole shebang onto the ramp and pulled it out of the water.

This boat, which was yellow, had a hole in it which we hadn't noticed at first; however it was a streamlined looking vessel. It had USAF printed clearly on the side, a few barnacles were attached here and there but it certainly didn't look as if it had been underwater since World War 2. We wondered how on earth it had come to be on the bottom of the lagoon and why? Containers were set into four compartments in its deck; two were there but two were missing – little did we know what they had been used for. We were to find out more about those missing containers in the weeks to come.

Shortly after this find an 84-foot (25.6 metres) luxury yacht from New Zealand with a gregarious captain and crew sailed in for a brief visit. They plied us with beer, wine, rum-spiked coffee and lamb. We partied and clowned around with them but being on a delivery meant that they couldn't linger. Before they left the navigator presented us a stack of charts, charts we hadn't yet been able to obtain. In a letter I wrote to my mother I recounted the advice the navigator had given us: "He told us how to treat the natives in the South Sea Islands and which chiefs to ask for". Reading that now, 30 years later, it sounds absurd and hilarious at the same time! Sadly for Ray they set off with Patti aboard, leaving him to a hermit's existence. She had business to attend to and supplies to collect. Ray seemed to enjoy the solitude and kept himself busy with a variety of projects and occasionally we'd get together and he'd entertain us with his astonishing stories.

Early one morning we were alarmed to hear Ray yelling from the sea plane ramp close to our boat. We detected a note of panic in his voice and smartly hauled our sleepy bodies above decks. He was holding his ear from which blood was dripping, shouting that he needed help. Leaping into the dinghy we shot ashore and followed him at a run to his cabin.

There we were flabbergasted to see that he was in the process of attaching drums to his cabin, the idea being to float it across to another motu as he wanted a change of scenery. Unfortunately in the process of jacking it higher, it had slipped sideways and Patti's dog was now trapped under it and howling loudly. It was the only female dog on the island, the other dogs were male. Apparently when the accident happened, Ray had turned to run and call us for help and at that point one of the male dogs had leapt up at him as if to say "Don't go" and tore a large section of his ear right off. This was the ear he was holding with his dirty hand, the ear he wanted me to fix. He instructed Rob to save the dog and me to find the missing section of ear which he wanted me to stitch back on. There was no sign of this and we surmised one of the dogs had eaten it.

In the meantime Patti's poor dog died when Rob managed to get the weight of the cabin off it. I was extremely concerned about infection in the remainder of Ray's ear, being in a tropical climate, Ray's grubby hands and of course the bacteria introduced by the bite. None of us had any medication; no antiseptic, no antibiotics and no painkillers, but luckily we did have wound dressings. I immediately got water on the boil to try and clean the wound. Then we searched Ray's ship for any medication. I found a packet of sulphur powder and from my days as a medical technologist I remembered it to have powerful antibacterial and antifungal properties. I cleaned the remains of his ear as well as I could but was disturbed to notice a piece of cartilage hanging out. I didn't think that the skin would be able to grow around it and felt that maybe it needed to be trimmed. Of course Ray wouldn't hear of losing one extra millimetre of his ear so I cleansed it well with boiled water, packed it in sulphur powder, bandaged it up and held thumbs that it would heal properly.

Rob had the unpleasant, sad task of taking the dog's body out to sea for disposal as it was impossible to dig a hole in the hard coral to bury her. After the visiting yachtsman had dispatched the two dogs at sea (as mentioned earlier) we never saw any trace of them again so we knew her body would not wash back into the lagoon.

After contacting the U.S. Coast Guard in Hawaii, Rob explained what had happened to Ray and described the nature of his ear injury. After ascertaining that he was a citizen of the United States of America they asked us to clear the runway; they were coming in to 'rescue' him. As luck would have it the trade winds were blowing strongly on that particular day and for the pilot eyeing one crashed aeroplane lying next to the runway, discretion was the better part of valour and with that wise thought in mind, he decided against landing. This was after giving it a shot and scaring us into running for cover! Apparently wind shear is a major problem because as the pilot comes in to land, fighting the trade wind, the palm trees on either side of the runway create a windless pocket and the plane then suddenly veers off to one side as it dips into this pocket, before the pilot has time to take corrective action. The crashed Lockheed Loadstar was testament to this. At the best of times this airstrip presents a tight landing, further complicated by the thousands of seabirds wheeling in the air.

Rob spoke to the pilot or co-pilot on our handheld radio and they informed us that they would parachute a care package down to us. The contents did not have as many medical supplies as I had hoped for, containing only an anti-tetanus shot and a tube of antibiotic cream for Ray. However they had kindly included that day and the previous day's newspapers as well as a large, life-saving jar of coffee granules.

Ray, who had not come to observe the landing, was relieved as it turned out that he had no intention of going to Hawaii for treatment. I immediately administered the anti-tetanus shot, then the next thing I did was treat ourselves to a delicious cup of coffee, savouring each drop while perusing the newspaper. I didn't like the idea of keeping the remains of Ray's ear 'wet' with the antibiotic cream so I continued dusting it with the sulphur powder.

I cleaned and dressed his ear daily but after about a week or so most of the remaining ear had healed but the protruding cartilage was problematic and clearly had to be done away with. Ray agreed and asked us to help him with the removal of the offending piece. He had to steel himself for this as without painkillers or the correct equipment it was bound to be very painful. We were forced to use the only pair of scissors we had, a cheap pair of Chinese fold-up ones. Poor Ray chomped on a pillowcase, I sat on his chest and Rob gingerly tried to snip. The cartilage slipped sideways, Ray yelled, his body convulsed and I fell off.

We tried again, a lot more forcibly and for Ray painfully but this time Rob was successful and did a neat job. Within a week it had healed well and the only damage was to Ray's ego, salvaged by wearing his cap at a jaunty angle, hiding the disfigured ear. We cut the lightweight fabric of the parachute and sewed up an effective wind scoop for Moya which kept us cool for years to come.

In the evenings after supper we would sit in Moya's cockpit and enjoy the balmy night air or lounge in the main saloon and chat, play games like scrabble, backgammon, chess, cards, monopoly and so on, listen to the news which we could pick up from Honolulu on our shortwave radio, do odd jobs or I would sew.

This chapter wouldn't be complete without a description of one of our trips to Barren Island, the eastern-most island of the atoll. This was exploring at its finest and being a full day's outing we had to set off early while it was still comparatively cool. We would chug along in the dinghy across the lagoon heading for the causeway, Rob at the helm, while I sat in the bow enjoying the ever lush tropical scenery pass by. Navy would lie partly on my lap and partly on the seat with his tail wagging furiously, happily surveying the scene. Now and again the stillness of the lagoon would be broken by a glittering fish jumping high or a manta ray breaking the surface and landing with a heavy splash. Here and there a black tip protruded, moving slowly as sharks finned silently in the crystal clear waters. Periodically a happy Navy's wet tongue splashed across my cheek. Occasionally a large school of fish would pass beneath the dinghy and Navy would leap off my lap and run from side to side, looking over the edge, tail wagging madly and barking gruffly. Rob would yell at him to quieten down and he would jump onto my lap again.

Eventually we'd arrive at the causeway. This part was difficult, particularly if the tide was on the rise. The water from the inner lagoon poured through a narrow gap in the causeway and it was through this gap that we had to haul the dinghy. It was not easy to keep one's footing here. Rob would wade through to the inner lagoon, taking the painter with him. He would stand in the calmer water pulling the dinghy through the gap while I laboriously pushed from behind, bending low as I passed under the causeway bridge. This diminutive boat bucked and heaved its way through, our bodies straining with the effort of pushing and pulling. All of a sudden it would be over as the dinghy suddenly reached the peaceful water. Rob, Navy and I would then re-embark for the next leg of the journey.

This inner lagoon had a magical quality about it with its mirror-like surface and glimpses of white beach between clumps of vegetation. Here we felt that we were alone in the universe. It was difficult to imagine that there were cities out there, that wars were being fought and that the probability existed that we wouldn't be part of this forever. I would think about all of this while idly staring at the dinghy's wake, ever-widening ripples disturbing the glassiness of this tranquil, secure inner lagoon. In my notes I have written, "The sun is high in the sky now and burning down on us but our skin seems to have built up some sort of resistance to this attack and we simply turn a darker shade of mahogany". It was interesting to note that when we lived in Vancouver our skin was an almost translucent white.

It was hard work again when we got to the other side of the inner lagoon as we had to carry the dinghy over a strip of land to yet another lagoon. We left the little outboard engine on the beach there as we needed to reduce the weight we had to carry. The foliage was dark green, thick and luxuriant and blocked out the heat of the day. Before starting the hard work of getting the dinghy through this section we would scrounge around looking for coconuts which we invariably found almost immediately. We then lopped the tops off with our indispensible machete and drank the thirst-quenching liquid with appreciation. We always made sure that Navy got enough to drink as well and he loved the coconut water. When our thirst was satiated we'd split them down the middle and nibble on portions of coconut meat, taking chunks of it with us for snacks. Of course Navy got his fair share of this as well.

We would drag the dinghy over the tree roots at the intertidal zone, lift it up and start the difficult trek through the vegetation. We stopped for rests, had quiet chats, examined interesting little hermit crabs and then would pick the dinghy up and continue the strenuous journey. We'd finally break through the vegetation to a blazing hot, blindingly bright beach littered with chunks of coral. As our eyes adjusted we might notice a small chop on the final stretch of water we had to cross before reaching our goal, Barren Island, which lay dead ahead. A slight breeze often picked up but not enough to make us any cooler.

This third lagoon was teeming with life; plenty of turtles, ranging from small to enormous swam in the deeper patches, sharks and brightly coloured fish as big as us glided through the channels between the coral heads while prize game fish darted here and there, scattering shoals of smaller fish. Raucous boobies dived for fish or suffered attack by the scavengers of the sky, the frigate birds, who ate the distressed booby's disgorged meal even before it hit the water. The pretty terns hovered in groups of two or three, twittering curiously just above our heads.

We were wary of this stretch of water and kept Navy in the dinghy. The first section was too shallow to use the dinghy so we had to push it, machete in hand, as the pesky little black tips liked to zoom in for a close inspection and we feared one of them taking a test taste. As soon as we got to a deeper channel we'd hop into the dinghy with alacrity and row between the coral heads which infest this lagoon. Our excursions to Barren Island were so much about the journey; the destination to a lesser degree.

Perspiration dripping, we'd glide up to the sandbank that is Barren Island. We'd bottom the dinghy and fall overboard, lying on the sand in the shallows, the water cooling us marginally. If we felt brave enough we would don snorkel, mask and fins and navigate the channels, making sure to stick close to the protective coral heads. This was adrenalin-pumping stuff and well worth it because we understood that this was untouched nature, unsurpassed, and we were so fortunate to have found this special place and witness first-hand this pristine wilderness.

Then the treasure hunt would start in earnest! Barren Island had a surfeit of flotsam and jetsam that seemed to accumulate with every tide. Wandering along the water's edge in this perfect place with the sun shining down on us and a cooling breeze blowing was heavenly. In amongst the loads of bleached, weathered junk we found striking old bottles, perfectly wearable plastic sandals, sculptured looking driftwood, all manner of stunning shells, as well as items like old life-rings artistically trailing rotting bivalves, gooseneck barnacles or seaweed. Navy would sniff around for a while and usually end up lying in the shallows waiting patiently for us.

A little about the sandals; our feet had hardened up considerably as we were mostly barefoot. The one or two pairs of sandals we arrived with didn't last long given the terrain we walked on or clambered over daily. We were able to get sandals more or less our size on Barren Island and the mismatched colours didn't bother us. Of course they were rather degraded by the time they washed up on Barren Island so they didn't last long. Later on in the South Pacific we found out that the islanders squeezed a particular type of sea cucumber which forced it to eject a stringy, rubbery substance onto their waiting feet. This apparently protected their feet against the sharp coral.

By the time we got back to Moya the sun would be setting in a glorious display and we would be feeling happy, tired, well exercised and gorgeously bronzed. Who said life on a deserted island was boring?

Unfortunately, life being what it is there is no Utopia out there or anywhere else, much as we would love to think that we had found it. A small percentage of people seem to acquire criminal tastes when they are away from the confines of society and when they grasp that there are no police enforcing the rules out on the oceans and nobody who is likely to stop them from criminal behaviour or catch them once they have committed a crime.

You can literally get away with murder… or can you?

We heard about a shady episode that took place on the uninhabited atoll of Suvorov. A pair of yachties was overheard hatching a scheme which would see them murdering a lone sailor anchored nearby and stealing his boat under cover of darkness. The sailors who overheard this conversation armed themselves and moved aboard with the 'target' and thereby foiled the plot. The following day they all fled, terrified.

Then there was the anecdote of the elderly couple in Hawaii who were busy putting the finishing touches to their boat before setting off on a dream cruise into the South Pacific. They battled with the heavy work and were pleasantly surprised when a young man offered to help them. He was skilled with his hands and worked hard and became invaluable to the couple, who realised he would make the perfect deck hand for their voyage. They invited him along and were thrilled when he accepted. Finally the big day arrived and they cast off their mooring lines, expecting to have a trouble-free cruise with a sprinkling of adventure thrown in. Well, they got a whole lot more adventure than they had bargained on.

I'll fast forward here and tell you how this tale ended. The weather turned bad and a fishing vessel in distress put out a call for help. The rescue planes went out to search for the fishing vessel and were horrified to find a life raft bobbing in the tumultuous sea. A rescue operation was launched and the life raft yielded an elderly couple, thankfully still alive.

Apparently this is what happened; the perfect deck hand waited until Hawaii was no longer even a speck on the horizon before cold-heartedly informing the couple that he would be relieving them of their boat. Being a nice guy he would give them a choice, "Heads and I shoot you or tails, you get into the life raft to be set adrift". Tails it was and they lived to serve as a warning to all of us trusting yachtsmen and yachtswomen out there. We heard that their boat was never recovered.

Unfortunately we experienced a little of this criminal behaviour, but on a much smaller scale. We were witness to an incident we never anticipated would happen, perpetrated by the last people we would have suspected capable of such an action. A small weather station was operational on Palmyra, the power generated by solar panels. Now most yachties used wind chargers or solar panels to generate electricity on their boats and solar panels were very expensive at that time. Our 'friends' from two yachts went and stole the solar panels and then sailed off with them aboard! We were to hear later that one of them returned to Palmyra for a lengthy stay and he is actually portrayed in a positive light in various articles which were subsequently written about Palmyra.

It is interesting how perfectly nice, normal, law-abiding people in society can behave so out of character when faced with no consequences for their abhorrent actions in a 'lawless' situation, such as we encountered on this deserted island. It certainly makes one think!

—10—

… And Death On Palmyra

When we arrived on Palmyra, I found a bundle of newspaper clippings in the building known as the Quonset hut above the sea plane ramp, in retrospect such a synchronistic find. I've often thought about who the person was, who over time, gathered these articles and then left them behind. Judging by the wad of clippings, every newspaper was interested in the story, obviously a high profile case. I read these stories, stories that chronicled the apparent double murder of a yachting couple, the Grahams, committed six years earlier right there on Palmyra Island as well as the theft of their sailing boat, the Sea Wind. The articles went on to describe how this stolen boat had made landfall in Hawaii where it was recognised and reported to the authorities. What a coincidence that this boat should be recognised by someone, by a person who was familiar with the Grahams and their distinctive boat, even though it was painted a different colour.

I have been asked if the newspaper stories frightened me or raised my levels of suspicion towards other yachties or if I felt that we shouldn't remain for too long on a deserted island with help so far away. In truth nothing changed for me. I am a trusting person by nature and I suppose that my usual feelings of 'what will be will be' remained entrenched.

The strangest thing though, was that I knew with absolute certainty that I would find the remains of at least one of the Grahams. And I did. Not only that but I also located the sunken boat from which two of four containers had been taken, one of which turned out to be Muff Graham's coffin.

Often when Rob and I were out walking we would see bones and speculate about them but generally they didn't look like human bones; in all likelihood they were either fish or bird bones. As an ex-medical technologist I had studied anatomy and believed that I had a satisfactory idea as to what human bones looked like. Mac and Muff were often in my thoughts and I would find myself actively looking for traces of their passing, knowing that it was simply a matter of time before evidence of some description turned up.

The date, January 25, 1981, was an auspicious day for me, one that will never be forgotten, one that stirred a hornets' nest and gripped the American public's imagination and sympathies. This was the day that I chanced upon the remains of Mrs Eleanor (Muff) Graham, who, along with her husband, Mac, had been missing since 1974, presumed dead. This was the date that all doubts as to whether they were alive or dead were eradicated and suppositions laid to rest.

The night before I set out on my walk of exploration had been a wild one. The storm had exploded over the atoll with unusual violence and although we had tied Moya securely in place, we nonetheless carried out a few checks during the course of the night. The tempestuous rain pelted down and we could hear the hiss of the drops colliding with the surface of the lagoon. For once it was cool and we cuddled up, warm in our safe little rocking cocoon listening to the maelstrom outside.

We were reassured by the knowledge that we were secure in the protection of the lagoon. Shortly after our arrival we upped anchor and moored at the dolphins opposite the runway and after about a week we shifted from there and moored in the sheltered cove next to the seaplane ramp. We remembered how extremely unpleasant the conditions could be outside the shielding ring of coral motus, the crash of the surf on the outer reef testament to the ferocity of the weather that night.

In the morning the island had a washed out feel about it. The birds were subdued, we could see palms had been blown over and later in the forest we would find gigantic trees lying on their sides, surface roots like a vertical halo. These huge trees don't send roots down into the ground; instead they put out a network along the surface which provides a tenuous grip. There didn't seem to be any 'real' soil on Palmyra, soil that could provide deep tap roots with nourishment and a secure hold. One thing was for sure; we'd be eating palm heart for the next few days!

After breakfast Rob strung his hammock under the palms with the intention of reading, relaxing and delighting in the relatively cool morning air. We had acquired a duffel bag full of novels and Rob was currently engrossed in what I laughingly called 'doctor-doctor' novels. This was a man who previously stuck religiously to non-fiction only! How times change when faced with a literary drought.

Machete in hand and empty fabric hold-all over my shoulder I strode off with Navy, tail wagging, trotting along behind me. I intended exploring a section of the island I hadn't been to before as I hoped to find more Japanese glass floats washed ashore after the storm. As I write this story I catch glimpses of the remaining glass floats to the left of me, lying on the floor of my lounge, a tangible reminder of Palmyra.

As the morning progressed I did what I usually did; I swam, I ambled lazily along the shoreline, I pottered around, I examined interesting shells, I lopped the tops of coconuts and drank their refreshing liquid, I shared chunks of coconut with Navy, I meandered along occasionally singing with zero talent but great gusto and generally having a grand ol' time. By this stage I was quite a long way away from Rob and Moya but I was used to messing around on Palmyra on my own. I noticed that the tide was retreating further than normal so decided to go on to a part of Strawn Island usually covered by water. Here the naupaka bushes extended their branches over this area now patchy with shade and puddles. I glanced into their tangle of greenery while idly mulling over which route I should choose. I decided to stroll alongside this cool, leafy, green vegetation and see where it led me.

A soft warm breeze gently stirred the lagoon's surface, the omnipresent birds were Palmyra's 'muzak', I could hear the occasional splash of a fish as it breached the surface and the constant, distant low roar of the surf crashing on the outer reefs. I extracted my toes from the wet coral sand and headed in the direction I had chosen. As I glanced to the side a flash in the undergrowth about three metres away caught my eye. "What on earth is that?" I queried aloud as dear Navy cocked his head at the sound of my voice. It flashed again and this time I knew it was gold! I hurried over and peered into the snarl of branches and leaves. "Oh no, I've found Muff Graham!" was my first instinctive thought.

What I saw gave me the shivers and in the light of my sinister find the location suddenly took on an eerie atmosphere. In a heartbeat all the visual clues led me to believe that this was the skull of Mrs Graham that had me so transfixed. Shafts of sunlight penetrated the gloom and glinted off the gold tooth in the upturned skull that periodically rocked in a rapidly draining pool of water. The skull was small and charred with a hole near the crown, a woman's skull I thought, and the teeth, particularly the gold one, indicated dentistry I wouldn't have supposed an islander to have had.

Nearby was an open metal container lying on its side with a bone and a charred watch in the nearby lid, clearly a woman's watch. Rob says in his letter to my mom that the time-piece indicated 12 o 'clock. I don't recall this. A length of wire in the shape of the container with an empty loop the size of a chunk of coral was lying close by. The somewhat corroded box which was charred inside no longer had latches as they had rusted off. I recognised it as one of the missing boxes from the boat I had found and with a sense of horror realised that Mac was probably in the other missing container. Bones were littered in close proximity to the container and skull, amongst which seemed to be a femur; clearly the owner had not been a very tall person. When I looked at the way the bones were scattered it was clear that they had spilled from the box.

Years later in the courtroom in San Francisco the description I gave of this exact scene was evidence the defence attorney, Earl Partington, did not want to hear. Indeed, Mr Partington tried hard to insinuate that the bones had not been in the container at all and therefore it was impossible for them to have fallen out. He theorised that the container had been wedged into place by the overhanging vegetation growing into it. Before completing this chapter I read a book written by Buck Walker, the convicted murderer of Muff Graham and by his own admission he said that he had put Mac Graham into the other metal container and towed both 'coffins' into the lagoon for sinking and apparently he had told Mr Partington this. So clearly the bones had been in the container all along.

I scooped up the skull and gently placed it in my bag. Then I took one last look around, burning this macabre scene into my brain before dashing off to fetch Rob. It was imperative that we get here with the dinghy as this evidence had to be collected quickly because the incoming tide would wash it all away, for good. The very fact that I had found these remains, submerged for almost seven years, was against all odds and hopefully would go a long way towards solving the mystery of the Grahams' disappearance.

As I panted with exertion after the run, Rob eyed me sleepily from the comfort of his hammock. "You won't believe what I've found," I gasped, holding my bag up.

"A big shell?" he replied doubtfully.

"No, no, look, it's a skull," I gabbled while extracting it from my bag, "and you'd better come quickly before the tide comes in and help me collect the rest of the bones and the metal container that was the coffin."

Rob, being a fairly cool guy, seldom reacted strongly but at the sight of the skull he all but fell out of his hammock. We jumped into the dinghy and raced to the grisly site, getting it in as close as possible. We piled the bones into the 'coffin' which we lifted into the dinghy and continued searching the area until the tide came in and we were forced to stop. We were confident that we had gathered every visible trace of evidence. In a sombre mood, with our thoughts churning and the chilling cargo balancing on the seat between us, we silently made our way back to Moya.

While gliding across the lagoon's still waters I thought about the

Grahams. Like us, they were probably free-spirited sailors hoping to explore and enjoy all that Palmyra had to offer. If the newspaper articles were anything to go by, they had an exquisitely appointed boat, the Sea Wind, which they had meticulously provisioned for an extended voyage, so they certainly seemed like well-prepared and competent people. While still in Hawaii they set up a schedule of regular ham calls with a friend who was based there, a good thing too, as this was the friend who raised the alarm when Mac didn't keep to his scheduled call and tragically was never heard from again. Little did the ham radio operator from Hawaii know that his friends were dead and their boat 'pirated'!

The following morning we went back to the bone site, taking Ray and Patti Landrum as well as visiting yachtsmen, Fern and Jean Prince. We searched the area thoroughly and found a few extra bones – now scattered and some partially submerged. We put them with the other bones in the 'coffin'.

All who heard about the disappearance of the Grahams suspected foul play and they also suspected that the only other couple on Palmyra with the Grahams were the logical culprits, especially as the Grahams had been uneasy with them as evidenced by court testimony. The other couple being Stephanie Stearns and Buck Walker, Buck who by all accounts was a lazy, dope-smoking, low-life criminal and to top it all, was fleeing from the law. They had washed up on Palmyra like so much of the debris on her shores, in their supposedly ill-found, poorly provisioned sailing boat, the Iola. The Iola was apparently a much-patched, badly restored boat seemingly not terribly seaworthy and the cherry on top was no engine. To their and their boat's credit it must be said that they undertook the ocean crossing and safely reached their destination, Palmyra, which they called by her old name, Samarang. This was no mean feat.

According to courtroom testimony it seems that as soon as they met the Grahams they saw opportunity, the opportunity to sponge as much as they could off the Grahams, particularly food. Apparently they were useless at 'living off the land', so the Sea Wind with her impressive larder was highly desirable. Tensions soon flared between the two couples, with Mac

Graham being of the opinion that nobody would scare him off the island and Muff Graham wishing they could leave Palmyra as she felt nervous and uncomfortable about the situation.

Other yachties came and left, noting the unpleasant scenario; none of them had anything positive to say about Buck Walker. Eventually Walker and Stearns had to face bitter reality; their idea of living off the land on Palmyra wasn't working and they desperately needed supplies so they were forced to plan an upwind voyage in the leaky Iola to Fanning Island. This never happened.

Of course no one knows to this day what really transpired as Buck steadfastly and to his death in 2010, denied committing a double murder. Investigators pieced the scenario together and it would appear that the motive for killing the Grahams was to gain possession of their boat, which had ended up in the hands of Walker and Stearns. They sailed out of Palmyra on the Sea Wind and scuttled the ill-fated Iola.

In Hawaii they repaired (swordfish damage), repainted and even renamed the Sea Wind, 'Lokahi', a local word meaning 'unity, to be expressed with harmony'. The occurrence I found bizarre was the swordfish attack in which the Sea Wind sustained damage below the waterline before reaching her destination. Why on earth would a swordfish attack an item so much bigger than itself which didn't look or even smell like food? And is this why they went to Hawaii instead of somewhere else where there would be far less chance of either them or 'their' boat being recognised?

Walker, who had many previous convictions and Stearns, who both tried, unsuccessfully, to escape from the authorities in Hawaii maintained that the Grahams had disappeared in a dinghy accident while out fishing. Walker said he had found their overturned inflatable dinghy, engine still attached and although they both searched, they could not find the Grahams. Consequently they decided to take the Sea Wind and her contents for themselves; Stephanie was even spotted wearing one of Muff Graham's blouses.

They were arrested and charged with only the theft of the vessel because of the double jeopardy law. The fly in the ointment was the fact that there were no bodies despite a search carried out on Palmyra by a team sent by the U.S. Government. It was hoped that a body would turn up at a later stage that would make a murder charge more likely to succeed. They were convicted of the theft of Sea Wind; however Stearns only served seven months of her two-year term and was released in November 1977. Walker served five years of his 13-year term and then in July 1979 he escaped from the U.S. Penitentiary at McNeil Island, Washington.

The suggestion of modern-day piracy at a time where this was almost unheard of, the shocking thought of a possible double murder of well-prepared American people living out their dream on a deserted island paradise and the mystery surrounding the case resulted in this story capturing the public's attention in the U.S. and becoming common knowledge in Hawaii.

At about this point in my account I realised that I felt uncomfortable with the way the scenario had been presented in the courtroom. I simply didn't believe that Buck and Stephanie or any vaguely normal person would murder for food when the island had so much freely available. Possibly they did run out of staples like flour or sugar but there wasn't a snowball's chance in hell of starving on Palmyra with the abundance of eggs, tame birds, land crabs, hermit crabs and coconut crabs, shellfish, fish, turtles, coconuts lying around in their hundreds, possibly thousands as well as palm heart from storm-downed palms. Not only that but fresh water was freely available as was fuel and shelter. If you add to that all the items that were left behind on Palmyra you'd want for very little, as we discovered in the five months we were there.

I ruminated over why the body had been put into this metal container and not fed to the sharks. I knew that it couldn't be buried as the island was almost solid coral with not much in the way of soft earth. Years later I came to the conclusion that, as we had discovered with the manta ray and Palmyra's well-fed sharks, the meal was not disposed of in one 'sitting'. It took a few days and obviously the murderer/s couldn't take the chance of the unfinished remains washing ashore from either the sea or the lagoon and being spotted by new visitors to the island. A box weighted down by a rock or chunk of coral seemed to be a permanent solution, even more so if you then sunk a boat on top of the container!

There was so much fuel on Palmyra that my guess was the murderer/s probably filled the container up with fuel and ignited it in a misguided effort to obliterate the victim. The metal container measured roughly three feet long, two feet wide and two feet deep (approximately one metre long, point six of a metre wide and point six of a metre deep). Could a person's body be folded up in such a way that it would fit into this container, I mused. I thought it could and I felt that all the talk later at the court case of cutting up the body to fit was sensationalist and unnecessary.

Ray and Patti had spent the night at another island and when they returned the next morning we showed them my find. They were aghast as were the other pair of visiting yachties, and Ray immediately radioed the coast guard in Hawaii on his ship's CB radio. They patched us through to the FBI who asked a number of questions; the transmission was distorted and crackly and we kept losing them but eventually got our message across. They were quite insistent that we put the remains on shore and did not keep them on the boat with us. We found out later that this was for our protection as one of the suspects was an escapee at the time and the possibility existed that he could get to Palmyra and do away with the evidence. We set up a radio schedule for the next day and signed off. That night and every night until the FBI collected the remains we slept with one eye open, both ears on high alert and the loaded shotgun next to us.

The six of us speculated like mad as to what might have happened and where the other body might be. We knew that it would most likely be in the same container as the one I had found with the remains, the container from the USAF boat which was now lying on the sea plane ramp. So off we went that afternoon on a diving expedition to look for the other box, but to no avail despite hours of searching.

We listened to the Hawaii radio station, as was our habit at supper time, and the news broadcasts were filled with the account of my find and what it meant. We were in constant contact with the FBI and of course the whole world could listen in to our conversations including the escaped suspect!

In the meantime, while listening for radio broadcasts on 'our' story, we discovered that events were hotting up at home in South Africa. We heard on the news reports that armed terrorists were entering the country by the boatload. We worried about our families and hoped that they were okay. This was 1981; apartheid was alive and well. The last vestiges of this system would only come to an end in 1994 when free general elections would be held for the first time and the outstanding and exceptional Nelson Mandela would become president of our country.

Eleven days later the FBI arrived on a six-seater plane and landed on the old runway amongst the carnage they had created. Hundreds of birds were chopped up and hundreds of eggs were squashed, much to the unsuspecting pilot's horror. They filled us in on the background to this remarkable 'piracy' story and we learnt that Buck Walker, the prime suspect, had many previous convictions and was an escape artist of note. We showed them the site of my find and spent time searching for additional evidence, specifically any additional bones which might have surfaced with the changing tides.

At the time of my find I never did complete the walk I had set out to do, the glass float finding walk. The FBI guys scoured the area intently and then broadened their search to include the nearby waterline. I heard one of them hollering, "Hey look what I've found!" We all rushed to see what it was and there lay a few gorgeous, unbroken, perfect glass floats. Hrrmf, my luck – not that I needed any more bulky glass floats!

We discussed at length what forces caused the container to land up where it did and why now. Finding it was such a long shot and against all odds; I just happened to be there at exactly the right time. The next tide would in all likelihood have scattered and/or buried the bones and washed the container away. And if it weren't for that gleaming gold tooth I might never have become aware of what was in the drying shallows under the vegetation.

I surmised that the decomposing body had created gases which made the container buoyant, in spite of the few visible corrosion holes which might have been blocked with algae, seaweed or detritus of one sort of another. As the tide ebbed and flowed the 'anchored', buoyant container would have drifted from side to side over the years until the presumably now rusty wire broke free of its improvised coral anchor. That's when it floated up and it happened to float up during a severe storm, at spring tides. It would probably have been partially submerged with just enough visible above the water to catch the wind. The stormy winds blew it to the shore on the high tide and as the tide retreated the winds and possibly the low overhanging foliage kept it pinned there.

Almost three weeks later the skull was positively identified as belonging to Eleanor Graham. This identification was made by a forensic odontologist as a result of comparing her dental charts and X-rays, supplied by her dentist, to the actual skull, teeth and dental work. An indictment for felony-murder was brought against Stearns and Walker for first degree murder in the death of Muff Graham and the manhunt for Walker was started in earnest. Stearns turned herself in and the following day was released on a $100,000.00 bail. Walker was arrested in Arizona, seven months later after being on the run for over two years. He was brought to trial in June 1985.

Headlines screamed out the story, news broadcasts focused on it and even in South Africa billboards were hung on the streets proclaiming 'S A SAILORS FIND KEY MURDER EVIDENCE'. My mother collected one of these for me which I still have today!

I had agreed to the FBI's request that I give evidence at the future court case/s. As we voyaged on around the world the FBI kept tabs on us until the day they needed us. This day turned out to be many years later, after the births of both our children. At my request our flight to the U.S. for me to give evidence were made en-familie, with Rob entertaining the children when I appeared in court on June 1, 1985. The media went crazy and every detail was faithfully recorded by the media and devoured by the public. I was amused to note that even a description of what I was wearing to the courtroom was documented.

Walker and Stearns were tried separately by a jury so we flew to San Francisco on two occasions. Originally the trial venue was Honolulu but this was changed to San Francisco on the basis that pre-trial publicity had created a general attitude of bias against the defendants.

As a result of my find the legal processes ensued and Buck Walker was eventually convicted in 1985 for the murder of Muff Graham and sentenced to life in prison. Stephanie Stearns was acquitted; a controversial verdict. Walker, who denied that he killed the couple, wrote an 895 page book entitled 'Palmyra: The True Story of an Island Tragedy' in which he claimed that the Grahams died as a result of a love triangle that went tragically wrong. He served 22 years in prison and although he wasn't up for mandatory release until 2018 he was paroled in 2007, aged 69, because of advancing age and poor health. His freedom was short-lived as he died on April 26, 2010.

It shook me that four people could share the island, two were brutally murdered yet of the two remaining people, only one was found guilty. Did Stephanie honestly not have an inkling as to what was going on at the time of the murders? Many people assumed that she was the brains and Buck the brawn, but that theory flies out the window as apparently, while Buck was in prison, he was tested and found to have a high IQ. Maybe Stephanie didn't have a clue; only she would know. I tried to track her down so that I could get further insights into this tragedy but to no avail.

In the course of writing this book I trawled the internet for information on Buck Walker. I came across a startling post by a person calling himself or herself 'Masked Marvyl' stating that Muff was raped by Buck before being killed. Does somebody know something we don't? This certainly throws a new light on the crime; one that I don't think was investigated. Taking that thought further, it would be logical then for Buck to conceal this and the subsequent murders from Stephanie. Maybe this gave him the inspiration for the 'love triangle' story in the book he wrote while languishing in prison. It is food for thought!

This is the collection of posts I found on the following site:

http://aolanswers.com/questions/duane_buck_walker_palmyra_convicted_9512605516081

Judy Cooke asked: "Does anyone know how to get a hold of Duane "Buck" Walker, the convicted killer of the couple on Palmyra Island?"

Shawn answered: "I gave him a ride approximately two weeks ago. A friend of mine knows how to contact him. May I ask what this is concerning?"

Catmandhu answered: "He has his own website http://palmyramystery.com/web1/Page 1x.html where there's a link to email at the end. I suspect he'd get an email there...? You can also order his 900 page fictional account of "true" events. I am not sure why you'd want to contact the guy. If you read his website through, it's riddled with inconsistencies, denials, self-righteousness, blame on others (in other words, lawyers), and so on. It is a typical unapologetic denial of reality and responsibility, similar to the letter he drafted in prison to Mac Graham's sister that was supposedly written while on return to Hawaii. It is a shame he was let out since he already had 10 plus years of freedom, something he took from the Grahams, before being convicted."

Palmyrafan answered: "He is also on Facebook."

Salsalady answered: "Buck Walker passed away on April 26, 2010, in Lakeport, California."

MaskedMarvyl: "May I ask why you would give a ride to such an evil piece of scum? He raped and killed a woman, then dismembered her body and tried to burn it beyond recognition. He probably disposed of the husband the same way. It is nice to know that you do such good deads for psychotic rapists and murderers... (I think Manson needs some care packages, if you're interested)."

(I think he meant to say, "It is nice to know that you do such good <u>deeds</u> for psychotic rapists and murderers..." but I guess he had 'dead' on his mind.)

This story has intrigued and followed me for most of my adult life and eventually I did what I now wish I had done years ago – I ordered Buck

Walker's book. What a read; I couldn't put it down. I thought of little else; I was transfixed. It made the time that has elapsed between then and now telescope down until it seemed like yesterday that I was there on Palmyra – a strange sensation. In his book Buck comes across as a charismatic rogue, living life his way, with a flagrant disregard for the law. I laughed many times while reading it and under different circumstances he is probably a person I might have liked, had I met him and known nothing of his personal history. As I suspected Buck's account opened new thought processes in my mind and I am not altogether convinced that the outcome of this bizarre story was indeed correct.

I don't believe that he murdered Mac and Muff for either their boat or for food. Stephanie and Buck could very easily have hitched a lift off the island with visiting yachties and as I have already mentioned the island provided enough food. So what was the motive? Did Mac perhaps stumble across Buck's marijuana plants, maybe even destroy them? Did these two headstrong men have a disastrous fallout over a disagreement of sorts? Maybe Buck flirted openly with Muff… or more? I think that the possibility exists that Muff might have been done away with because she was witness to an incident that happened between Mac and Buck in which Buck emerged as the victor.

His book was apparently initially 2,000 pages long but thankfully Buck condensed it to 895 pages. I suppose when you are in prison for that long you can fill a lot of pages! There are inconsistencies and I'm sure some of it is self-serving, some of it outright lies, some probably faulty memories, but I'm just as sure that within the pages of his book there is some truth too. How do we now sift and distil this truth? We can't.

There is a lot of sex in his book, probably because he was deprived of that in prison so took his pleasure in writing about it instead. There is also shocking sensational stuff, like the following on page 831: "It has been the tradition since I have been at the U.S. Penitentiary at Lompoc, California these past 12 years for the warden to treat the inmate population to barbecue picnics twice a year. Since the first one, I have never attended. I skip the camaraderie of my fellow desperadoes for the hermitage of my cave-like cell. The heavy greasy smell of searing meat reminds me of the smells I once smelled of human bodies burning – it winds up into my nostrils to permeate my soul with a sickness."

When I turned the last page of his book I felt ill at ease, distraught even. My find had resulted in this fellow human being incarcerated for the bulk of his adult life. Did he really have a fair trial? I don't know. After mulling it over and over I came to the conclusion that I did the right thing in reporting my find and testifying in court. In the same situation I would do the same again.

Malcolm Graham's body has never been found. I know that if his body had been found the circumstances might have been established. Unlikely as it is, I truly hope that one day some sea gypsy like me stumbles across Mac's remains.

RIP

—11—

In Conclusion

Looking back I feel that I have been extremely fortunate to have done all these things I have written about and all the other activities that didn't find their way into this book. I have special memories and many photos, I have forged long-lasting friendships and I have seen and done much that many others haven't had the opportunity to do or possibly the desire to do. Best of all is that there is a limitless supply of exciting challenges and adventurous getaways out there just waiting for one. Dream it and you can do it, no matter what your age! That's my motto.

It does have its downside though, in that I constantly feel slightly restless, a strangely uncomfortable stirring of the soul (for lack of a better word), an urge to 'go', anywhere, by any means, into the unknown… or maybe it's just the way I'm wired. 'Settling down' is anathema and occasionally I feel like an alien living here in suburbia trying to 'fit in', to do what's considered normal amongst my cultural group. I struggle with this everyday drudge even though I give it my all in terms of family responsibilities, socialising, positive thinking, self-improvement studies and generally trying to get my mind to accept the lifestyle I have to pursue in order to 'fit in'.

My family and friends, who I adore, are loving, interesting and supportive and without them life would be so much harder. Of course the initial stages of motivating myself to do these trips, especially those I do by myself, is challenging but once the first hurdle is overcome I thoroughly enjoy all the aspects – the planning, the execution and the resulting gratification.

I feel that somewhere along the line we've chosen the wrong path. We work long hours because we feel we have to, to get paid with money we spend on stuff we don't need. Our babies are largely bottle-fed, our children get brought up by a nanny or day mother, and we don't have time to spend with our teenagers, let alone our partners and elderly parents. Apart from the general decay in civilised behaviour, blood pressure, cholesterol and stress levels are high, obesity, drug and alcohol use, divorce, teenage pregnancy, suicide and murder are on the increase and like lemmings we carry right on. Why do we think that having the latest cell phone, pair of shoes, car or hairstyle is so important? Why do we not get taught at school about time to think, time to play, time for others, time to do nothing at all? How often have you said "I'm too busy," or heard other people say "I'm too busy"? Our society is 'rich' in so many ways, yet it is time impoverished.

It's seldom that we come across people who are completely satisfied with what they have and with their lives in general. Being contented with what we have, no matter how meagre, could be what being successful all is about.

Is the state of dissatisfaction simply human nature? It is argued that this state of dissatisfaction is necessary because it drives us on to progress. All this progression has poisoned our planet and to a large degree ourselves. We are now seeing earth-friendly green initiatives being put into place in an effort to heal the world but in my opinion society also desperately needs healing. Greed, power, wealth, is what it's all about. We have lost faith in each other, our leaders, our institutions and our governments.

At the end of the day, when we've worked our youth and our middle age away, when we're in a state of senescence and when ailments and illness are most likely to happen, what do we do? We retire! Terrific, now that the body is on the sclerotic, downhill slide how are we supposed to do the fun stuff? I suppose the idea then is to sit around, surrounded by the items you've accumulated. At this stage a lot of people won't go out there and follow their aspirations because they've had little experience at it and are now too timid or feel too old or infirm to try something new.

My mother, who is 83, mentioned that now that she is old she often looks back in time and ruminates on distant and not-so-distant memories. I asked her what her over-riding thoughts about her life were now. Her answer shook me although it shouldn't have. I should have known and it makes me sad. She said life had passed her by and that she had missed out. I probed as to why she felt that way and her response was, "All I can remember is working". Is this the average person's fate?

Of course the choice to strike out for the unknown takes a certain amount of courage; we might have to wave goodbye to security, throw caution to the wind, leave our comfort zone, family, pets, insurance policies, medical aid scheme, gym contract, cosy home and regular income behind… all in the name of a profound, body and mind-refreshing, life-affirming adventure!

The 'rat race', the major social affliction of our times; people who are off to enjoy what's left of their lives or those few souls who opt out when they still have many good years ahead of them generally refer to themselves as opting out of the rat race. I suppose the thing I miss most when I'm in the rat race, sitting in an air-conditioned office, is being able to absorb the sun's rays, being pummelled by the wind, walking in the rain, feeling freezing cold or boiling hot, muscles aching with fatigue, perspiration dripping, gazing at the clouds drifting by and generally being in touch with what's happening outdoors and in turn, being in touch with my body. My weekend, the allotted two-day allowance, doesn't satisfy me.

I like the way my body feels after being outdoors, especially if I've exerted myself. The feeling of aching, tired muscles is a happy, healthy fatigue. I enjoy being hammered when riding in the dirt, being filthy, having my hair knotted in the wind, getting caked in salt at sea, shivering with cold on high mountains or being drenched in a downpour. I sleep well; I wake up feeling phenomenal with my energy levels high. Even if I haven't exerted myself, simply being outdoors makes me feel good, skin tight from the sun, with a rosy glow, languid and relaxed. The heat of the sun warms me as well and I feel sexy and loving. I think it's the contrasts that do it for me.

I actually shouldn't but do feel guilty when I take off on one of my (therapeutic) forays but periodically I have to do them. If I don't, this sense of life not being worth living intrudes into my daily consciousness. Going away, adventuring, and hiking in the wild is my way of maintaining a feeling of normal but to keep those around me happy and to keep from being labelled selfish, I try to balance work and play. (Of course work still outweighs play!)

There are no easy answers to the numerous queries raised by our societal ills and it's very easy to criticise, which I don't enjoy doing unless I can be constructive and come up with answers. I can't, only offer food for thought. For many people in regular eight-hour jobs, flexi-time or working from home certainly would help. In this age of instant communication where being on site is not a necessity, companies should be looking at decentralising their operations. Making activities in-house, in a totally non-corporate, relaxed setting would possibly be another option, home-from-home.

Maybe we should think about becoming less 'Westernised'. We lead insular lives where the single family home is the norm and which I am beginning to feel might be to our detriment. Also single people tend to live alone which, as a single person, I know can be isolating, compounding feelings of loneliness. I think we should consider the merits of the extended family or a communal lifestyle where sharing, caring, helping, learning to get along and so on are par for the course. Our social skills would be vastly improved and apart from the many benefits this offers I'm sure it would help bring the divorce rate down. The incidence of illness would be reduced as a result of way less stress and when one is sick there will always be someone to keep an eye on you. Also, it's a lot more cost effective to live if expenses are shared and resources are equitably pooled. The quality of life would be improved. I know that many of you will be rolling your eyes and saying, "Hell no, I could never live with my mother-in-law", and yes, there are negatives but if correctly structured I feel that the plusses could outweigh the negatives.

Why do we have to have ownership of so much? Whatever happened to sharing? Is it because people are not as trustworthy as they might have been in the past or have we become distrusting, selfish or acquisitive, or maybe it's simply because of our insulated lifestyles? Sharing would take a little of the strain off the earth, definitely a 'green' contribution.

Another bugbear of mine is pollution (of the self-inflicted variety) which has become a fact of life and I feel powerless in the face of it. We are bombarded by advertisements proclaiming the benefits of surrounding ourselves with cleaning agents, disinfectants, insect-killing sprays, odour-disguising aerosols (they should be called air polluters not air fresheners), vaporisers and powders, the benefits of taking pills, supplements, tonics, high-energy drinks and food-substituting milkshakes. Even in countries where the water is fine people are persuaded into believing the bottled variety must be better, probably one of the greatest cons of the 20th century! The plastic bottles require about 47 million gallons (approximately 178 million litres) of oil per year to produce and the resulting plastic waste is about 1.5 million tons per annum!

Talking about cons the greatest con in the last few years has to be the balance bracelet which supposedly improved one's balance, strength, flexibility and performance. Athletes were targeted as prime candidates and it would appear that many people were 'caught' by these unsubstantiated claims. They actually supposed that it worked and gave them the edge by wearing it. Of course they probably did have the edge because they believed it strongly enough, the powerful placebo effect.

I could drone on and on here but the point is why do we buy it? Why do we believe it all to be true? Why do we allow ourselves to be subjected to this nonsense on TV, and see it in magazines, posters, illuminated billboards, and so on? Those who rebel against this media bombardment or who think about it or question it are seen as being to some extent, peculiar. A person whose comment made me ponder his IQ said to me, by way of constructive criticism, "I don't know why you have to question what you are told, it's so annoying – why can't you accept", so IQ aside, it seems that having an enquiring mind can be irritating to some people. I think human beings enjoy being 'part of the group', or 'one of the crowd', so being keen to do what the next man does or says is simply human nature. That's why advertising works.

We need to remind ourselves to approach life logically, to have enquiring minds and not to accept blindly. We should be able to examine the evidence and weigh up the pros and cons rationally. Most important is the ability to make informed decisions and openly express what we feel, even if others don't always agree with us or if it goes against mainstream thinking.

Intense belief in anything seems to work for the believer; in other words the power of mind over matter, as mentioned earlier. I am of the opinion that anyone can enjoy tremendous benefits by exercising mental discipline, employing positive thinking, living a healthy and honest life, not allowing stress to get a stranglehold and achieving enough rest and playtime.

With playtime in mind let me relate the following incidents. I do think that having a partner to share my life with would be nice and to that end a bunch of single girlfriends and I had a brief fling with internet dating. Oh my, what an eye-opener! I cyber chatted with a few potentials and eventually arrangements were made and I met them face-to-face.

The first message I received was from a person whose photograph showed a nice-looking, distinguished guy. After swapping a few e-mails we agreed to meet for coffee at a central restaurant where I was surprised to see what looked like the father of the person in the photograph walking towards me, smiling. After the initial introduction was over I impolitely blurted out, "The photograph you used on the website doesn't look like you."

"Oh that was taken about 20 years ago," he replied, with a straight face. I found this unsettling and after a stilted chat which bored me silly he said, "I'd love to see you again."

I couldn't understand why as the meeting had been awkward, we didn't gel at all and he had misrepresented himself by posting a 20-year-old photograph on the dating site, so I simply said, "No, I don't think this will work for me. Goodbye."

I persevered and once again accepted an invitation to meet for coffee in a restaurant. This time the person was as nice looking as his up-to-date photograph indicated. Strangely we were both dressed exactly the same; black shirt, black jeans and black boots. While waiting for the coffee to arrive he told me about himself. He continued telling me about himself over that first cup of coffee; the monologue persisted over the second cup and I found my attention wandering. I realised that he was talking at me rather than to me and before he ordered yet another cup I tried to make my escape. He would have none of it as he hadn't finished, so insisted I stay while he drank a (by now) tongue-corrugating third cup. I was beginning to despair as his caffeine-fuelled diatribe seemed set to continue indefinitely.

As he neared the end of his coffee I got up and excused myself. He too stood up, we paid the bill and he followed me out to my car, still talking. Desperation was settling in but I eyed my car with a sense of relief. I opened the door to get in but he held it open and continued talking while I sat dumbly in the driver's seat. Eventually I had to be rude and pulled the door closed. His parting words which invoked a sense of déjà vu were, "I'd love to see you again."

"What!" I replied, flabbergasted. I had hardly managed a word in edgeways and he knew nothing about me! Exhaling audibly I managed to drive off without fitting in a further response. I don't think he noticed.

In the meantime, having had similarly dismal encounters, my friends cleverly decided to have a party and invite all the singles they had chatted to on the site. That way we wouldn't have to go through the tedious one-on-one sifting process. This time I met a sporty person who invited me out a few times. It was relatively affable but luckily before anything got off the ground I discovered that he was the insanely jealous, possessive type. That marked the end of that and we all gave up on the idea of internet dating!

All of this and listening to my friends' love stories had me thinking. I deliberated the fickleness of some individuals who are in love today and out of love tomorrow. It doesn't work that way for me but I've discovered that this powerful word, 'love', gets bandied around and used ad nauseum. Is it lack of command of the English language perhaps where love also means like, want, enjoy, desire, care for, need, fond of, keen, fancy, lust for, attracted to and so forth, or does its inappropriate use (often ultimately hurtful), simply indicate a supremely shallow attitude/person? To me it's a commitment word in a relationship, a cementing word, a word that holds promise, a sincere word that should only be used when genuinely meant, not used with gay abandon, here today, gone tomorrow… and then maybe picked up again a few months down the line for use on another sucker.

Back to my tale once more, my biking days seem to be limited as a result of my two injuries while biking. In themselves they are not bad but it seems that at my age when you fall off, you hurt yourself. I always thought that 'slowing down' as you get older was a myth but it seems that the body just isn't as bouncy or resilient or heals as quickly as when one is younger. I have sold my Yamaha XT660R but I am keeping the Yamaha TTR250 for the time being, 'just in case'. When my arm heals I hope to still ride but maybe I will have to accede to the softer option, on the beaten track instead of mostly off the beaten track!

For those of you who are interested in doing a long, border-crossing motorcycling trip there are a few suggestions as to what you should consider learning how to do. Although my intentions were good, I didn't learn how to do all of this before I left:

- Repairing a puncture
- Removing front and rear wheels
- Replacing brake pads
- Replacing brake fluid and bleeding the brakes
- Replacing fuses

- Adjusting clutch and brake cables
- Replacing or fixing a broken chain
- Adjusting the suspension
- Preparing the bike for transport

Of course an essential tool kit and essential spares are a necessity. As far as riding technique goes, you'll pick up what you need to know along the way.

After many discussions and seeing it for myself, I believe that if you are planning to over-land on a motorbike in a Third World country, keep it small and choose a bike that's lightweight and manoeuvrable. You can't ride very fast on most of the roads, especially if you plan to use minor roads, spares for small bikes are more readily available, you don't stick out like a person likely to dish out hand-outs and anyway I think that pootling along and taking in everything around you is quite satisfying.

On my journeys I occasionally wished I was on my bigger bike but in retrospect those times were few and far between and I will be sticking to the smaller bike for all my future missions.

At this point the sailing (cruising) lifestyle still holds tremendous allure but doing it on my own does not. This is something one can enjoy doing at any age. Living on a yacht is simple; no rates, no utility bills, no traffic jams, and it is satisfying and carefree. The big minus is leaving family, pets and a comfortable home behind. I sail locally with friends which I find gratifying, but sailing to distant islands and atolls, the more out-of-the-way the better, is what I enjoy doing the most. I have a bucket-list of islands and destinations in my mind that I hope to achieve one day; my early cruising years have whetted my appetite.

The long time that I spent away from 'civilisation' while on board Moya and then Energy had unexpected consequences; I missed out on years of news, music and movies and later I'd hear about a news item, a song or see a movie on TV that everybody else but me seemed to know about. I don't think I ever quite 'caught up' although that was unimportant.

While cruising I never kept a diary or took any photos. I did write long letters to my mother that I can now refer to and over the years I have given the odd presentation about my cruising lifestyle. I have on a few occasions written about the Palmyra incident so as a result the life that I led over this period and all its tales has remained clear in my memory. The Palmyra saga has become part of my life as it keeps resurfacing at the most unexpected times. I still own the same cheap pair of Chinese fold-up scissors that Rob used to trim Ray Landrum's ear on Palmyra. It is now looking a little rusty but I treasure it and haven't the heart to throw it away so I keep in my hiking first aid kit and it's still useful for cutting (actually 'hacking' is the honest word here) Elastoplast and so on.

Discussing Vincent Bugliosi's book 'And the Sea Will Tell'

Ten months after leaving Palmyra it was once again in the news. This time the report, rather embellished I thought, was about a trimaran, the Sisyphus that had been dismasted but managed to enter Palmyra's lagoon. It was reported that the 'shipwrecked' father and his two young children were marooned on this deserted island with only an eccentric hermit (Ray) for company. Anyway, using Ray's rig they radioed for help but the coast guard was in no hurry to launch an expensive rescue operation for people whose lives were not in any danger, and who in fact simply needed transport off the island, not rescuing. Public sympathies were stirred and an amount was raised which enabled a mercy flight by a Honolulu pilot to 'rescue' the hapless family. To add to the father's problems was a small matter of a large sum of money he owed in the United States, a problem he was forced by the authorities to address once he was back in 'civilisation'.

The twist in this tale was Ray's involvement. Being an entrepreneurial man and a survivor to beat any contestant in any TV show, he mulled over the good fortune eyeballing him from the lagoon. He set about repairing the boat and apparently successfully piloted the trimaran to Hawaii. (This was about five months later.) I would love to meet Ray again, as apart from being splendid to see him, I have so many questions that need answering.

Somewhere along the line an American friend found his way to Palmyra for the sole purpose of relieving the last remaining dog, Navy, of his lonely island existence. He was taken to Los Angeles where he visited a vet. He underwent a thorough examination and pronounced healthy, although the vet was mystified at the state of his teeth which had been worn down to stubs. My friend fed him soft foods and Navy lived out his remaining days in the lap of luxury, mostly on the rear seat of my friend's luxurious Cadillac. One day I received the sad news that Navy had gone to doggy heaven. One of his main heart valves was no longer functioning correctly and although medication has been given to him, it didn't really work. When it was realised that he was uncomfortable he was taken for the last time to the vet who administered a one-way

anaesthetic so that he wouldn't have to suffer. He died while being lovingly stroked by my friend; a gentle way to go and preferable to starving to death on Palmyra as a result of his worn-down teeth.

On a lighter note my friend described a comical incident that occurred in Los Angeles when Navy was confronted by a bitch in heat for the first time in his life. He instinctively grasped that certain behaviour was anticipated of him but being an elderly lad he wasn't sure as to what it was. That smell was driving him crazy but oh dear, what to do? So he spun in circles, he sniffed again, he whined, he pawed the soil but this wasn't doing the trick so he rolled over onto his back, paws airborne, all to no effect. In truth it did have an effect, a huge effect on my friend who was holding his sides with laughter.

I dream of Palmyra. I long to go back to Palmyra and would love the opportunity to contribute in a small way to the important work that is being done there. The rat eradication programme will make a visible difference and I am thrilled that the island is being assisted to its 'au naturel' state. I consider myself extremely privileged to have had the opportunity to spend a small portion of my life there and to have explored it as thoroughly as I did. At the time I knew I was privileged and would often sit alone on the beach of one of her many motus, thinking about life elsewhere and how extremely fortunate it was that I was sitting right there. I also appreciated that it couldn't last forever and I tried to take mental snapshots of the beauty around me, snapshots which have remained forever locked in my mind.

My daughter, Lara, is now working as a physicist in a job she is passionate about. Her boyfriend, Clayton, is an environmentalist and together they share their home with two energetic dogs. Lara informs me that these are the only grandchildren I'm likely to see! Lara and Clayton still hanker after the good times they had on our journey to Malawi and will no doubt go on more motorcycling trips at a later stage. We all agreed that in retrospect the best part of that journey was at the end of each day when we would relax together in an exotic location after a hard day's biking and watch the sun set, while recounting the day's stories and sipping ice cold local beer.

Life has not been easy for my middle son, Thana. He lives a very private life in another city and sadly we do not see him often. I wish he would let me help him or that he could come to terms with his personal demons and at least achieve a measure of peace but it seems that this will be a long road he'll have to walk himself. My love and support for him remain on standby, always there waiting for his acceptance. His passion is medicinal plants and he has become a walking encyclopaedia on this subject. His other passion is physics and as a result his workspace is a curious mix of cogs, wheels, magnets, strange inventions, small tools, computer bits and bobs and incongruously a solar-charged nodding plastic flower. He has a large scar across his big toe, a reminder of those long-forgotten sailing days.

Justin, my youngest son, lights up our home with his wit, good humour and out-the-box ideas. His school marks remain consistently good despite his adamant refusal to study much more than is absolutely necessary. Computer gaming is his passion at the moment and that's our only real area of conflict. He spends hours in his darkened room tapping away at lightning speed. I'm still old fashioned enough to believe that sports and fresh air are invaluable to a growing person. He's at an age now where, when he's not gaming on his computer he's socialising with his friends, fitting in a touch of soccer and of course girls have become important. I can feel the empty nest syndrome hanging around there on the horizon so I cherish my time with him.

My ex-husband, Rob, seems to have settled down with his fourth wife. They live in the U.S. and have a son, a half-brother Lara and Thana would love to meet. Sadly there seems to be little chance of that. Judging by an e-mail Rob's current partner sent me I gather 'old' families are threatening to 'new' families. Thana last saw his father when he was eight years old, despite my later trying to arrange a reunion. Rob never visited South Africa or his children again but Lara flew to the U.S. and met with her dad when she was 20 years old. Happily they got on extremely well and enjoyed each other's company. My heart breaks when I see my children's pain at not having their father involved in their lives. Such is life, this we have to accept.

I have been offered a crewing position from South Africa to Brazil and then into the Pacific Ocean and beyond on a 47-foot (approximately 14 metres) Ron Holland designed sailboat, an offer I have happily accepted. Time frames are vague so who knows if and when it'll come about. The owner and skipper is a good friend of mine and this could be the voyage of a lifetime (as all my other voyages have been). If it materialises and if it's what I hope it will be and as exciting as I think it will be, you'll hear all about it in my next book.

Letters From School

One of the schools I spoke at, Glenwood Preparatory, sent me notes written by the Grade Sixes who had attended my presentation. I have included some of these messages here, a small selection from a modest mountain of letters.

These were special to me as the children embraced the tale with enthusiasm and keen interest making my presentation a memorable one. This particular presentation was entitled 'Pirates' and was based on my sailing ventures.

Their teacher wrote, "Dear Sharon, Our grateful thanks for coming to talk to our Grade Sixes. They were totally enthralled by your very entertaining talk. We were inundated with questions when we got back to our classes. You have certainly given them a different perspective on life and its countless possibilities. Thank you. Carmel."

Talking to Grade Sixes was particularly rewarding. At another school my allocated hour ran over into the lunch break and eventually the school bell rang signalling the end of school. Instead of rushing out of the classroom the children called in their parents who were waiting outside. Eventually the room was packed with children, teachers and parents!

Before doing these presentations I worried that I would lose the youngsters' interest. I had never done a presentation before so I wasn't quite sure as to how to go about it. Eventually I decided that I needed to capture their attention from the word go, so I dressed the part and took props with me. It turned out to be unnecessary but undoubtedly created an element of surprise and entertainment. And it was such fun for me too! I so enjoyed the flood of interested questions before, during and after my talk.

Dear Sharon Jordan

We had so much fun with you. I really enjoyed the talk. I liked it when you went up that lovely cave. also when your son and daugter were born ~~on~~ in diffemt countries.

Thank you

Nokuthula Mphambukel

Dear Sharon Jordan

We thank you for the lovely talk you gave us about your trip around the world it was nice especially when you showed u some interesting objects which some of us have not seen it was nice and mostly I enjoyed the part where you ~~we~~ went to the caves under water and about the dogs that ate sharks and wish you all the best with your family.

Yours Sincerly
Vukani Mabaso

Dear Sharon.......

Thank you for coming to our school and sharing your fabulous stories with us they were most enjoyable. The one that I thought was the most exciting one was when you went into the cave with lace coral all over the walls and sea snakes on every ledgeledge you tried to rest on. What I found the most interesting was that your daughter was born in Australia and your son was born in Brazil. What I found most terribly disgusting was when one of the dogs that you had found on one of the islands ripped a man that was on another yacht's ear off. What amaized me was that you could still remember all of these wonderful stories.

Your sincerely

Jason Cook 6 Swan

Dear Sharon

I thought your stories were great, you must be a very brave person to do what you did. You must be a great mother and wife!

I would like to go on a ship and sail all around the world, go to places that no one knows about and going to see all the different animals around the world just like you.

All the things you have done are amazing but the one thing that must have been great was all the different fish you saw. The size, the colours all those fish you saw must have been big, wide and beatiful. I would have loved to see that.

I would also like to live on a un-inhabited Island where there is no rushing car, no pollution at all just **MYSELF** and the beatiful animals.

Yours Sincerely

Christin Meistre

6S

This youngster seemed to have run out of commentary in his search for descriptive words and he even forgot to write his name at the bottom.

Dear Sharon

Thank you for spending your time with us; giving us an interesting talk on your life, sailing around the world, discovering new things, dead bodies, skeletons and caves as well as many other interesting items. I found you stories extensively remarkable My personal favourite was the story about how the two dogs intellegently caught the sharks in the lagoon and the about how your son, when he was only two years old, cut his toe right down to the bone! Ir must been ~~inerct~~ incrediblay painful. Most of all I would like to say thank you for all your time, it is ~~thegaul~~ thoroughly appreciated, your talk was interesting, ~~infieo~~ and highly amazing

Dear Sharon

I really liked your story. I found it most interesting. When you told us your story, I could mostly imagine what had happened to you. I really liked the part when you went Xm? meters underwater to go to a cave and found sea serpants. I also liked it when you told about the dogs and how they find there food. I liked it when You found the bones of dead people. I found it most interest when you tried looking for treasure under the water. I will never forget your story because it was the best story ever!!

Yours Sincerely
Kyle Pillay

Dear Sharon

Thank you so much for giving up your time and coming to talk to all the grade sixes about your wonderful experience out at sea.
I really enjoyed the part about how the dogs caught ~~there~~ food and how they survived out on the island. I think you are extremely brave to do this whole experience and also to go into that underwater cave, I don't think I would have been able to. You have been a very big role model to me and when I am older I would like to do something similar to what you did. Thank you so much.

Yours sincerely
Sharnaé Zimmermann.

Dear: Sharon

Thank you for your excellent ~~pormoma~~ stories. I really enjoyed them. Your adventures were amazing. ~~Maybe~~ One of these days I will ~~tak~~ mabe ~~go~~ sail to an island to have an adventure. I can't believe what kind of foods you ate. Snails and coconuts! Coconuts is okay but snails are discusting. It would be awesom if you found treasure like gold or sliver. I must say what you did was very risky because there are so many dangers when traveling on the opened sea, but I think it paid of. You must of had a whole lot of fun. I bet you miss it. I really enjoyed the storie ~~of~~ about the cave you must be really brave to do something like that.

Yours sincerely
Somesh Naidu 6S

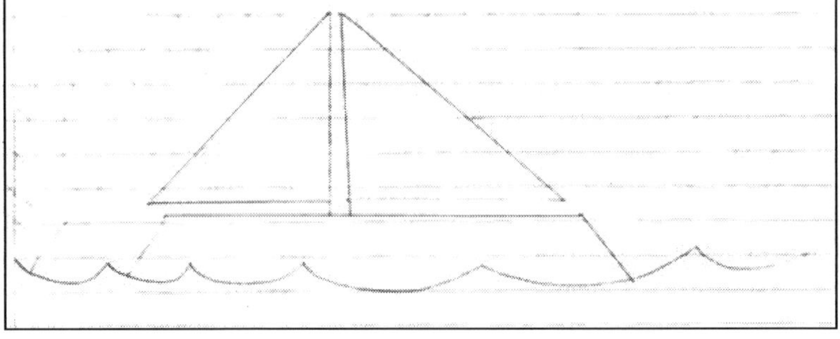

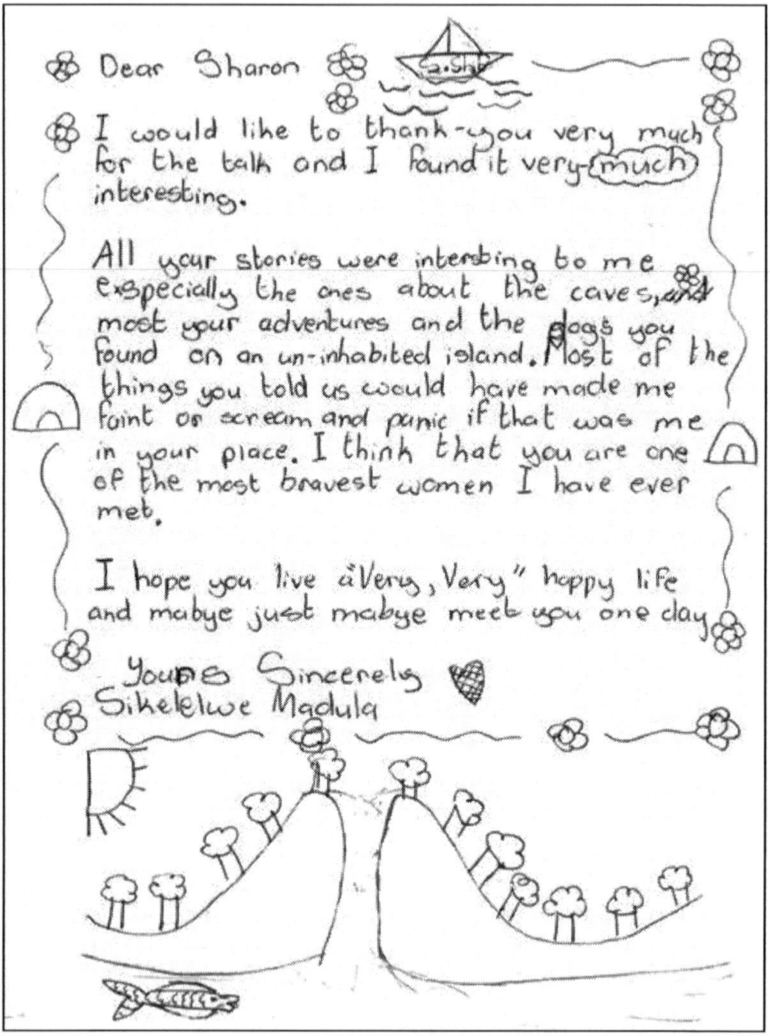

Dear Sharon

I would like to thank-you very much for the talk and I found it very much interesting.

All your stories were intersting to me especially the ones about the caves, and most your adventures and the dogs you found on an un-inhabited island. Most of the things you told us would have made me faint or scream and panic if that was me in your place. I think that you are one of the most bravest women I have ever met.

I hope you live a"Very, Very" happy life and mabye just mabye meet you one day

Yours Sincerely
Sikelelwe Madula

Dear Sharon...

I'd like to thank you for coming to our school. You haven't sailed for a long time, yet when you told us the stories it was like you sailed yesterday. The adventures you went on was amazing. I don't think I would have been brave enough to do what you did. When you went through the tunnel in Tonga it must have been absolutley ~~amazing~~. astonishing. You tell the stories with such great detail. I can only imagine how it must have been to see the lace coral. It must have been beautiful, wonderful, attractive, gorgeous, delightful and absolutley marvelious in every way. I can ~~only~~ only with I had a memory like yours. You are amazing.

Yours sincerely
Ashleigh Biggar